The Control of Aggression

The Control of Aggression

Implications from Basic Research

John F. Knutson, editor

Routledge
Taylor & Francis Group
LONDON AND NEW YORK

First published 1973 by Transaction Publishers

2 Park Square, Milton Park, Abingdon, Oxfordshire OX14 4RN
711 Third Avenue, New York, NY 10017

Routledge is an imprint of the Taylor & Francis Group, an informa business

First issued in hardback 2017

Library of Congress Catalog Number: 2006047811

Library of Congress Cataloging-in-Publication Data

Conference on Current Concerns in Clinical Psychology (7th : 1971 : University of Iowa)
The control of aggression : implications from basic research / edited by John F. Knustson.
p. cm. -- (Current concerns in clinical psychology ; 6)
Includes bibliographical references and indexes.
ISBN 0-202-30952-5 (alk. paper)
1. Aggressiveness--Congresses. I. Knutson, John F. II. Title.

BF575.A3C57 1971a
155.2 32--dc22

2006047811

ISBN 13: 978-0-202-30952-1 (pbk)
ISBN 13: 978-1-138-52122-3 (hbk)

Contents

Acknowledgements

Many people participated in the development of this volume, and it is a pleasure to acknowledge their contributions. The National Institute of Mental Health, through Training Grant MH-5062, supported the Current Concerns in Clinical Psychology Symposium, upon which six of the chapters are based. The Department of Psychology of the University of Iowa hosted that Conference and provided considerable support. Professor Rudolph W. Schulz, chairman of the department, interrupted a demanding schedule to provide the time and effort which put the finishing touches on the symposium.

I would like to thank the American Psychological Association, Brain Research Publications, Inc., Academic Press, Soumalainen Tiedeakatemia, Prentice-Hall and Perganon Press for the permission to reproduce essential figures.

The preparation of the manuscript was aided immeasurably by Susan P. Schrader, who checked references, and Barbara Pethick who brought considerable skill to the tasks of proofing, indexing, and typing.

The editing of a book often results in intrusions into the lives of the editor's family as well as his own. This book was no exception. I am especially grateful for the gracious manner with which my wife, Claudia, and my daughter, Amy, adjusted to disrupted evenings, weekends, and vacations.

The Control of Aggression

Introduction

JOHN F. KNUTSON

The Seventh Annual Conference on Current Concerns in Clinical Psychology was devoted to the issue of aggression control. This volume, with one exception (chap. 7), is made up of the papers presented at that conference and forms part of the Current Concerns in Clinical Psychology series. The series reflects the dual nature of clinical psychology: its concern both with basic research and with the application of its findings to practical problems. And so it is with the present volume on aggression.

Aggression is a timely topic of concern. The news media are continuous sources of information on aggressive and violent behaviors committed within any number of different contexts: multiple murder, urban riot, military atrocities, assault, and other individual and collective aggressive behaviors. The melange of aggressive and violent events confronting the public daily has given impetus to a number of responses, one of which is marked anxiety. The spreading fear of being a potential victim in a violent episode is apparently causing a large segment of the population to become radically defensive; many individuals literally lock themselves in homemade fortresses (*Life* 1971). Responding to the apparent pervasiveness of increasing anxiety in the face of the apparently increasing frequency of violence, *Life* magazine conducted a survey to investigate readers' feelings of safety and precautions taken to insure their personal safety (*Life* 1971). In a subsequent issue, the magazine provided information on how to avoid attackers and on optimal self-defense (*Life* 1972). Other examples of analyses of aggression in the popular press include comments by movie critics on the potential influence of cinematic violence (e.g., Kael 1972) and questions by syndicated columnists on the role of aggressiveness in the survival of the species (e.g., Harris 1972). With the continuous exposure to, report of, or commentary on violence, it is not surprising that considerable impetus is given to efforts to understand the causes of aggression or to control aggressive behavior.

Political responses directed toward understanding aggression have included the appointing of fact-finding commissions (e.g., National Commission on the Causes and Prevention of Violence 1969; Surgeon General's Scientific Advisory Committee on Television and Social Behavior 1972). A political response directed ostensibly at control of aggression has been the push for law-enforcement legislation, with the concomitant increase in the popularity of so-called law-and-order candidates.

With this apparent increase in the frequency of aggressive and violent behavior and public concern about it, it is not surprising that the applied behavioral scientists, such as clinical psychologists, are often asked to offer suggestions in the development of programs for its control.

Before applied psychology can respond to the current popular demands to control aggression, it seems necessary to establish that the science of psychology has a current concern for aggressive behavior and, more importantly, has empirically based information upon which to develop that response.

Prior to the last decade, research in psychology had been notably unconcerned with aggression. Prior to the late 1950s only three major developments within psychology had been addressed to analyses of aggressive behavior, including, certainly, Freud's (1933) theory that a drive toward death and destruction was an essential part of human nature. Although Freud's hypothesis was later largely rejected by psychoanalysis, some characteristics of the hydraulic-instinct model have been retained and enhanced through the popular publications of Lorenz (1966) and Ardrey (1966). Even if the Lorenz (1966) and Ardrey (1966) position has been strongly criticized by the scientific and academic communities (see, e.g., Montagu 1968), its popularity with the general public has been considerable. The second major early consideration of the subject took place within the area of psychological testing in the efforts to understand and predict aggressive behavior through the use of tests. Most of the research on aggression during the 1930s, 1940s, and 1950s involved the use of projective techniques and objective tests of personality. These methods have continued to be used in recent studies of personality and attempts to predict aggressivity on the basis of assessment techniques (e.g., Blumenthal 1972; Megargee 1966; and Olweus 1969). The third early development, and perhaps the one having the greatest impact on psychological research on aggression, was the frustration-aggression hypothesis. Originally formulated by Dollard, Doob, Miller, Mowrer, and Sears (1939), then modified by Miller (1941) and reconsidered by Berkowitz (1969), this basic position has probably been more instrumental in generating psychological laboratory research on aggression than any other early consideration of aggressive behavior.

Research based upon hydraulic-instinct theories of aggression, psychological assessment procedures in aggression, and the frustration-aggression hypothesis continues. In addition, the popular *Zeitgeist*, technological developments in research, advances in the understanding of behavior in general, and new strategies of research have all combined to provide a burgeoning of new research on aggression during the last ten years. Consequently, the currency of the topic of control of aggression is based upon concerns of the public and the applied psychologists, as well as basic-research developments in the laboratories of behavioral biologists and psychologists.

The goals of this book are to offer considerations of aggression based upon research and to present productive research paradigms that might be useful in continued research on aggressive behavior. Each of the papers included attempts to provide an individual data-based analysis of aggressive behavior and to provide, in addition, an explication of the research tactics used to obtain the data. It would be presumptuous for the editor of such a volume to suggest that the information provided will solve the pressing demands suggested above. He might more reasonably expect to promote research in this area and perhaps to gather a data base from many different laboratories. The value of this book may be tied ultimately to its influence on human behavior and specifically on human aggression. Yet, three chapters are based primarily on nonhuman subjects, and three chapters are based on data on human subjects. One chapter reports an attempt to adapt a theoretical research paradigm to both human and nonhuman subjects, after which however, the authors chose to do research on animal aggression. Interspecies generalizations without empirical demonstrations of interspecies similarity and differences are suspect. However, several chapters reflect across-species similarities, which may ultimately result in empirical demonstrations that add to our understanding of human as well as nonhuman aggression.

In the first chapter, Moyer distinguishes among eight different kinds of aggressive behavior, noting their functional values and stimulus-bound characteristics. Using data on animals, primarily, he builds a case for a physiologically based model of different kinds of aggression. Moyer then reviews research on the control of aggressive behaviors in which brain lesions, central nervous system stimulation, hormonal manipulations, and pharmacotherapy are used.

Denenberg explores the influence that pre- and postweaning environments and neonatal hormones have on naturally occurring intraspecific aggressive behavior in the mouse and in the rat, and on interspecific aggression in the rat. His chapter also shows that the influences of the early-experience variables are determined to a large degree by the genotype of the subjects. Closely related to the Denenberg chapter is the one by McClearn and DeFries, in which, using the laboratory mouse as the prototype, they examine two aspects of the interrelationship between genetics and aggression: First, phenotypic aggressive behavior determined by the manner in which various genotypic characteristics interact with the environment to control interorganism interactions; second, the importance of dominance and aggression in determining the characteristics of the gene pool and, hence, the potential aggressive characteristics of progeny.

The chapter by Ulrich, Dulaney, Arnett, and Mueller reviews two classes of aggressive behavior: aggression maintained by positive reinforcement and aggression elicited by painful stimulation. While their research was based on nonhuman subjects, they report a series of experiments in which attempts were made to adapt their model of aggression to humans. Despite some support for their model, the authors encountered difficulties in attempting to adopt their strategy with humans.

Berkowitz bases his analysis of aggressive behavior on classical conditioning principles. In his model classical conditioning is viewed as an essential process by which social stimuli and symbols acquire the properties necessary to instigate aggressive behavior or to direct the aggressive behaviors of a sufficiently stimulated subject. His data are almost exclusively laboratory based. In contrast, Patterson and Cobb used a fine-grain observational procedure for an in situ analysis of the behavior of deviant and nondeviant children. They describe the control of social stimuli for classes of noxious behaviors in boys in the initial part of a program designed to build a social learning theory of human aggression.

Bandura, who did not attend the conference, has provided a chapter in which he considers the development of, provocation to, and maintenance of human aggressive behavior. His multifaceted social learning theory of aggression is based on data concerned with imitation, positive reinforcement, aversive stimulation, and self-reinforcement.

Each chapter with the exception of the last one, by the editor, is an independent unit capable of being considered in isolation. However, it is hoped that by publishing these papers together, the import of the book as a unit will exceed the sum of its parts. To that end the final chapter is addressed to recurring problems in aggression research, as well as to a consideration of the points of agreement and disagreement among the contributors.

References

Ardrey, R. *The Territorial Imperative.* New York: Atheneum, 1966.

Berkowitz, L. "The Frustration-Aggression Hypothesis Revisited." In *Roots of aggression*, edited by L. Berkowitz New York: Atherton Press, 1969.

Blumenthal, M. D. "Predicting Attitudes toward Violence." *Science* 176 (1972): 1296–1303.

Dollard, J.; Doob, L.; Miller, N.; Mowrer, O., and Sears, R. *Frustration and Aggression*. New Haven, Conn.: Yale University Press, 1939.

Freud, S. *New Introductory Lectures on Psycho-Analysis*. New York: Norton, 1933.

Harris, S. "Fitted, Not Strongest, Survive." *Des Moines Register*, January 24, 1972, p. 16.

Kael, Pauline. "The current cinema: Stanley Strangelove." *New Yorker* 47 (1972): 50–53.

Life. "Fortress on 78th Street." November 19, 1971, pp. 26–35.

Life. "Mugging: The U.S. Puts New Muscle into a Campaign Against Street Robbers Who Can "Hit" a Victim in Seconds." January 28, 1972, pp. 28B–34.

Lorenz, K. *On Aggression*. New York: Harcourt, Brace, & World, 1966.

Megargee, E. I. "Undercontrolled and Overcontrolled Personality Types in Extreme Antisocial Aggression." *Psychological Monographs*, vol. 80 (3, whole no. 611) (1966).

Miller, N. E. "The Frustration-Aggression Hypothesis." *Psychological Review* 48 (1941): 337–42.

Montagu, M. F. A. *Man and Aggression*. New York: Oxford University Press, 1968.

National Commission on the Causes and Prevention of Violence. *To Establish Justice, To Insure Domestic Tranquility, Final Report*. Washington, D.C.: Government Printing Office, 1969.

Olweus, D. *Prediction of Aggression*. Stockholm: Scandinavian Test Corporation, 1969.

Surgeon General's Scientific Advisory Committee on Television and Social Behavior. *Television and Growing up: The Impact of Televised Violence*. Washington, D.C.: Government Printing Office, 1972.

Kenneth E. Moyer received his bachelor's degree from Park College and his Ph.D. from Washington University. After completion of the Ph.D., Dr. Moyer joined the faculty of Carnegie Institute of Technology. He is currently professor of psychology at Carnegie-Mellon University. In 1954 Professor Moyer served as a consultant on higher education to the government of Norway. He is a fellow of the Division of Psychopharmacology, American Psychological Association, and a fellow of the American Association for the Advancement of Science. In addition to his extensive research on the physiological bases of aggression, Professor Moyer's research interests include endocrinology, emotion, and avoidance behavior.

1

The Physiological Inhibition of Hostile Behavior

K. E. MOYER

It is appropriate and timely that we further our understanding of methods of aggression control: We live in a society in which violence and aggression are rampant, and, if society as we know it is to survive, methods of aggression control must be found. With reference to the effects of violence in our culture, the National Commission on the Causes and Prevention of Violence (1969) concluded after two years of study:

> Violence in the United States has risen to alarmingly high levels. Whether one considers assassination, group violence, or individual acts of violence, the decade of the 1960s was considerably more violent than the several decades preceding it and ranks among the most violent in our history. The United States is the clear leader among modern, stable democratic nations in its rates of homicide, assault, rape, and robbery, and it is at least among the highest in incidence of group violence and assassination.
>
> This high level of violence is dangerous to our society. It is disfiguring our society—making fortresses of portions of our cities and dividing our people into armed camps. It is jeopardizing some of our most precious insitutions, among them our schools and universities—poisoning the spirit of trust and cooperation that is essential to their proper functioning. It is corroding the central political processes of our democratic society—substituting force and fear for argument and accomodation. [P.xv]

Six hundred years before the birth of Christ the prophet Ezekial had the same concerns when he wrote, "The land is full of bloody crimes and the city is full of violence" (Ezek. 7:23).

Every sixty-eight seconds between the years of 1820 and 1945 a man has died at the hands of a fellow man as a result of violence ranging from murder to war (Boelkins and Heiser 1970; Richardson 1960).

Thus, it appears that man's hostility to man and his concern about that behavior is as old as man himself. Aggressive behavior is not new; what is new is the dramatic increase in man's destructive capacity. On the international scene, as we have often been told, man has the ability to translate hostile impulses into the instant obliteration of all mankind, all other life on the planet, and perhaps the very planet itself. At the level of the local tavern, the temporary loss of hostility control caused by alcohol can result in death because of the ready availability of the lethal handgun. Only a technologically advanced civilization could provide its politicians with a hydrogen bomb and every second home with a gun (Newton and Zimring 1970).

There seems to be little doubt that the trend in violent crime in the United States is on the way up and is accelerating. After a serious consideration of the many possible sources of error in predictions based on crime statistics, Graham (1969, p. 385) comes to the following conclusion: "Most experts now believe that this rapid surge in crime, with its new heavy component of crimes of violence, will continue and perhaps will accelerate, at least for the next ten years."

Aggression and the Population Increase

Projections beyond the next ten years must be tentative, at best, but there appears to be good reason to believe that interpersonal aggression is going to increase before it decreases. A "population explosion" now seems inevitable. According to Ehrlich (1968, p. 11), one of the more visible population biologists, "The battle to feed all of humanity is over. In the 1970's the world will undergo famines—hundreds of millions of people are going to starve to death in spite of any crash program embarked upon now."

It is obvious that the population growth rate of approximately 2 percent per year cannot continue indefinitely. At that rate, the world population will double by the beginning of the next century. Several authors have calculated the absurd consequences of a theoretical continuation of such a birth rate (Augenstein 1969; Ehrlich 1968; Taylor 1968). In five hundred to six hundred years, each individual would have 1 square yard of the surface of the earth to call his own, and in six thousand years, the mass of people would exceed that of the known universe.

The population problem will, of course, be solved. In time, the death rate will begin to exceed the birth rate. How soon that will happen will depend on many factors. However, if we can place any faith in the pessimistic prognosis of Ehrlich (1968), it is unlikely that any or all of the possible projected solutions are going to be sufficiently effective to prevent a massive population increase within the life span of the reader of this volume. It also appears highly likely that an aggression explosion will accompany the population explosion.

Unless drastic preventive measures are taken, extreme crowding will provide the environmental conditions that breed violence (see Moyer 1972): Significant increases in population size will foster aggressive behavior by magnifying man's deprivation and frustration levels, decreasing his personal space, increasing his information overload, increasing social disorganization, increasing the absolute number of violence-prone individuals, and, finally, by increasing the absolute number of young males (the group that overwhelmingly commits the greatest amount of violent crime). As the population pressures grow, the caldron of violence, hostility, and aggressive behavior will seethe and boil with increasing fury. Thus, man's survival depends on more effective methods of hostility control.

Models of Aggressive Behavior

The assumptions made about the underlying causes of hostility determine, in large measure, the kinds of control techniques considered. One prevalent theory of aggression takes the position that there are no internal impulses to aggressive behavior and that all hostile tendencies are learned. When the proponents of this position consider methods of control, they concern themselves exclusively with the manipulation of the external environment. Scott (1962) and Hinde (1967), for example, made no mention of the possibility of aggression control through changes in the individual's internal environment. Other theorists, such as the ethologists as represented by Lorenz (1966) and the psychoanalytic school as recently represented by Storr (1968), emphasize the concept of internal impulses to aggressive behavior. However, these impulses are conceived in terms of "aggressive energy," which is closely linked with the energy of ambition, love, and other positive attributes. The recommendations of these schools for aggression control are therefore confined to suggestions for the redirection of this aggressive energy, and the possibility of the reduction of hostile tendencies per se are not seriously considered. They suggest, in fact, that the elimination of aggressive tendencies would be a disasterous step, resulting in diminution of many of man's most positive attributes—such as artistic creativity, scientific endeavors, and even love: "Thus, intra-specific aggression can certainly exist without its counterpart, love, but conversely there is no love without aggression" (Lorenz 1966, p. 217).

Here, a different model of aggressive behavior will be presented briefly: an interaction model that deals with both the external provocations and the internal impulses to hostile behavior. The implications of this model for the control of aggression will then be considered; and it will be seen that this different way of looking at the problem implies different solutions and that these different solutions are fraught with both benefits and dangers.

Kinds of Aggression

Several years ago I postulated a number of different kinds of aggressive behavior and attempted to classify them on the basis of the types of stimuli that would elicit a hostile response (Moyer 1968). Definition of the kinds of aggression on that basis alone now appears too restrictive: The kinds of aggression vary on a number of different dimensions, and all of them must be considered in the definition of each kind (see Moyer 1972). The types of stimulation that will elicit attack are usually different for each kind of aggressive behavior. Thus, aggression may be considered as stimulus bound. In many classes of aggression the stimulus situation to which the animal reacts with hostility is remarkably specific. For example, a male mouse will attack another male, but will generally not attack a female or a juvenile (Scott and Fredericson 1951). A rat will attack a strange member of the same species, but will seldom react aggressively to a member of its own group (Barnett 1963; Eibl-Eibesfeldt 1961). The mouse-killing laboratory rat will seldom attack a rat pup and can be readily handled by the experimenter.

There are also obvious differences in response patterns shown by animals in different aggression-inducing situations. Predatory aggression in the cat involves little if any emotional display. The attack is careful, silent, and deadly. In irritable or fear-induced aggression, however, the animal may explode in a flurry of scratching and biting (Hutchinson and Renfrew 1966; Roberts and Kiess 1964; Wasman and Flynn 1962). Male deer confront one another with lowered head and the locking of antlers. Attacks by predators, however, are met by striking out with the front hooves (Tinbergen 1953).

Sex is another dimension on which the kinds of aggression may vary. In most species certain types of aggressive behavior are restricted to a particular sex. For example, intraspecific fighting in many animal species is, in general, restricted to the male, but aggressive behavior in defense of the young is primarily a female characteristic (King 1963).

The neurological and endocrine bases of each of the different kinds of aggression may overlap, but can be differentiated. In the now classic study of Egger and Flynn (1963), it was shown that electrical stimulation of the lateral hypothalamus of the cat resulted in a typical predatory attack on a rat, while the experimenter was ignored. However, if the cat was stimulated in the medial hypothalamus, the animal ignored the rat in its cage and manifested well-organized aggressive responses toward the experimenter. Recently, Chi and Flynn (1971) have shown that the neural systems underlying these two different kinds of directed attack are different. Although there is much more to be learned, differential physiological bases for several kinds of aggression have been summarized (Moyer 1968).

The evidence indicates that it may be useful to classify aggressive behaviors as follows: predatory, intermale, fear induced, maternal, sex related, irritable, and instrumental. Instrumental aggression differs from the others in that it is a learned response that occurs in a given situation because it has been reinforced in the past. Thus, instrumental aggression does not have a specific physiological basis other than in the sense that learning has a physiological basis.

It is unlikely that the classification system suggested above is the most useful one that can be devised, and it should be modified as research provides more insight into the mechanisms of hostility. It is clear, however, that there are different kinds of aggression, and an understanding of that concept is important to any efforts directed at the control of hostile behavior. As indicated below, some control measures are effective in some instances of aggression, but are ineffective in others. This is undoubtedly accounted for, in part, by the fact that the underlying mechanisms are different.

A Physiological Model of Aggression

In this section an attempt will be made to identify the types of mechanisms peculiar to different kinds of aggression (see Moyer 1971, 1972).

There is now abundant evidence that there are neural mechanisms for aggressive behavior. When these innately organized neural systems are active in the presence of particular stimulus complexes, the organisms behave in a destructive manner toward those stimuli. Thus, aggressive behavior is stimulus bound just as eating behavior is stimulus bound (Moyer 1969). As indicated above, it has been shown that a cat can be induced to attack by brain stimulation. However, whether it attacks an available rat or the experimenter, depends on which neural system is activated.

The type of stimulation required to elicit a particular kind of aggressive behavior may be quite restricted and, even though a neural mechanism for aggression is active, the hostile behavior will not be manifest unless the appropriate external stimulus is available. For example, a monkey stimulated in the anterior hypothalamus showed no increase in irritability and did not manifest any increased tendency to attack the experimenter or inanimate objects. However, when the animal was stimulated in the presence of a dominant male monkey, a vigorous and intense attack ensued. Only the male monkey was attacked, and the stimulated male showed no tendency to attack a female monkey that was also in the cage. The attacks by the experimental monkey were so intense that after a number of trials the dominance relationship was reversed (Robinson, Alexander, and Bowne 1969).

There are now several reviews of the literature on brain mechanisms related to aggression which convincingly demonstrate that there are neural systems for aggression and that the different kinds of aggression have separate representations in the brain, although they may overlap (Flynn et al. 1970; Kaada 1967; Moyer 1971).

For obvious reasons, most of the experimental work on the neural basis of aggressive behavior has been done on animals, and one must be careful about generalizing data obtained from animal research to humans. However, the evidence clearly supports the proposition that man's evolution has not eliminated his neural systems for aggression. A number of cases demonstrating aggression as a result of the activation of particular neural systems are presented in *Violence and the Brain* by Mark and Ervin (1970). Other cases have been reported by Ervin, Mark, and Stevens (1969); Sem-Jacobsen (1966); and Sem-Jacobsen and Torkildsen (1960). The now classic case reported by King (1961), can be used as an example. A mild-mannered female patient became aggressive, verbally hostile, and threatened to strike the experimenter when she was electrically stimulated in the region of the amygdala. When the current was turned off, her mild manner returned and she became apologetic for her behavior. She did not report a sensation of pain but indicated that it was unpleasant to feel so hostile. This patient's hostile feelings and behavior could be activated and deactivated simply by throwing the switch.

A number of experiments suggest that the neural systems for hostility are held in check by inputs from suppressor systems in other parts of the brain. It has been shown, for example, that the docile laboratory rat becomes irritable and aggressive if the olfactory bulbs are lesioned (Bernstein and Moyer 1970; Karli, Vergnes, and Didiergeorges 1969). Increases in irritability and aggressive behavior in cats has been reported after hypothalamic and amygdaloid lesions (Wheatly 1944; Wood 1958). There is also considerable clinical evidence that brain damage in man as a result of traumatic epilepsy and brain tumors may result in significant alterations of behavior, including a propensity for aggression at the slightest provocation (Moyer 1969). It has also been shown that the activation of the aggression suppressor areas in the brain results in an inhibition of ongoing aggressive behavior.

The thresholds for the activation of the neural systems for aggression wax and wane over time, and the sensitivity of these systems is, in part, related to various blood constituents. The system for intermale aggresion is regulated in part by the androgen level in the blood stream (Beeman 1947; Collias 1944), and the periodic tension and irritability in some women appear to be related to the premenstrual hormone balance (Dalton 1964; Hamburg, Moos, and Yalom 1968; Janowsky, Gorney, and Mandell 1967).

Although little is known about the physiology involved, it is well recognized that frustration and stress, especially if prolonged, result in a facilitation of irritable and aggressive behavior. This may be due in part to the particular hormonal balance which is characteristic of the stress syndrome. Both the adrenal cortex and the thyroid are intimately involved in the stress syndrome, and dysfunctions of either gland lead to increases in irritability (Cleghorn 1957; Gibson 1962).

An aggressive response, like any other response, can be influenced by learning. If aggression is reinforced, the probability that it will recur in similar situations is enhanced; and, if it is punished, the tendency for aggression to occur in that particular situation is decreased. Because of man's exceptional learning ability, his tendencies to hostility are more easily modified by experience than are the tendencies of the rest of the animal kingdom. Further, because of man's capacity for symbol manipulation, the kinds of stimuli that are capable of eliciting aggression are more varied and his methods of aggression expression are more diverse than those found in other animals.

In summary, the model briefly outlined above indicates that aggressive behavior is determined by a complex interaction of external, internal, and experiential factors. This should provide for three distinct approaches to the important practical problem of aggression control. First, the external environment can be modified to reduce the kinds of cues that instigate aggression. The environment can also be modified to reduce the levels of stress, frustration, and deprivation responses. Second, individuals may be taught to inhibit their aggressive tendencies. Finally, it should be possible to manipulate the individual's internal environment, directly affect the physiological substrates for aggression, and thereby block aggressive tendencies.

Although I will limit myself to a discussion of the last approach, this does not indicate that the other control methods are ineffective or unimportant.

Hostility Inhibition by Brain Lesions

If there are distinct neural systems that are responsuble for the different kinds of aggressive behavior, it should be possible to reduce or eliminate a type of behavior by disrupting the neural system. There is now a great deal of evidence that such a procedure is possible.

Since there are a number of different kinds of aggression and the neural substrate of each involves several brain structures, it is not surprising that surgical taming can be accomplished by placing lesions in a number of different brain areas. The reduction in one or another kind of aggression has been reported after lesions in the posteromedial hypothalamus (Sano 1966), anterior thalamic nuclei (Schreiner and Kling 1953), dorsal medial thalamus (Spiegel and Wycis, 1949), midbrain (Brown and Hunsperger 1963), lateral hypothalamus (Karli, Vergnes, and Didiergeorges 1969), the cingulate cortex (Glees et al. 1950; Kennard 1955; Ward 1948), and in the orbital frontal cortex (Butter, Snyder, and McDonald 1970).

The structures of the temporal lobe have received the greatest amount of attention in attempts to understand the neurological basis of hostility through the lesioning process. The surgical taming resulting from temporal lobe lesions has been known since Kluver and Bucy reported that vicious rhesus monkeys were converted to friendly playful animals by a radical, bilateral ablation of the temporal lobes (Kluver and Bucy 1937, 1938, 1939). A number of studies have now shown that lesions in the amygdala tend to eliminate or at least raise the threshold for several different kinds of aggressive responses. Irritable aggression is dramatically reduced. Cats subjected to this operation do not become aggressive even when suspended by their tails and generally roughed up (Schreiner and Kling 1953). Predatory aggression is also eliminated by bilateral amygdalectomy. This has been demonstrated for both the cat (Summers and Kaelber 1962) and the rat (Woods 1956). Amygdalectomized animals manifest a significant reduction in fear reactions and are consequently less inclined to behave aggressively when cornered (Rosvold, Mirsky, and Pribram 1954; Schreiner and Kling 1953, 1956).

Man can also be "cured" of certain types of violence-prone tendencies by brain lesions. As with animals, lesions in a variety of brain areas have been shown to be effective in the reduction of pathological hostility in man. These have included radical temporal lobectomy (Terzian and Ore, 1955), cingulectomy (Le Beau 1952; Tow and Whitty 1953), and lesions in posterior hypothalamus (Sano 1962), thalamus (Spiegel et al. 1951), fornix, and upper mesencephalon (Sano 1966), frontal lobes (Liddell 1953), and amygdala (Heimburger, Whitlock and Kalsbeck 1966; Mark and Ervin 1970; Narabayashi and Uno 1966; Narabayashi et al. 1963; and Schwab et al. 1965).

Temporal lobe lesions in man have been extensively used to control epilepsy, which cannot be controlled with drug therapy. In general, this operation is effective in seizure control but does not reduce the patient's psychiatric problems, with the significant exception of those problems that relate to excessive hostility (Bailey 1958; Falconer et al. 1958).

Although lesions in many of these areas do significantly reduce tendencies to hostility, they also have some unfortunate side effects. In the case reported by Terzian and Ore (1955), both temporal lobes were removed, and the result was an exact reproduction of the well-known Kluver-Bucy syndrome, including rage and fear reduction, loss of recognition of people, increased sex activity, bulimia, and serious memory deficiencies.

A general sedative effect and temporary loss of spontaneity has resulted from posterior hypothalamic lesions, and in some cases aggressive behavior has been temporarily increased by temporal lobe lesions (Sawa et al. 1954; Woringer, Thomalske, and Klingler 1953).

More recent surgical techniques for the reduction of hostility have eliminated many of the side effects by the use of much smaller and more precise stereotaxic lesioning techniques. Lesions 8–10 millimeters in diameter have been produced by an injection of 0.6–0.8 milliliters of oil to which lipiodol had been added (Narabayashi and Uno 1966; Narabayashi et al. 1963). These authors report that 85 percent of fifty-one patients showed a marked reduction in emotional excitability and a normalization of their social behavior. It should be emphasized that, except for the reduction in hostility, none of the signs of the Kluver-Bucy syndrome resulted from the bilateral destruction of the amygdaloid nuclei.

Similar results have been reported by Heimburger, Whitlock, and Kalsbeck (1966). They have lesioned approximately half of the amygdala using cryosurgery. This operation has resulted in dramatic improvement in some patients and an overall improvement in twenty-three of twenty-five patients. Destructiveness, hostility, and aggression toward others were the behavior symptoms most frequently improved by the operation. The improvement in two of the patients was so great that they were released from mental institutions. Others were moved from solitary confinement to open wards. Some of them were observed to smile and laugh for the first time in their lives after the operation. Heimburger, Whitlock, and Kalsbeck (1966, p. 169) conclude, "Stereotaxic amygdalotomy is a safe and relatively easy procedure for treatment of a select group of patients who have previously been considered untreatable."

Similar results have been reported by Schwab et al. (1965),

and by Mark and Ervin (1970). They use a very promising technique of implanting forty-eight pairs of recording electrodes bilaterally through the limbic system. Then they carry out a program of recording and stimulation over a period of several weeks in order to localize and limit as much as possible the precise area that, when destroyed, will relieve the symptoms. A radio-frequency lesion is then made through the indwelling electrodes. Ervin indicates that there is good reason to believe from their observations that the neural and neurochemical substrates for the motor seizure and for the interseizure assaultive and aggressive behaviors are different. It is possible to eliminate the one without affecting the other (Ervin, personal communication).

Hostility Control by Brain Stimulation

If there are suppressor systems in the brain which send inhibitory fibers to the neural substrates for aggression, it should be possible to prevent both feelings of hostility as well as hostile behavior by the chemical or electrical activation of suppressor systems. This has been repeatedly accomplished in both animals and man and thus provides another method for the direct physiological control of hostility.

Flynn et al. (1970) have experimentally determined a number of brain areas that, on stimulation, block attack behavior in the cat. Delgado (1960, 1967), working with monkeys, has reported that electrical stimulation of the caudate nucleus makes a normally vicious rhesus monkey sufficiently docile that the experimenter can put his finger in the animal's mouth without fear of being bitten. As soon as the current is turned off, the monkey once again becomes as savage as ever. These reports emphasize that the hostility reduction is not produced by a generalized motor inhibition. The monkey shows good coordination and no loss of response to sensory stimulation during caudate stimulation.

Delgado (1963, 1965) has also studied the effects of the activation of the aggression-suppressor systems on the normal social hierarchy in a colony of monkeys. This was accomplished by using a system that permitted the remote activation of the stimulating electrode through a radio transmitter that sent signals to a receiver bolted to the skull of the experimental monkey. Stimulation of the caudate nucleus of the top animal in the hierarchy inhibited his spontaneous aggressive behaviors. The other monkeys in the colony began to react to him differently. They made fewer submissive gestures and were generally less fearful. As a result, the position of the stimulated monkey in the social hierarchy fell.

During a later phase of the above experiment the activator button for the transmitter was placed in the cage. It was then possible for other monkeys in the colony to activate the transmitter and thus gain control over the caudate stimulation of the "boss" monkey. One of the submissive animals learned to press the button during periods when the boss monkey showed aggressive tendencies. When the dominant monkey made threatening gestures, the smaller one would frequently look him straight in the eye and press the button, thereby directly calming him down and reducing his hostile tendencies.

Feelings of hostility and overt aggressive behavior in man can also be inhibited by the activation of suppressor systems. Violent manic patients have been made cooperative, communicative, and tractable by direct stimulation of an area in the ventromedial frontal lobes and of the central area of the temporal lobe. There is also evidence that one stimulation session of about fifteen minutes had a prolonged effect, permitting the patient to be calm and free from uncontrollable aggressive tendencies for as long as a day (Sem-Jacobsen and Torkildsen 1960).

For obvious reasons, the locations of the rage-suppressor systems in man have not as yet been systematically investigated, but the available data on both animals and men seems to indicate that a number of different brain areas send inhibitory fibers to the neural substrates for hostility. Although he does not give statistics, Heath (1963) indicates that the inhibition of violence by brain stimulation has been accomplished in his clinic in a large number of patients. Much of his work has been concerned with the stimulation of the septal region through implanted electrodes and cannulas; and he has shown that a number of unpleasant affective states, including depression, pain, and rage, can be inhibited by direct septal stimulation. A violent, agitated, threatening, psychotic patient can receive direct septal stimulation and have his behavioral state instantly changed to one of happiness and mild euphoria. The subject is unaware that he has received the stimulation and, on questioning, is unable to explain the rapid shift in his mood state (Heath 1963).

Sweet, Ervin, and Mark (1969) report a case in which electrical stimulation of the medial amygdala resulted in pain and the subject's communication that he felt he was losing control. This was the same type of feeling he had previously experienced just prior to episodes of violent attack. The examiners stimulated this particular area only twice for fear that they, the patient, or both might sustain injury. Stimulation at a point in the amygdala just 4 millimeters lateral to that point, however, resulted in the patient's reporting feelings of extreme relaxation, and he related it to the type of feeling one experiences under demerol; he felt as though he were "floating on a cloud." During this favorable mood the patient, although previously frequently violent, showed no rage reactions. After a series of stimulations to the "relaxation" area, the patient's mood state remained positive for a period of eight to thirty-six hours. By providing periodic sessions of stimulation it was possible to keep the patient free from his attacks of uncontrollable rage for a period of three months. However, the patient continued to need this controlling stimulation. As a result, the decision was made to make small bilateral lesions in the medial amygdala, which, on stimulation, had induced the feeling of loss of control. A two-year follow-up of this patient revealed no further rage episodes.

Another violent patient responded well to stimulation of the right amygdala. Both his mood and thought content improved significantly after a session of stimulation, and the effects were long lasting. This patient's response was so favorable that the electrodes were removed and he was discharged. He remained free of both violent behavior and seizures for an entire year, during which he led a normal life and held down a good job. Unfortunately, he subsequently relapsed.

Heath (1954) has developed a transisterized, self-contained unit that the patient can wear on his belt. This unit, which generates a preset train of electrical pulses, could be connected to an electrode implanted in one of the hostility-suppressor systems.

The patient would then have available to him what might be described as an "antihostility button." Whenever he had irrational aggressive feelings, he could press his antihostility button and convert his mood into one of calm and equanimity.[1]

One of the problems with the self-controlled antihostility device is that the patient may very well not recognize when his feelings of hostility are irrational and inappropriate. He may regard his aggressive-mood state as being both justified and laudable. It is therefore necessary, if the patient is not to be either sedated, or straightjacketed, or both, to activate the hostility-suppressor system with an override mechanism that bypasses the self-controlled antihostility button. This, too, is now technologically feasible.

The patient, like the monkeys in the experiment described above, can be equipped with a radio receiver, which, when activated by a tuned transmitter, will close the circuit and provide brain stimulation through an implanted electrode. If the electrode is implanted in an aggression-suppressor system, the patient's hostile behavior can be brought under control from a considerable distance, limited only by the range of the transmitter. The technical feasibility of this approach is demonstrated by the fact that four patients at Massachusetts General Hospital have already been equipped with radio receivers connected to implanted electrodes. The activation of brain areas through these electrodes has resulted in a variety of effects, including "pleasant sensations, elation, deep thoughtful concentration, odd feelings, super relaxation and colored vision" (Mark et al. 1969). Although hostility control with this device has not yet been reported, there is every reason to believe that it would be possible.

Delgado (1969) has recently reported that a radio receiver unit has been miniaturized so that it is now about the size and shape of a half-dollar. The entire unit can be connected to the electrodes in the appropriate brain areas and then implanted un-

1. This device, as far as I know, has not yet been used in the control of hostility. It has, however, been used with a narcoleptic patient, who, whenever he felt himself drifting off to sleep, could reach down and press his "on" button and once again become alert. His friends soon learned that they could press the button to get him back into the conversation if he fell asleep too rapidly to press it himself (Heath 1963).

der the skin. Thus, there is no need for the electrode wires to penetrate the skin, and that source of possible irritation and infection has been eliminated. Also, as soon as the hair grows back after the operation, the patient will look no different from any other individual, and he will no longer be conspicuous because he wears a radio on his head.

The above examples provide evidence for the direct control of man's hostility by man. However, there is now evidence that it may one day be possible for man's hostility to be controlled by a computer. Delgado (1969) has implanted electrodes in the brain of a chimpanzee and connected them to a transmitter-receiver which was bolted to the subject's head. With this arrangement it was possible to make EEG recordings from depth electrodes, as well as to provide remote stimulation of deep brain sites. It was then determined that spontaneous spindles from the amygdala were correlated with excitement and attack behavior, and that stimulation in the area of the central grey resulted in a negative response in the chimp. A computer was then programmed to differentiate the spindle waves from other EEG responses and to activate the electrode implanted in the central grey on the occurrence of the amygdaloid spindles. A reduction in the amount and frequency of spindle waves from the amygdala resulted. Within two hours the amount of spindling was reduced by one-half, and after a few days the spindles were essentially eliminated. The behavior of the chimpanzee also changed. He became considerably more docile, had less appetite, and became somewhat lethargic. This behavior change persisted for a two-week period without further stimulation.

The interpretation of this experiment is not yet clear. Until the procedure is applied to humans, it will not be possible to know what kinds of subjective experiences are associated with either the spindles or the stimulation of the central grey. Central grey stimulation has been associated with the experience of pain and thus may be undesirable as a locus for stimulation in the control of aggression. However, it has been shown that under certain circumstances violent behavior is preceded and accompanied by particular EEG tracings from the depths of the temporal lobe, particularly the amygdaloid and hippocampal regions (Mark and

Ervin 1970). As indicated above, stimulation in several brain areas results in an inhibition of hostility, with the substitution of some positive affect. Thus, it appears that the basic mechanisms for the computer control of hostility in humans have already been demonstrated. It is obvious, however, that much more research needs to be done before such a procedure becomes practical.

The inhibition of aggressive behavior by the stimulation of the brain may last from hours to months. As yet, there is very little information on mechanisms underlying such a prolonged effect. If this finding is substantiated by further research, the ultimate in the control of pathological aggression may come with the development of a technique for the stimulation of precise .brain areas without the necessity of surgery. Such a devise is not beyond the realm of possibility. A stereotaxic lesioning method is now available (Baltimore Instrument Company, Baltimore, Maryland) which involves the use of two parabolic reflectors that focus sound energy in such a way that only at the point of intersection of the two sources will there be an effect. With this instrument it is possible to produce precise lesions without opening the skull. According to one of the developers of this instrument, there is the possibility that it could be modified to use as a stimulator (C. Dickey, personal communication). If and when this technique is developed, it would be possible for the pathologically hostile individual to keep his destructive tendencies under control by the periodic stimulation of his aggression-suppressor systems. The mechanics would be less onerous than the daily insulin injection of the diabetic.

Hostility Inhibition by Hormone Manipulation

If, as indicated in the physiological model of aggression, the neural systems for hostility are sensitized by particular hormone balances, an adequate understanding of these interactions should lead to a rational hormonal therapy for certain kinds of hostility. It has been repeatedly demonstrated that certain types of fighting in animals can be reduced or eliminated by the reduction of androgens in the blood stream by castration (Beeman 1947; Seward 1945; Sigg 1969; Urich 1938). There is evidence that the same operation in humans has been useful in the control of some violent sex criminals (Hawke 1950; LeMaire 1956). However, in one study of 102 legally castrated males in Norway, the opertation did not appear to have a general pacifying effect in disturbed mental cases (Bremer 1959).

It has been suggested that some of the antiandrogenic substances such as A-Norprogesterone (Lerner, Bianchi, and Borman 1960), chlormadinone acetate (Rocky and Neri 1968), and cyproterone acetate (Neumann et al. 1968), might be useful in the control of sex-related hostility (Neuman, Elger, and Von Berswordt-Wallrabe 1967). To date there is not sufficient evidence to make a judgment on that hypothesis. Edwards (1970), has shown that although cyproterone acetate has a potent anti-androgenic effect on the seminal vesicles of mice, it does not reduce androgen-dependent aggressive behavior in those subjects. There is some reason to believe that cyproterone acetate may act as an anti-androgen on non-neural tissue, but as an androgen on some hypothalamic structures (Davidson and Bloch 1969; Edwards 1970). Thus, the net effect of this substance may be to enhance hostile behavior.

There is some evidence that estrogenic hormones may function to mask the sensitizing effects of the androgens on the central nervous system. Suchowsky, Pegrassi, and Bonsignori (1969) reports that the fighting behavior of isolated male mice can be completely blocked by estradiol, and that pregnane derivatives appear to have a more prolonged effect on the inhibition of this particular aggression syndrome. It is, of course, a long way from mouse to man, and there is very little evidence that the female hormones can be used to inhibit human hostility. There are, however, some case studies to indicate that such an approach may be feasible. Sands (1954), has used stilboestrol to promote the control of aggressive tendencies in adolescents and young adults, and Dunn (1941) reports the effective use of the same preparation with an intractable prisoner.

The hormonal control of feelings of irritability and hostility has also been accomplished in women manifesting these symptoms during the premenstrual period. These women can be made less prone to hostility by the administration of progesterone (Dalton 1964; Greene and Dalton 1953).

Pharmacotherapy and Hostility Inhibition

The complexity of the problem of the physiological control of hostility is well illustrated by the attempts to use drugs for that purpose. A single pharmacological agent may dramatically reduce the hostile tendencies of one individual; it may just as dramatically increase the expressions of aggression by a second individual; and it may have no effect on these tendencies in a third. Kalina (1962), for example, has quite successfully used diazepam to eliminate the destructive rampages of psychotic criminals. However, DiMascio, Shader, and Harmatz (1969), report that the same drug may result in assaultive and destructive behavior. Previously quiet patients were seen to break up office furniture shortly after being placed on the drug. DiMascio, Shader, and Harmatz also refer to cases of violence and even murder presumed to result from the "paradoxical rage reaction" induced by the ingestion of this "antihostility" compound.

The above finding is not surprising when one recognizes that there are a number of different kinds of aggressive behavior and that each of them has a different physiological basis. Similar effects have been reported in animal studies. In an excellent review article by Valzelli (1967), a table is presented which shows the effects of eighty compounds on aggressive behavior in different species. These results indicate that some drugs block one kind of aggression and facilitate another within the same species, and that a given drug may inhibit aggression in one species but facilitate it in another. Further, there are wide individual differences in the susceptibility to the taming effects of various drugs.

In man, the problem of predicting which drug will be effective in the inhibition of hostility in a given individual is an even more difficult problem. Aggressive behavior has many causes and can result from a variety of neural and endocrine dysfunctions. There are not, as yet, good diagnostic tests that permit a rational pharmacotherapeutic approach to hostility control. However, in spite of this lack of perfect predictability in the matching of a particular drug to a particular patient, there are now a large number of substances which are useful in the management of aggression. It is already possible to reduce or eliminate much of the irrational, nonadaptive hostility found in psychotic, neurotic, and in ostensibly normal individuals.

Space does not permit a review of the extensive literature on the use of drugs in the control of aggression, but some examples can be cited. All of the phenothiazines appear to have some hostility-control effects over and above their purely sedative actions, although this is not true for all patients (Ban 1969; Goodman and Gilman 1966). Perphenazine and thioridazine are particularly useful in this respect. The former has reduced the level of aggressiveness in depressed patients (Pennington 1964), mental defectives (Mises and Beauchesne 1963), sex criminals (Buki 1964), and hostile alcoholics (Bartholomew 1963). Thioridazine has been useful for the control of epileptic psychotics (Wolpowitz 1966), disturbed adolescents (Rosenberg 1966), and hyperkinetic children (Alderton and Hoddinott 1964).

Sodium diphenylhydantoin has improved the behavior of children with severe temper tantrums (Zimmerman 1956). It has reduced the anger, irritability, and tension of private psychiatric patients (Turner 1967), and has made both prisoners and juvenile delinquents more tractable (Resnick 1967).

Hyperactive children have particular difficulty with aggressive impulse control, and a number of drugs have now been shown to reduce this symptom without sedation. They include the amphetamines (Heath and Buddington 1967), benadryl (Fish 1960), and haloperidol (Barker and Fraser 1968).

Finally, in spite of the fact that some of the minor tranquilizers such as chlordiazepoxide and diazepam do occasionally produce the paradoxical rage reactions mentioned above, they are valuable hostility-control agents for many patients (De Craene 1964; Denham 1963).

Another class of minor tranquilizers including meprobamate and tybamate also appear to be effective in reducing general irritability, as well as the aggressive symptoms associated with premenstrual tension (Ban 1969).

Some Limitations

Considering the evidence presented so far, there can be no doubt that it is possible to control a number of different kinds of aggressive behavior through physiological manipulations. However, it should be emphasized that all aggression is not subject to that type of control. Some destructive, criminal, and antisocial behavior is not derived from feelings of anger and hostility. It is learned just as courtesy and table manners are learned. There is a vast literature on the influence of learning on the aggressive-behavior patterns. In chapter 5, Berkowitz, deals with many of the mechanisms involved. This is the major emphasis in *Violent Men* by Hans Toch (1969) and in *The Subculture of Violence* by Wolfgang and Ferracuti (1967). There can, of course, be no doubt that individuals learn to do what is expected of them and that there are many subcultures in our society and in the world in which some forms of violence are expected. Claude Brown (1965) expresses this with literary impact in *Manchild in the Promised Land.*

> I was growing up now, and people were going to expect things from me. I would soon be expected to kill a nigger if he mistreated me, like Rock, Bubba Williams, and Dewdrop had.
>
> Everybody knew these cats were killers. Nobody messed with them. If anybody messed with them or their family or friends, they had to kill them. I knew now that I had to keep my respect in the neighborhood. I had to keep my respect because I had to take care of Pimp and Carole and Margie. I was the big brother in the family. I couldn't be running and getting somebody after some cat who messed with me. [P. 126].

These hostile tendencies have been referred to earlier as instrumental aggression: aggression in which the individual engages because it is, in one way or another, rewarded. The physiological basis of instrumental aggression is diffuse and not localized in particular brain structures. Its neurological basis is the same as that for other habit patterns. At the current level of sophistication in the biological sciences, it is not possible to alter specific habit patterns physiologically, and there is no evidence that such tendencies are even on the distant horizon. Hostile feelings can be "cured" but hostile habits must be replaced by other habits.

Summary

A physiological model of aggressive behavior is presented in which it is suggested that there are different kinds of aggression. Aggressive behavior directed toward particular stimuli results when certain innate neurological systems in the brain are active. The sensitivity of these neurological systems and the ease with which they can be activated is a function of the interactions of a number of different variables, including inhibitory neural systems, facilitating neural systems, and certain blood constituents. All of these mechanisms interact with behavior components, which are learned.

The implications of this model for the control of aggression are considered and evidence is presented to demonstrate that hostile behavior can be physiologically inhibited by several methods. The neural systems for aggression can be surgically interrupted, with the result that the individual loses his hostile tendencies. Those neural systems which suppress the aggression systems can be directly activated through implanted electrodes, with the result that feelings of hostility are replaced with more positive affect. Finally, the neural systems for aggression can be desensitized by altering the blood chemistry, either through endocrine manipulations or by pharmacotherapy using drugs that function as relatively specific antihostility agents.

References

Alderton, H., and Hoddinott, B. A. "A Controlled Study of the Use of Thioridazine in the Treatment of Hyperactive and Aggressive Children in a Children's Psychiatric Hospital." *Canadian Psychiatric Association Journal* 9 (1964): 239–47.

Augenstein, L. *Come, Let Us Play God.* New York: Harper & Row, 1969.

Bailey, P. "Discussion." In *Temporal Lobe Epilepsy,* edited by M. Baldwin and P. Bailey, p. 551. Springfield, Ill.: Charles C. Thomas, 1958.

Ban, T. A. *Psychopharmacology.* Baltimore: Williams & Wilkins, 1969.

Barker, P., and Fraser, I. A. "A Controlled Trial of Haloperidol in Children." *British Journal of Psychiatry* 114 (1968): 855–57.

Barnett, S. A. *A Study in Behavior.* London: Metheun & Co., 1963.

Bartholomew, A. A. "Perphenazine (Trilafon) in the Immediate Management of Acutely Disturbed Chronic Alcoholics." *Medical Journal of Australia* 1 (1963): 812–14.

Beeman, E. A. "The Effect of Male Hormone on Aggressive Behavior in Mice." *Physiological Zoology* 20 (1947): 373–405.

Bernstein, H., and Moyer, K. E. "Aggressive Behavior in the Rat: Effects of Isolation and Olfactory Bulb Lesions." *Brain Research* 20 (1970): 75–84.

Boelkins, C. R., and Heiser, J. F. "Biological Bases of Aggression." In *Violence and the Struggle for Existence,* edited by D. N. Daniels, M. F. Gilula, and F. M. Ochberg. Boston: Little, Brown & Co. 1970.

Bremer, J. *Asexualization.* New York: Macmillan Co., 1959.

Brown, C. *Manchild in the Promised Land.* New York: Macmillan Co., 1965.

Brown, J. L., and Hunsperger, R. W. "Neuroethology and the Motivation of Agonistic Behaviour." *Animal Behavior* 11 (1963): 439–48.

Buki, R. A. "The Use of Psychotropic Drugs in the Rehabilitation of Sex-deviated Criminals." *American Journal of Psychiatry* 120 (1964): 1170–75.

Butter, C. M.; Snyder, D. R.: and MacDonald, J. A. "Effects of Orbital Frontal Lesions on Aversive and Aggressive Behaviors in Rhesus Monkeys." *Journal of Comparative and Physiological Psychology* 72 (1970): 132–44.

Chi, C. C., and Flynn, J. P. "Neural Pathways Associated with Hypothalamically Elicited Attack Behavior in Cats." *Science* 171 (1971): 703–5.

Cleghorn, R. A. "Steroid Hormones in Relation to Neuropsychiatric Disorders. In *Hormones, Brain Function and Behavior,* edited by H. Hoagland. New York: Academic Press, 1957.

Collias, N. E. "Aggressive Behavior among Vertebrate Animals." *Physiological Zoology* 17 (1944): 83–123.

Dalton, K. *The Premenstrual Syndrome.* Springfield, Ill.: Charles C. Thomas, 1964.

Davidson, J. M., and Bloch, G. J. "Neuroendocrine Aspects of Male Reproduction." *Biology of Reproduction Supplement* 1 (1969): 76–92.

De Craene, O. "Nervoses et therapeutique tranquillisante." *Scalpel* 117 (1964): 1044–50.

Delgado, J. M. R. "Emotional Behavior in Animals and Humans." *Psychiatric Research Reports* 12 (1960): 259–71.

——. "Cerebral Heterostimulation in a Monkey Colony." *Science* 141 (1963): 161–63.

——. *Evolution of Physical Control of the Brain*. New York: American Museum of Natural History, 1965.

——. "Brain Research and Behavioral Activity." *Endeavour* 26 (1967): 149–54.

——. "Aggression in Free Monkeys Modified by Electrical and Chemical Stimulation of the Brain." Paper presented at the Symposium on Aggression, Interdepartmental Institute for Training in Research in the Behavioral and Neurologic Sciences, Albert Einstein College of Medicine, New York, June 5, 1969.

Denham, J. "Psychotherapy of Obsessional Neurosis Assisted by Librium: Topical Problems of Psychotherapy." *Supplementum ad acta Psychotherapeutica et Psychosomatica* 4 (1963): 195–98.

DiMascio, A.; Shader, R. I.; and Harmatz, J. "Psychotropic Drugs and Induced Hostility." *Psychosomatics* 10 (1969): 27–28.

Dunn, G. W. "Stilbesterol Induced Testicular Degeneration in Hypersexual Males." *Journal of Clinical Endocrinology* 1 (1941): 643–48.

Edwards, D. A. "Effects of Cyproterone Acetate on Aggressive Behaviour and the Seminal Vesicles of Male Mice." *Journal of Endocrinology* 46 (1970): 477–81.

Egger, M. D., and Flynn, J. P. "Effect of Electrical Stimulation of the Amygdala on Hypothalamically Elicited Attack Behavior in Cats." *Journal of Neurophysiology* 26 (1963): 705–20.

Ehrlich, P. R. *The Population Bomb*. New York: Ballantine Books, 1968.

Eibl-Eibesfeldt, I. "The Fighting Behavior of Animals." *Scientific American* 205 (1961): 112–22.

Ervin, F. R.; Mark, V. H.; and Stevens, J. "Behavioral and Affective Responses to Brain Stimulation in Man." In *Neurobiological Aspects of Psychopathology*, edited by J. Zubin and C. Shagass, pp. 54–65. New York: Grune & Stratton, 1969.

Falconer, M. A.; Hill, D.; Meyer, A.; and Wilson, J. L. Clinical, Radiological, and EEG Correlations with Pathological Changes in Temporal Lobe Epilepsy and Their Significance in Surgical Treatment." In *Temporal Lobe Epilepsy*, edited by M. Baldwin and P. Bailey, pp. 396–410. Springfield, Ill.: Charles C. Thomas, 1958.

Fish, B. "Drug Therapy in Child Psychiatry: Pharmacological Aspects." *Comparative Psychiatry* 1 (1960): 212–27.

Flynn, J.; Vanegas, H.; Foote, W.; and Edwards, S. Neural Mechanisms Involved in a Cat's Attack on a Rat. In *The Neural Control of Behavior*, edited by R. Whalen, R. F. Thompson, M. Verzeano, and N. Weinberger. New York: Academic Press, 1970.

Gibson, J. G. "Emotions and the Thyroid Gland." *Journal of Psychosomatic Research* 6 (1962): 93–116.

Glees, P.; Cole, J.; Whitty, C.; and Cairns, H. "The Effects of Lesions in the Cingular Gyrus and Adjacent Areas in Monkeys." *Journal of Neurology, Neurosurgery and Psychiatry* 13 (1950): 178–90.

Goodman, L. S., and Gilman, A. *The Pharmacological Basis of Therapeutics.* New York: Macmillan Co., 1966.

Graham, F. P. "A Contemporary History of American Crime." In *Violence in America: Historical and Comparative Perspectives*, edited by H. D. Graham and T. R. Gurr, pp. 371–85. Vol. 2. A Report to the National Commission on the Causes and Prevention of Violence. Washington D.C.: U.S. Government Printing Office, 1969.

Greene, R., and Dalton, K. "The Premenstrual Syndrome." *British Medical Journal* 1 (1953): 1007–14.

Hamburg, D. A.; Moos, R. H.; and Yalom, I. D. "Studies of Distress in the Menstrual Cycle and the Postpartum Period." In *Endocrinology and Human Behaviour*, edited by R. P. Michael. London: Oxford University Press, 1968.

Hawke, C. C. "Castration and Sex Crimes." *American Journal of Mental Deficiency* 55 (1950): 220–26.

Heath, R. G. "Behavioral Changes Following Destructive Lesions in the Subcortical Structure of the Forebrain in Cats." In *Studies in Schizophrenia*, edited by R. G. Heath et al., pp. 83–84. Cambridge, Mass.: Harvard University Press, 1954.

——. "Electrical Self-Stimulation of the Brain in Man." *American Journal of Psychiatry* 120 (1963): 571–77.

Heath, R. G., and Buddington, W. "Drugs for Stimulation of Mental and Physical Activity in *Drugs of Choice, 1968–1969,* edited by W. Modell. Saint Louis: Mosley, 1967.

Heimburger, R. F.; Whitlock, C. C.; and Kalsbeck, J. E. "Stereotaxic Amygdalotomy for Epilepsy with Aggressive Behavior." *Journal of the American Medical Association* 198 (1966): 165–69.

Hinde, R. A. "The Nature of Aggression." *New Society* 9 (1967): 302–4.

Hutchinson, R. R., and Renfrew, J. W. "Stalking Attack and Eating Behavior Elicited from the Same Sites in the Hypothalamus." *Journal of Comparative and Physiological Psychology* 61 (1966): 300–367.

Janowsky, E. S.; Gorney, R.; and Mandell, A. J. "The Menstrual Cycle: Psychiatric and Ovarian-adrenocortcal Hormone Correlates: Case Study and Literature Review." *Archives of General Psychiatry* 17 (1967): 459–69.

Kaada, B. "Brain Mechanisms Related to Aggressive Behavior." In *Aggression and Defense: Neural Mechanisms and Social Patterns*, edited by C. D. Clements and D. B. Lindsley, pp. 95–134. Vol. 5, *Brain Function*. Los Angeles: University of California Press, 1967.

Kalina, R. K. "Use of Diazepam in the Violent Psychotic Patient: A Preliminary Report." *Colorado GP* 4 (1962): 11–14.

Karli, P.; Vergnes, M.; and Didiergeorges, F. "Rat-Mouse Interspecific Aggressive Behaviour and Its Manipulation by Brain Ablation and by Brain Stimulation." In *Aggressive Behaviour*, edited by S. Garattini and E. G. Sigg, pp. 47–55. New York: Wiley, 1969.

Kennard, M. A. "The Cingulate Gyrus in Relation to Consciousness." *Journal of Nervous and Mental Disease* 121 (1955): 34–39.

King, H. E. "Psychological Effects of Excitation in the Limbic System." In *Electrical Stimulation of the Brain*, edited by D. E. Sheer, pp. 477–86. Austin: University of Texas Press, 1961.

King, J. A. "Maternal Behavior in Peromyscus." In *Maternal Behavior in Mammals*, edited by H. L. Rheingold, pp. 58–93. New York: John Wiley & Sons, 1963.

Kluver, H., and Bucy, P. C. "Psychic Blindness and Other Symptoms Following Bilateral Temporal Lobectomy in Rhesus Monkeys." *American Journal of Physiology* 119 (1937): 352–53.

——. "An Analysis of Certain Effects of Bilateral Temporal Lobectomy in the Rhesus Monkey, with Special Reference to Psychic Blindness." *Journal of Psychology* 5 (1938): 33–54.

——. "Preliminary Analysis of Functions of the Temporal Lobes in Monkeys." *Archives of Neurology and Psychiatry* 42 (1939): 979–1000.

LeBeau, J. "The Cingular and Precingular Areas in Psychosurgery (Agitated Behaviour, Obsessive Compulsive States, Epilepsy)." *Acta Psychiatrica et Neuroligica* (Copenhagen) 27 (1952): 305–16.

LeMaire, L. "Danish Experience Regarding the Castration of Sexual Offenders." *Journal of Criminal Law and Criminology* 47 (1956): 294–310.

Lerner, L. J.; Bianchi, A.; and Borman, A. "A-Norprogesterone an Androgen Antagonist." *Proceedings of the Society for Experimental Biology and Medicine* 103 (1960): 172–75.

Liddell, D. W. "Observation on Epileptic Automatism in a Mental Hospital Population." *Journal of Mental Science* 99 (1953): 731–48.

Lorenz, K. *On Aggression*. New York: Harcourt, Brace & World, 1966.

Mark, V. H., and Ervin, F. R. *Violence and the Brain*. New York: Harper & Row, 1970.

Mark, V. H.; Ervin, F. R.; Sweet, W. H.; and Delgado, J. "Remote Telemeter Stimulation and Recording from Implanted Temporal Lobe Electrodes." *Confina Neurologica* 31 (1969): 86–93.

Mises, R., and Beauchesne, H. "Essai de la perphénazine chez l'enfant, et l' adolescent." *Annales medico psychologiques* 2 (1963): 89–92.

Moyer, K. E. "Kinds of Aggression and Their Physiological Basis." *Communications in Behavioral Biology* 2 (1968): 65–87.

——. "Internal Impulses to Aggression." *Transactions for the New York Academy of Sciences* 31 (1969): 104–14.

——. *The Physiology of Hostility.* Chicago: Markham, 1971.

——. *The Psychobiology of Aggression.* New York: Harper & Row, forthcoming.

Narabayashi, H.; Nagao, T.; Saito, Y.; Yoshida, M.; and Nagahata, M. "Stereotaxic Amygdalotomy for Behavior Disorders." *Archives of Neurology* 9 (1963): 1–16.

Narabayashi, H., and Uno, M. "Long Range Results of Stereotaxic Amygdalotomy for Behavior Disorders." *2nd International. Symposium Stereoencephalotomy, Confina Neurologica* 27 (1966): 168–71.

National Commission on the Causes and Prevention of Violence. *To Establish Justice, to Insure Domestic Tranquility, Final Report.* Washington D.C.: Government Printing Office, 1969.

Neumann, F.; Elger, W.; and Von Berswordt-Wallrabe, R. "Intersexuality of Male Foetuses and Inhibition of Androgenic Functions in Adult Animals with a Testosterone Blocker." *German Medical Monthly* 12 (1967): 1–17.

Neumann, F.; Von Berswordt-Wallrabe, R.; Elger, W.; and Steinbeck, H. "Activities of Antiandrogens: Experiments in Prepuberal and Puberal Animals and in Foetuses." In *Testosterone: Proceedings of the Work Shop Conference, April 20–22, 1967, Tremsbuettel,* edited by J. Tamm, pp. 134–43. Stuttgart: Georg Thieme Verlag, 1968.

Newton, G. D., and Zimring, F. E. *Firearms and Violence in American Life.* Washington D.C.: National Commission on the Causes and Prevention of Violence, 1970.

Pennington, V. M. "The Phrenotropic Action of Perphenazine Amytriptyline". *American Journal of Psychiatry* 120 (1964): 1115–16.

Resnick, O. "The Psychoactive Properties of Diphenlylhydantoin: Experiences with Prisoners and Juvenile Delinquents." *International Journal of Neuropsychiatry* suppl. 2,3 (1967): S20–S47.

Richardson, L. F. *Statistics of Deadly Quarrels.* Pittsburgh: Boxwood, 1960.

Roberts, W. W., and Kiess, H. O. "Motivational Properties of Hypothalamic Aggression in Cats." *Journal of Comparative and Physiological Psychology* 58 (1964): 187–93.

Robinson, B. W.; Alexander, M.; and Bowne, G. "Dominance Reversal Resulting from Aggressive Responses Evoked by Brain Telestimulation." *Physiology and Behavior* 4 (1969): 749–52.

Rocky, S., and Neri, R. O. "Comparative Biological Properties of SCH 12600 (6-chloro 4,6 pregnadien 16-methylene 17-α-ol-3,20-

dione-17-acetate) and Chlormadinone Acetate." *Federation Proceedings* 27 (1968): 624.

Rosenberg, P. H. "Management of Disturbed Adolescents." *Diseases of the Nervous System* 27 (1966): 60–61.

Rosvold, H. S.; Mirsky, A. F.; and Pribram, K. H. "Influences of Amygdalectomy on Social Behavior in Monkeys." *Journal of Comparative and Physiological Psychology* 47 (1954): 173–78.

Sands, D. E. "Further Studies on Endocrine Treatment in Adolescence and Early Adult Life." *Journal of Mental Science* 100 (1954): 211–19.

Sano, K. "Sedative Neurosurgery: With Special Reference to Posteromedial Hypothalamotomy." *Neurologia Medico Chirrurgica* 4 (1962): 112–42.

——. "Sedative Stereoencephalotomy; Fornicotomy, Upper Mesencephalic Reticulotomy and Posteromedial Hypothalamotomy." *Progress in Brain Research.* Vol. 21B, pt. B, *Correlative Neuroscience: Clinical Studies.* Amsterdam: Elseiver, 1966.

Sawa, M.; Ueki, Y.; Arita, M.; and Harada, T. "Preliminary Report on the Amygdaloidectomy on the Psychotic Patients, with Interpretation of Oral-emotional Manifestation in Schizophrenics." *Folia Psychiatrican et Neurologica Japonica* 7 (1954): 309–29.

Schreiner, L., and Kling, A. "Behavioral Changes Following Rhinencephalic Injury in Cat." *Journal of Neurophysiology* 16 (1953): 643–58.

——. "Rhinencephalon and Behavior." *American Journal of Physiology* 184 (1956): 486–90.

Schwab, R. S.; Sweet, W. H.; Mark, V. H.; Kjellberg, R. N.; and Ervin, F. R. "Treatment of Intractable Temporal Lobe Epilepsy by Stereotactic Amygdala Lesions." *Transactions of the American Neurological Association,* 90 (1965): 12–19.

Scott, J. P. "Hostility and Aggression in Animals." In *Roots of Behavior,* edited by E. L. Bliss. New York: Harper & Row, 1962.

Scott, J. P., and Fredericson, E. "The Causes of Fighting in Mice and Rats." *Physiological Zoology* 24 (1951): 273–309.

Sem-Jacobsen, C. W. "Depth-electrographic Observations Related to Parkinson's Disease." *Journal of Neurosurgery* 24 (1966): 388–402.

Sem-Jacobsen, C. W., and Torkildsen, A. "Depth Recording and Electrical Stimulation in the Human Brain." In *Electrical Studies on the Unanesthetized Brain,* edited by E. R. Ramey and D. S. O'Doherty, pp. 275–90. New York: Hoeber, 1960.

Seward, J. P. "Aggressive Behavior in the Rat. I. General characteristics; age and sex differences." *Journal of Comparative Psychology* 38 (1945): 175–97.

Sigg, E. B. "Relationship of Aggressive Behaviour to Adrenal and Gonadal Function in Male Mice." In *Aggressive Behaviour,* edited by S. Garattini and E. B. Sigg, pp. 143–49. New York: John Wiley & Sons, 1969.

Spiegel, E. A., and Wycis, H. T. "Physiological and Psychological Results of Thalamotomy." *Proceedings of the Royal Society, Medical Supplement* 42 (1949): 84–93.

Spiegel, E. A.; Wycis, H. T.; Freed, H.; and Orchinik, C. "The Central Mechanism of the Emotions." *American Journal of Psychiatry* 108 (1951): 426–32.

Storr, A. *Human Aggression.* New York: Atheneum, 1968.

Suchowsky, G. K.; Pegrassi, L.; and Bonsignori. "The Effect of Steroids on Aggressive Behaviour in Isolated Male Mice." In *Aggressive Behaviour,* edited by S. Garattini and E. B. Sigg, pp. 164–71. New York: John Wiley & Sons, 1969.

Summers, T. B., and Kaelber, W. W. "Amygdalectomy: Effects in Cats and a Survey of Its Present Status." *American Journal of Physiology* 203 (1962): 1117–19.

Sweet, W. H.; Ervin, F.; and Mark, V. H. "The Relationship of Violent Behaviour to Focal Cerebral Disease." In *Aggressive Behaviour,* edited by S. Garattini and E. G. Sigg, pp. 336–52. New York: John Wiley & Sons, 1969.

Taylor, G. R. *The Biological Time Bomb.* New York: New American Library, 1968.

Terzian, H., and Ore, G. D. "Syndrome of Kluver and Bucy Reproduced in Man by Bilateral Removal of the Temporal Lobes." *Neurology* 5 (1955): 378–80.

Tinbergen, N. "Fighting and Threat in Animals." *New Biology* 14 (1953): 9–24.

Toch, H. *Violent Men.* Chicago: Aldine Publishing Co., 1969.

Tow, P. M., and Whitty, C. W. "Personality Changes after Operations on the Cingulate Gyrus in Man." *Journal of Neurology, Neurosurgery and Psychiatry* 16 (1953): 186–93.

Turner, W. J. "The Usefulness of Diphenylhydantoin in Treatment of Non-epileptic Emotional Disorders." *International Journal of Neuropsychiatry* 3, suppl. 2 (1967): S8–S20.

Urich, J. "The Social Hierarchy in Albino Mice." *Journal of Comparative Psychology* 25(1938): 373–413.

Valzelli, L. "Drugs and Aggressiveness." *Advances in Pharmacology* 5 (1967): 79–108.

Ward, A. A. "The Cingular Gyrus: Area 24." *Journal of Neurophysiology* 11 (1948): 13–23.

Wasman, M., and Flynn, J. P. "Directed Attack Elicited from Hypothalamus." *Archives of Neurology* 6 (1962): 220–27.

Wheatley, M. D. "The Hypothalamus and Affective Behavior in Cats." *Archives of Neurology and Psychiatry* 52 (1944): 296–316.

Wolfgang, M. E., and Ferracuti, F. *The Subculture of Violence.* London: Tavistock, 1967.

Wolpowitz, E. "The Use of Thioridazine (Mellaril) in Cases of Epileptic Psychosis." *South African Medical Journal* 40 (1966): 143–44.

Wood, C. D. "Behavioral Changes Following Discrete Lesions of Temporal Lobe Structures." *Neurology* 8, suppl. (1958): 215–20.
Woods, J. E. " 'Taming' of the Wild Norway Rat by Rhinencephalic Lesions." *Nature* 178 (1956): 869.
Woringer, E.; Thomalske, G.; and Klinger, J. "Les rapports anatomiques du noyau amygdalien et la technique de son extirpation neurochirurgicale." *Review neurologique* 89 (1953): 553–60.
Zimmerman, F. T. "Explosive Behavior Anomalies in Children of an Epileptic Basis." *New York State Journal of Medicine* 56 (1956): 2537–43.

Victor H. Denenberg received his bachelor's degree from Bucknell University and his Ph.D. in experimental psychology from Purdue University. After receiving his Ph.D., he remained on the faculty at Purdue until becoming professor of biobehavioral sciences and psychology at the University of Connecticut in 1969. In addition, his experiences include a research associate position with the Human Resources Research Office, a year at the Subdepartment of Animal Behaviour, Cambridge University, and a Carnegie fellow and visiting investigator at the Roscoe D. Jackson Memorial Laboratory. He was president of the International Society of Developmental Psychobiology in 1970. Professor Denenberg's research has assessed the effects of early experience, maternal behavior, hormones and behavior, and the ontogeny of behavior.

2

Developmental Factors in Aggression

VICTOR H. DENENBERG

A number of studies investigating early developmental determinants of aggression in the mouse and the rat have been carried out since 1963 at our laboratories at Purdue University and at the University of Connecticut. When we began this research we were not interested in the analysis of aggression per se: instead, we were manipulating early social variables in the mice. Since fighting is one of the species-specific characteristics of the mouse, it seemed appropriate to use aggression as one of our endpoints. In other words, our major interest was upon early social experiences rather than upon aggression. However, our initial studies produced such exciting findings that we began a program of research concentrating upon developmental determinants of aggression.

Unfortunately, a synthesis of our findings cannot be presented in a coherent framework. Such an approach would probably not be realistic; because our data, as well as that of many others, strongly indicate that aggression is determined by multiple factors and that no single "theory" of aggression will be sufficient to incorporate the many diverse phenomena extant in the literature. Instead, what these studies will show is that even within an animal's early developmental history there is evidence for at least three or four different mechanisms that may act to influence ag-

This research was supported in part by research grant GB 27511X from the National Science Foundation.

gressive behavior. One may argue that there may be some final common pathway underlying each of the sets of studies; in theory one might hope to find a single set of mechanisms that would allow us to integrate much of what we know about aggression during early development. However, that is doubtful: we know that the various procedures we use have different effects at different times in early development, and it is hard to conceive of a single mechanism that would be independent of the temporal dimension.

The Measurement of Aggression

When we investigate aggression in animals we are working with an ethologically meaningful variable, that is, a variable that is species specific, is rooted in the evolutionary history of the species, and has adaptive value in enabling an animal to survive and, therefore, to pass on its genes. In short, aggression is a natural behavior for any animal species.

One of the very great advantages of working with natural behavioral units is that we are in a better position to make cross-species comparisons and generalizations than when we work with the more complex behavioral units usually studied by psychologists. Consider, for example, measures of learning and motivation. Aside from the serious question concerning the philosophical and conceptual basis of such comparisons (Lockhard 1971), it is tremendously difficult, if not impossible, to do comparative studies in the areas of learning and motivation because of our inability to equate units of measurement. These problems are minimized when we work with species-specific behaviors. For example, while the particular behavior patterns may differ grossly from one species to another, all of us can agree on what we mean by aggressive behavior, although this may include such diverse events as interspecific predator-prey aggression and intraspecific dominance fights. The critical thing in aggression is the function of the act rather than its form, and by knowing the behavior of the species in question we are able to identify that function.

In addition to the greater ease of doing a comparative analysis across species, we are also in a far better position to look at underlying physiological mechanisms. For example, the male hormone, testosterone, is one of the critical endogenous chemicals that act to influence an animal's aggressive behavior. At another level, odors, or pheromones, may also have a profound effect upon exciting or inhibiting aggressive behavior.

Thus, by using a behavior that occurs naturally in a species, we are on better philosophical and logical grounds for making cross-species comparisons, both at the behavioral and biological levels. This may be called the comparative *ethology* of aggression, in contrast with the comparative *psychology* of aggression.

To refer to the comparative ethology or psychology of aggression is to consider in particular the measurement procedure. When aggression is studied in an ethological context the experimenter intervenes as little as possible in the behavior of the species. Obviously, when animals are studied in the wild there is essentially no intervention. When we turn to laboratory animals, however, there is, by definition, experimental involvement. Nevertheless, this can be minimized so that the animals under investigation have an opportunity to exhibit their natural behavior, often called "spontaneous" behavior. For example, to study aggression in the mouse all that is necessary is to place two strange males together. If we do this, there is a good likelihood that a "spontaneous" fight will ensue. We may increase that probability by such procedures as isolating the animals beforehand or placing one animal in another's home cage. The important thing is that the experimenter has to do virtually nothing except place two animals togetter in order for the behavior to occur. At the level of predator-prey relationship, the same principle is seen: when a cat and a mouse are placed together, there is a good likelihood that the cat will attack the mouse. In other words, when we approach the study of aggression from a naturalistic point of view, as experimenters we try to set conditions so as to give the animal's biological behavior the opportunity to express itself.

This method contrasts sharply with the one employed by those interested in the comparative psychology of aggression, in which artificially contrived laboratory procedures are used to induce aggressive behavior—for example, aggression induced in rats by electrical shock to the feet or induced when two animals are forced to compete for one pellet of food. These situations bear little resemblance to an animal's experiences in its natural setting. Thus, the very serious question is raised as to the meaning (i.e., validity) of such measurement procedures, as well as to their degree of generality within a species or among species.

I do not maintain that artificially contrived procedures are without value, but that those individuals who employ such psychological measures of aggression have the scientific responsibility of demonstrating that their measurement procedures provide information about aggressive behavior in animals in a natural setting. Because the procedure induces attack is not sufficient justification for labeling the response "aggression." That would be analogous to proclaiming that a particular test item is indeed a measure of "intelligence" because it requires verbal understanding and some mathematical reasoning to solve the problem. In both instances the frame of reference is that of the experimenter, not the animal. We have to view our measurement procedures from the animal's vantage point, not our own, if we hope to make progress in the study of aggressive behavior. Research with animals should make much greater strides toward an understanding of aggression when we use natural units of behavior in our studies. This position might be modified when those persons who use artificially contrived laboratory procedures to induce aggression can demonstrate the validity of their procedures in providing a better understanding of naturally occurring aggressive behavior.

These various considerations led us to choose behavioral endpoints in which we interfered minimally with our animals: intraspecific fighting in the mouse brought about when mice are allowed to interact with each other after a brief period of isolation, mouse killing by rats when the two species are placed together, and killing of rat pups by adult male rats when they are placed together. In each instance, the role of the experimenter is limited to placing the animals in physical contiguity with each other. Other than that we do nothing. Whether one animal "chooses" to attack another or to kill another is not a function of experimentally manipulated external events, but instead, is presumably a function of endogenous processes which have an important biological foundation. Anchoring behavioral measurements in the animal's biology is a more powerful approach to the understanding of aggressive behavior.

Turning now to our research studies, I will describe (1) a set of experiments investigating the effects of various peer-group combinations in the mouse during early development upon subsequent mouse-mouse aggression; (2) studies in which intraspecific fighting was reduced by manipulating the maternal variable with mice; (3) research in which early social interaction between the rat and the mouse modified the rat's mouse-killing response in adulthood; and (4) experiments investigating the adult male rat's response of killing baby rat pups, showing how this is modified by early hormonal manipulations.

Effects of Early Peer-Group Interactions upon Later Aggression in the Mouse

A number of studies have been completed in which we investigated the effects of early social experience in the mouse upon the animal's later aggressive behavior (Denenberg, Hudgens, and Zarrow 1964, 1966; Hudgens, Denenberg, and Zarrow 1967, 1968; Paschke, Denenberg, and Zarrow 1971). Our main interest in these experiments was in manipulating the maternal variable, but in several of these studies we also manipulated the kinds of peers with which the young mouse associated both before and after weaning. Before weaning mice were raised either in litters or in isolation. After weaning they were either segregated in cages with other mice, reared in isolation, or placed together with rats. When adult, the males were tested for fighting behavior.

To study fighting we take two adult mice and place them in a box measuring 11.75 by 15 by 16.25 inches, which is divided into two equal-sized compartments by means of a removable plywood guillotine door. There are wood shavings on the floor, and each compartment is covered by a fiber-glass top having externally refillable food and water supplies. Each mouse is placed in a separate compartment, where he remains alone for several days. After this, testing begins by removing the partition between compartments, thus allowing the animals to interact with each other. This interaction continues for a six-minute interval unless a fight occurs, in which case the session is terminated five seconds after the fight starts. The animals are then separated into their individual compartments and the partition is restored. This procedure is continued for seven days. The presence or absence of fighting is recorded for each testing session.

In these experiments two animals from different litters but with the same experiential history are given the opportunity to fight each other. Table 2.1 is a pooled summary of the fighting statistics from five experiments in which the C57BL/10J mouse was used.

Two things stand out from an examination of table 1. First, the absence of peer-group interaction between birth and weaning leads to a significant increase in adult aggression, regardless of the nature of the postweaning peer-group interaction. Second, the presence of same-species peers after weaning results in enhanced aggression in adulthood, regardless of the social experience the mice had before weaning. Interestingly, being reared with rats as social cage mates did not have any major effect upon the animal's aggressive behavior against other mice, as compared with being reared in isolation. The key variable was the presence or absence of conspecific cage mates.

TABLE 2.1 *Incidence of fighting among C57BL/10J mice as a function of different preweaning and postweaning peer-group combinations*

	Postweaning Peers		
Preweaning Peers	*mice*	*none*	*rats*
Mice	45%	0%	13%
	(96)	(17)	(30)
None	78%	46%	31%
	(18)	(24)	(16)

NOTE: Figures in parentheses = *N*.

SOURCES: Denenberg, Hudgens, and Zarrow (1964, 1966); Hudgens, Denenberg, and Zarrow (1967, 1968); Paschke, Denenberg, and Zarrow (1971); see text for explanation of data.

Therefore, even in an animal that fights spontaneously, there can be considerable variability in aggression as a function of the particular social-peer combinations during early life. An even greater effect was produced by the maternal variable.

Effects of the Mother upon Aggression

As indicated above, the variable of major interest in our studies on aggression in the mouse was the maternal variable. We manipulate this variable by having the neonatal mouse reared either *(a)* by a mouse mother which may be his natural mother or a foster mother or *(b)* by a lactating rat. Although it belongs to a different species, the rat is also a rodent, and its maternal behavior is similar enough to that of the mouse to insure that the newborn mouse is maintained and properly cared for.

The real importance of fostering mice to rats is that this is an experimental procedure that allows us to investigate the effects of the postnatal maternal environment independent of the animal's genetic and prenatal determinants. In nature, the genetic, prenatal, and postnatal variables are all thoroughly confounded, and thus it is not possible, when examining an adult behavior pattern, to determine the relative contributions from these different potential sources of variance. However, this confounding is nullified by having the mouse reared by a rat mother. If we find that such an animal behaves quite differently from control mice, we may then conclude that the postnatal maternal environment is a significant determinant of the animal's subsequent behavior. That is exactly what we have found in our studies. These data have recently been reviewed rather extensively (Denenberg 1970), here, I will go over part of these data more briefly, restricting myself to a comparison of the effects of the rat mother with those of the mouse mother. In some of these experiments we also manipulated various peer-group combinations, but most of those data have been dealt with in the section above.

In all of our studies our control group consists of mice reared by a mouse mother, with mouse peers present before and after weaning except when the animal is placed in isolation prior to aggression testing. In our first study (Denenberg, Hudgens, and

Zarrow 1964) we compared control mice with mice reared by rat mothers and with rat pups as peers before and after weaning. We found that 44 percent of our control animals fought when placed in our fighting-box situation as adults (*N* = 16 pairs), while none of the twelve pairs of experimental animals fought.

We were quite surprised by this finding, because we did not think it would be that easy to turn off such an important species-specific behavior as aggression. After all, this behavior pattern is particularly critical in the evolutionary history of the species as a survival mechanism. Thus, we immediately set about to replicate the experiment with additional controls. In our first study, we had confounded the rat mother with the presence of rat peers. In our second study (Denenberg, Hudgens, and Zarrow 1966), our experimental group consisted of litters of mice fostered to a lactating rat mother who had had all her rat pups removed. Thus, both the experimental and control groups had the experience of same-species peers both before and after weaning, and the only difference between the two groups was that one was raised by a rat mother and the other by a mouse mother. In this study we found that 77 percent of our thirteen pairs of control aniamls fought, while only one of the eleven pairs of experimental animals had a fight (9 percent).

Thus we had replicated our original finding and had eliminated the peer variable at the same time. One thing we had not done was determine whether the act of fostering was critical, since in our first two studies our control mice had been reared by their natural mothers, while our experimental animals had all been fostered. Our third experiment (Hudgens, Denenburg, and Zarrow 1967), then, was in part a replication of our second study, except that we fostered litters of newborn mice either to lactating mouse mothers or to lactating rat mothers. In that experiment we found that 39 percent of our control animals fought (based upon twenty-three pairs of animals), while none of the twenty-one pairs of experimental animals fought.

The third experiment clearly established the reality of the phenomenon, that is, that species-specific aggressive behavior could be readily attenuated by varying the nature of the mother. We then performed a rather complicated factorial experiment in which we varied the nature of the mother (rat or mouse), the composition of the preweaning peer-group environment, and the kinds of postweaning peer environment (Hudgens, Denenberg, and Zarrow 1968). Part of those data have been summarized in table 1. For purposes of this presentation, the only relevant information concerns the maternal variable. Here we found that only 11 percent of our control animals fought (based upon 27 pairs). We have no way of explaining the cause of this sharp drop in fighting incidence. However, we also had two different experimental groups reared by rat mothers, one with eight pairs, and another with seven pairs. In both instances we found that no animal fought. Thus, in all four experiments we found a higher percentage of control animals fighting.

I shall digress briefly: In addition to studying aggression in these experiments, we were also investigating the open-field activity of our mice, and we routinely found that our experimental animals were less active in the field than were our controls. Our findings of reduced fighting and reduced open-field activity for our experimental animals suggested that these animals may have been less emotionally reactive. This suggested that the pituitary-adrenal axis of the experimental animals may have been modified by their maternal experiences. Thus, we carried out an experiment investigating the hormone corticosterone and did find that experimental animals, when compared with controls, released less of the hormone into their blood when exposed to a novel stimulus (Denenberg, et al. 1968). However, in order to do that experiment, it was necessary to shift from the C57BL/10J mouse to the Rockland Swiss-Albino animal. We then carried out a set of studies using the Swiss-Albino mouse to investigate the effects of maternal variables upon open-field performance and the plasma corticosterone response (see Denenberg 1970 for review of this material).

It was during this series of studies that we developed our rat "aunt" preparation. The reason for using the rat aunt was to ascertain whether the differences obtained in the offspring's behavior was a function of the adult rat's behavior toward the mice between birth and weaning, or whether it was a function of the nature of the rat mother's milk, which is known to differ biochemically from the milk of the mouse mother. The basis for our aunt preparation stemmed from a report by Rosenblatt (1967) that adult virgin rats who were continually exposed to infant rats eventually acted maternally toward them and would engage in all the maternal behaviors observed in a lactating mother except that these animals had no milk to nurse the young. Thus, we placed a pregnant mouse and a virgin rat together in the same cage. The mouse gave birth to her litter and nursed them competently, while the rat took over the other caretaking duties of the mother. Using our endpoints of open-field performance and corticosterone, we found that the rat aunt was almost as effective an agent as the rat mother for modifying the mouse's subsequent performance. All these studies were carried out with the Swiss-Albino mouse, and none of them involved the measurement of aggression.

Once we had worked these techniques out, we then did a comparative study using both the rat aunt and the rat mother arrangements with the C57BL/10J and the Swiss-Albino mouse. One of our endpoints was our aggression test (Paschke, Denenberg, and Zarrow 1971). For the C57BL/10J mouse we found that 82 percent of our control animals fought (based on 17 pairs), while only 17 percent (12 pairs) of the mice raised by rat mothers and 36 percent (11 pairs) of those raised in the presence of rat aunts fought. These latter two groups did not differ significantly from each other, but both were significantly different from the control group. This permits us to conclude that it is the behavior of the rat mother or aunt toward the young between birth and weaning which is the critical determiner that leads to attenuation of fighting.

For our Swiss-Albino animals, however, a different picture emerges. Eighty percent of our forty pairs of control mice fought, while 82 percent of the albino mice reared by a rat mother (17 pairs) and 84 percent of those reared in the presence of a rat aunt (19 pairs) fought. Obviously, none of these differences is significant.

It is apparent that there is a major interaction between the mouse's genotype and the postnatal maternal environment. Although one may hope for simplicity and wish that the Swiss-Albino had had its aggression reduced in a manner similar to the C57BL/10J, anyone who believes in evolutionary processes and in the importance of genes should not reasonably expect environmental variance to be that powerful. One of the interesting challenges facing us now is to unravel this genotype-environment interaction.

Another facet of our research involved interspecific aggression.

Modification of the Rat's Mouse-killing Response by Early Social Interaction

In our studies in which we reared weaning mice and rats together for varying periods of time, the two species coexisted peacefully. Our mice survived and thrived in this social situation and, as indicated above, were used in a variety of experiments concerning maternal factors and peer-group interactions. Although this was an unnatural setting, these results seem reasonable to those of us who believe that early social interactions among organisms tends to reduce aggression. However, this almost "intuitive" feeling was at variance with some experimental facts. There is a literature that documents that the adult male rat can very efficiently and very effectively kill mice when the two species are placed together (e.g., Myer 1964, 1968). But our rats did not kill our mice, suggesting that the early social interactions between the two species had acted to attenuate this response. In this regard Kuo's (1930, 1938) classical research—in which he reared various species together during early development, including the rat and the kitten—supported the idea that early social interactions will prevent aggression. On the other hand, we had no knowledge as to whether our particular strain of rats were mouse killers. Therefore, we conducted an experiment to investigate this particular problem (Denenberg, Paschke, and Zarrow 1968).

When weaned at twenty-one days, experimental male Purdue-Wistar rats were placed into cages with C57BL/10 mice in social groups consisting of two rats and two mice or three rats and one mouse. They remained together until fifty-seven days of age, at which time the rats were removed and placed into social groups of ten in cages in our rat-colony room. These animals remained in their rat world until ninety days of age, when we conducted our critical test. Our control rats had, of course, been reared in this same rat-colony room in groups of ten from the time of weaning.

The critical test consisted of placing a rat and a mouse together in a plastic cage and leaving them for twenty-four hours. Each rat was exposed to a black mouse (C57BL/10, but not to one of those used during the early socialization experience) and one white mouse (Rockland Swiss-Albino). Half the rats were exposed to the black mouse first, and the other half were exposed to the white one first.

Of our forty control rats eighteen (45 percent) killed one or two mice. There was no difference in the percentage of animals killing a black mouse and those killing a white mouse. How does this compare with our experimental animals who had spent their early life living with a black mouse? None of our twenty experimental animals killed either a black or a white mouse.

An independent confirmation of the Denenberg Paschke, and Zarrow (1968) finding was reported by Myer (1969). His experimental Long-Evans rats were repeatedly exposed to mice from the time of weaning until they were 150 days old. During the equivalent interval control rats were not exposed to mice. At 150 days all rats were individually housed for a period of ten days and were then tested for mouse killing. Fifty-four percent of the controls killed mice, as contrasted with only 9 percent of the experimentals. The rats were then maintained in their rearing cages for an additional two months, during which time they were not exposed to mice. On a retest Myer found that 73 percent of the controls killed, while only 14 percent of the experimental rats were killers.

Thus, both experiments demonstrate that early social interaction will suppress or inhibit mouse killing. It is important to note that Denenberg Paschke, and Zarrow (1968) used the Wistar albino rat, while Myer used the Long-Evans hooded rat, thus giving us a fair degree of generality across different rat strains. Both experiments also demonstrate that the blocking of the killing response is not merely an immediate consequence of having lived with mice, but is a condition that will persist over a period of one to two months.

Finally, both experiments have important implications for instinct theories of aggression. Lorenz (1966) has argued that the deprivation experiment is the critical design needed to determine whether a behavior is instinctive. In such an experiment the animals are reared in conditions where they are never exposed to a critical stimulus event (in this case, mice), and then their behavior is observed when they are first presented with this stimulus. Both Denenberg, Paschke, and Zarrow (1968) and Myer (1969) found in their experiments that rats that had never previously seen mice would, indeed, attack and kill them upon first exposure. In Lorenz's sense, then, mouse killing is instinctive. However, both experiments demonstrated that rats exposed to mice in early life were unlikely to kill mice. The behavior, then, is "noninstinctive." It is apparent from these data that, in order to understand an animal's behavior, not only is it necessary to remove or subtract experiences, as one does in a deprivation experiment, but it is also necessary to add experiences, as we and Myer did with our experimental groups. When we consider these data, as well as those presented in the previous two sections, our conclusion is one that we have suggested previously: "rather than use an instinct-learning classification, we feel that a more fruitful approach to an understanding of behavior is within a developmental framework in which the organism's behavior at any point in time is viewed as a function of the animal's accumulated experiences as well as his genetic background" (Denenberg, Paschke, and Zarrow 1968, p. 39).

Early Hormonal Factors Affecting the Rat's Pup-killing Response

The final set of experiments were initiated by a serendipitous observation. You will recall that mouse pups reared in the presence of rat aunts were markedly less aggressive than control mice. We were interested in determining whether this was a function of being raised with a female rat, or whether a male rat would also reduce aggression, since Rosenblatt (1967) had reported that male rats will also act maternally toward rat pups after an exposure period of approximately one week. Thus, we decided to investigate a rat "uncle" preparation. In order to sensitize our male rats to act maternally, we were going to expose them to rat pups over a period of a week until we could elicit maternal behavior. Much to our surprise we found that the initial response of our male rats on being presented with newborn pups was to calmly proceed to kill them. This was not the aberrant behavior of a few males, but was observed rather commonly. We were not aware of any reports in the literature concerning a phenomenon like this, although Rosenblatt (personal communication) told us that he had also observed a similar event in his colony. Since Adult virgin female rats do not kill newborn pups when presented with them, while adult males do, this form of aggression appeared to be worthy of investigation. The first conjecture was that the killing response of the male could be under the control of neonatal sex hormones during early infancy, since these hormones have been shown to have a marked effect upon a variety of sex-related behaviors (Levine and Mullins 1966; Young, Goy, and Phoenix 1964).

We carried out a set of experiments to test the hypothesis that the rat's pup-killing behavior was under the organizing influence of testosterone in infancy (Rosenburg et al. 1971). If this were true, then castration in adulthood should not attenuate the pup-killing behavior. Thus, in our first experiment, we took five known male rat-pup killers, castrated them, and observed their subsequent behavior. All five continued to kill pups. In addition, five naive adult males were castrated and were then exposed to rat pups. Three of the five killed. Thus, circulating amounts of testosterone in the blood of the adult animal was not a determinant of the killing response.

We then investigated the effects of castrating males at two days of age upon their adult pup-killing behavior. Sham-operated controls and undisturbed controls were part of the experimental design. The sham controls and unoperated controls, which did not differ from each other in our various experiments, were pooled to give us one control group against which to compare the effects of neonatal castration. We carried out three experiments on neonatal castration and the summary statistics are as follows: over all experiments fifty-seven of ninety-nine control animals (57.6 percent) were pup killers, while only fourteen of eighty-two castrated animals (17.1 percent) killed infant rats.

Neonatal testosterone clearly influences the killing pattern. However, in one of our experiments we have found that it did not matter whether the males were castrated at two days, ten days, or fifteen days of age. Castration at any of these ages was equally effective in reducing pup killing. These data are at variance with the research on the effects of the male hormone upon sexual behavior, in which it has been shown that castration must be done within the first five days of life in order to feminize the male. Here, there is no evidence for a critical period for this phenomenon; it is likely that what we have here is a prepubertal event rather than a neonatal one. In this set there was one final experiment. We were able to feminize males by castrating them in infancy. The obvious question was whether we could masculinize females by injecting them with the male hormone during early development. Of twenty-nine females that received the testosterone injection at two days of age, seven were killers (24.1 percent), while five of fifty-one controls (9.8 percent) killed. This difference is not significant. In combining the two groups, we find that among females in our population 15 percent (12 of 80) will kill rat pups upon first exposure. Interestingly, this value of 15 percent is very similar to the value of 17.1 percent that we obtained with the castrated males, thus suggesting that we had fully "feminized" the males by our early castration procedure. Our inability to masculinize the females is quite a puzzling phenomenon, which requires further investigation.

Conclusions

These studies may be summarized as follows:

1. Preweaning and postweaning peer-group interactions among mice influence intraspecific fighting. Depending upon the particular peer combinations, fighting behavior may be either enhanced or depressed.

2. When mice are reared with a rat mother or in the presence

of a rat aunt, this will markedly reduce intraspecific aggression in one strain, but does not have any effect upon a second strain.

3. Social interaction between mice and rats after weaning drastically reduces the rat's mouse-killing behavior.

4. Neonatal castration of the male rat will significantly reduce its rat-pup killing behavior in adulthood, but testosterone injections to neonatal females do not make them pup killers.

One thing stands out quite dramatically in this series of studies, one that I wish to emphasize strongly: in each of these sets of experiments, we are able to reduce naturally occurring aggressive behavior. This applies intraspecifically in the usual type of fight used to establish a dominance relationship, as well as interspecifically in a predator-prey context, and it also applies to the intraspecific pup-adult relationship. I submit that these findings are particularly encouraging in indicating that it is possible to modify and attenuate aggressive behavior in mammals; they offer hope that we can find ways of reducing aggression in man. I hold no brief for the position that man is "inherently aggressive" and that combative behavior and war is a necessary part of his behavioral repertoire. If these studies with animals have any degree of generality, they certainly indicate that naturally occurring aggressive behavior in mammalian species may be controlled.

These studies emphasize early experiential and hormonal determinants as affecting subsequent aggressive behavior; they should not be taken to mean that only these kinds of determinants can reduce aggression. But they suggest that it may be wise for us to attend to early developmental determinants, especially at the level of social interactions, as one particularly useful tool to help us reduce and alleviate aggressive behavior.

References

Denenberg, V. H. "The Mother as a Motivator." in *Nebraska Symposium on Motivation, 1970,* edited by W. J. Arnold and M. M. Page. Lincoln, Neb.: University of Nebraska Press, 1970.

Denenberg, V. H.; Hudgens, G. A.; and Zarrow, M. X. "Mice Reared with Rats: Modification of Behavior by Early Experience with Another Species." *Science* 143 (1964): 380–81.

——. "Mice Reared with Rats: Effects of Mother on Adult Behavior Patterns. *Psychological Reports* 18 (1966): 451–56.

Denenberg, V. H.; Paschke, R. E.; and Zarrow, M. X. "Killing of Mice by Rats Prevented by Early Interaction between the Two Species." *Psychonomic Science* 11 (1968): 39.

Denenberg, V. H.; Rosenberg, K. M.; Paschke, R.; Hess, J. L.; Zarrow, M. X.; and Levine, S. "Plasma Corticosterone Levels as a Function of Cross-species Fostering and Species Differences." *Endocrinology* 83 (1968): 900–902.

Hudgens, G. A.; Denenberg, V. H.; and Zarrow, M. X. "Mice Reared with Rats: Relations between Mothers' Activity Level and Offspring's Behavior." *Journal of Comparative and Physiological Psychology* 63 (1967): 304–8.

——. "Mice Reared with Rats: Effects of Preweaning and Postweaning Social Interactions upon Adult Behavior." *Behaviour* 30 (1968): 259–74.

Kuo, Z. Y. "The Genesis of the Cat's Response to the Rat." *Journal of Comparative Psychology* 11 (1930): 1–35.

——. "Further Study on the Behavior of the Cat toward the Rat." *Journal of Comparative Psychology* 25 (1938): 1–8.

Levine, S., and Mullins, R. F., Jr. "Hormonal Influences on Brain Organization in Infant Rats." *Science* 152 (1966): 1585–92.

Lockard, R. B. "Reflections on the Fall of Comparative Psychology: Is There a Message for Us All?" *American Psychologist* 26 (1971): 168–79.

Lorenz, K. *On Aggression.* New York: Harcourt Brace & World, 1966.

Myer, J. S. "Stimulus Control of Mouse-killing Rats." *Journal of Comparative and Physiological Psychology* 58 (1964): 112–17.

——. "Associative and Temporal Determinants of Facilitation and Inhibition of Attack by Pain." *Journal of Comparative and Physiological Psychology* 66 (1968): 17–21.

——. "Early Experience and the Development of Mouse Killing by Rats." *Journal of Comparative and Physiological Psychology* 67 (1969): 46–49.

Paschke, R. E.; Denenberg, V. H.; and Zarrow, M. X. "Mice Reared with Rats: An Interstrain Comparison of Mother and "Aunt" Effects." *Behaviour* 38 (1971): 315–31.

Rosenberg, K. M.; Denenberg, V. H.; Zarrow, M. X.; and Frank, B. L. "Effects of Neonatal Castration and Testosterone on the Rat's Pup-killing Behavior and Activity." *Physiology and Behavior* 7 (1971): 363–68.

Rosenblatt, J. S. "Nonhormonal Basis of Maternal Behavior in the Rat." *Science* 156 (1967): 1512–14.

Young, W. C.; Goy, R. W.; and Phoenix, C. H. "Hormones and Sexual Behavior." *Science* 143 (1964): 212–18.

Gerald McClearn completed his Ph.D. degree at the University of Wisconsin. His experience includes fellowships at the Institute of Animal Genetics in Edinburgh, Scotland and Gauthen Laboratory in London. Presently Dr. McClearn is the director of the Institute for Behavioral Genetics at the University of Colorado. His research has covered the broad spectrum of behavior genetics.

Professor John C. DeFries received his bachelor's degree in agriculture from the University of Illinois. Subsequently, he completed both the M.A. and Ph.D. in quantitative genetics at the University of Illinois. After completing the Ph.D., he remained on the faculty of the University of Illinois until 1967, when he joined the faculty of the University of Colorado. Dr. DeFries is currently professor in the Institute of Behavioral Genetics, and a lecturer in the Department of Biology and the Department of Psychology at the University of Colorado. In addition, he has been a research fellow at the University of California, Berkeley, and visiting professor of genetics at the University of Hawaii. In 1969 Professor DeFries was invited as a visiting lecturer to the N.A.T.O. Advanced Studies Institute in Psychogenetics at the University of Birmingham, England. He is currently editor of Behavior Genetics.

3

Genetics and Mouse Aggression

G. E. McCLEARN AND J. C. DeFRIES

The causes of aggression are currently being examined with an unprecedented vigor, impelled by the urgency of many of our contemporary social problems. The social, behavioral, and biological sciences are all concerned with this evaluation, and the data and concepts from their respective domains are being invoked in the attempt to understand the causes of violence. Unfortunately, a residual from the old nature-nurture controversy impedes the exchange of ideas and concepts among these various disciplines. There often appears to be among social scientists an implicit (and sometimes explicit) belief that any point conceded to biological factors is one point less for social and environmental factors. This attitude reflects a dichotomous view of behavioral determination which is as unwarranted as it is widespread. There is no merit in the old proposition that pits "nature" against "nurture" as logically incompatible forces. On the contrary, genes and environmental forces interact from the moment of conception. Thus, the effects of a given genetic difference between people may be greater or less depending upon the environmental circumstances in which they reside. Similarly, the impact of an environmental agent depends upon the hereditary nature of the individual upon whom it impinges.

Because we now recognize both the genetic and environmental sources of influence, it becomes necessary to distinguish the phenotype, that is, the trait as we measure it, from the genotype, which is the array of hereditary factors that influence the phenotype. The appropriate conceptual model is one of many genes and many environmental sources, all of which contribute to the total variation of the phenotype. The classical Mendelian situation is then seen to be simply a limiting case where only one gene is involved and where the environmental influence is relatively small. In the multiple factor, or polygenic situation, a key index is the proportion of the total phenotypic variance that is due to genetic differences among the individuals in that population. In a simplified statement, we may say that the phenotypic variance (V_P) is equal to the genetic variance (V_G) plus the environmental variance (V_E). The degree of genetic determination is given by the ratio V_G/V_P. This ratio is sometimes referred to as the heritability of the trait, although technically this term should be reserved for a special variant of the ratio, which places in the numerator only additive genetic variance (Falconer 1960). It can be seen that this perspective is not simply tolerant of both environmental and genetic explanations; it is the case that the importance of one source cannot be evaluated without a simultaneous assessment of the importance of the other source.

The mechanism of genetic determination is also sometimes misunderstood, with genetic influence regarded as somehow alternative to the general physiological, biochemical functioning of the organism. In point of fact, it is through the nervous system, through the endocrine system, and through all of the organ systems comprising the body that the genetic influence is exerted.

Heredity and Aggression in the Mouse

The most extensive research on the genetic mechanism in aggressiveness and dominance behavior in experimental animals has been conducted with the laboratory mouse and, in particular, involves comparison of highly inbred strains. It is therefore necessary to make a brief statement concerning the methodology appropriate to the study of these animals. Highly inbred strains are, as the name implies, a product of intensive inbreeding, with inbreeding defined as the mating of individuals more closely related than would be expected by chance in a population. The degree of inbreeding employed in generating inbred strains in research animals is very much more intense than the minimum requirement of this definition, however. In fact, inbred strains are maintained by sib mating, and each generation is the progeny of a single male and his sister. After a sufficient number of generations (usually regarded to be about 20), animals within such inbred strains will have approached a condition of genetic homogeneity in that each mouse will be genetically like each other mouse (except for the sex chromosomes, of course). Inbred strains thus represent a sort of crystallization of a particular genotype, and it is possible to obtain replicate individuals upon demand. Therefore a researcher can employ a number of variables on different naïve samples from a particular strain, content in the knowledge that the basic material of the research, the experimental animal itself, has remained unchanged from one experiment to the next.

The probability that such separate breeding groups would come to be genetically alike for all of the different genes is negligibly small. Thus, if two or more such inbred strains, which have no breeding history in common, are reared under the same environmental circumstances and tested under constant environmental circumstances, then any differences that appear between these strains must be attributable to differences in ther genotypes. Such a demonstration of strain differences serves only as an indicator of genetic influence, and more detailed examination of the mode of hereditary transmission requires the study of generations derived from crossing of the inbred strains. Inbred strains are also useful, however, in the provisional testing of hypotheses about correlated characteristics. For example, hypotheses concerning physiological mechanisms involved in the determination of a trait or process can be tested by choosing strains that differ on the process in question and examining the level of the hypothesized related trait.

Several situations have been employed in the assessment of mouse aggression. We may begin by considering spontaneous fighting in "matches" arranged by taking animals from their home cages and placing them in a fighting chamber. The type of behavior that can occur in such a contest is illustrated by the following seven-point scale (as modified from Lagerspetz 1964, pp. 40–41), one or another variation of which has been used in numerous investigations:

0. No interest in each other except occasional slight nosing
1. Frequent vigorous nosing. No blocking, shoving, or crowding or any other display of hostility
2. Occasional blocking, shoving, or crowding
3. Frequent blocking, shoving, or crowding of opponent. The aggressor keeps after the other animal throughout the period
4. Slight wrestling and/or assuming a dancing position in which the animals clasp each other while standing nose to nose
5. Fierce wrestling. They jump, roll, and turn all over the cage very rapidly
6. Fierce wrestling. An animal bites the other hard enough to draw blood.

It must be emphasized that the fighting behavior involved in the scale is almost completely restricted to males. Females very rarely show aggression in this type of situation.

This description points up one of the basic difficulties in research on social processes in experimental animals. Unlike the circumstances in which one assesses an animal's activity, or learning performance, or some similar trait by placing the animal in an objective, standard, constant situation, in studies of social interactions such as aggression it is necessary to pit one animal against another. Since both are capable of change over time, one is faced with a shifting standard. The aggressive behavior of a particular mouse is likely to be rather different when he confronts another aggressive mouse than when he confronts a submissive one. A solution to this problem is usually attempted by pairing each animal with a number of opponents in "round robin" fashion. Ginsburg and Allee (1942) and Scott (1942) employed this basic technique in the first observations of strain differences in aggression. Ginsburg and Allee (1942) found that animals of a strain called C57BL were superior to a strain called C3H, which in turn were superior to a strain called BALB in ability to win fights. This order of superiority is not immediately obvious when the bouts are first begun, but develops only after a series of encounters.

In order to test the possibility that the C57BL mice were more aggressively successful than the others because they were reared by C57BL mothers rather than because they were themselves C57BL, Ginsburg and Allee (1942) performed cross-fostering experiments in which C57BL and BALB litters were split, with half of each being foster reared. Such change in maternal environment produced no effect on aggression. However, the importance of environment was indicated in three other observations. In the first instance, a number of fights were staged between mice within the same strain. In these intrastrain bouts hierarchies developed with one dominant mouse, some very submissive animals, and some intermediate ones who shifted about in aggressiveness from time to time. This pattern was produced in all three strains studied, but it was noted that the most stable hierarchy was established in the C57BL strain. Because each of these animals can be regarded as being genetically like every other animal of the strain, it is clear that the individual differences in hierarchy position cannot be attributed to genetic differences. Presumably a small environmental difference, such as might exist with respect to the point of uterine implantation, subsequent nutritional status differences, and so on—things either unrecognized or beyond the power of the experimenter to regulate or control—must account for these individual differences.

Experience with aggression was shown in this same series of experiments to be an important environmental determinant. In an attempt to modify the behavior of aggressive animals, they were repeatedly exposed to defeats by even more aggressive animals. When returned to their regular group of contenders, these formerly aggressive and dominant animals were seen to be very much reduced in aggressiveness. Similarly, it proved possible, although rather more difficult, to increase aggressiveness of submissive animals by exposing them to a series of victory experiences in confrontations with even more submissive animals.

Although Ginsburg and Allee (1942) found that members of the C57BL strain were more aggressive than those of the BALB strain, contrary results have been reported by other investigators. Scott (1942), for example, has described a particular substrain designated C57BL/10 as being "pacifist." More recently, Tellegen, Horn, and Legrand (1969) have reported that mice of another substrain, the C57BL/6J, rarely fight vigorously when attacked and, thus, were suitable standard victims in an experiment designed to test the reinforcing properties of opportunity for aggression by BALB/cJ mice.

In the Ginsburg and Allee (1942) studies, a relatively high level of illumination was employed (a 60-w lamp placed 19 inches above the floor of the test cage). In each of two experiments designed to test the hypothesis that level of illumination will differentially influence aggressive behavior of these inbred strains of mice, Klein, Howard and DeFries (1970) paired C57BL (pigmented) males with BALB/c (albino) males under two levels of illumination. In both experiments, under high illumination, C57BL males won about 90 percent of the bouts that resulted in submission. In contrast, under low illumination, C57BL males won only about 40 percent of the bouts. This finding of a highly significant interaction between strain and level of test illumination may explain the apparent inconsistency in the literature concerning the aggressive behavior of these two strains of mice.

With a different technique, Southwick and Clark (1968) surveyed aggressive behavior in fourteen inbred strains of mice. After a period of individual isolation, young adult males were placed in groups of four of like strain and, for a period of one hour, observations were made on tail rattling, chasing, attacking, fighting, and social grooming. Large strain differences were observed in all of these measures. For example, the mean latency to attack was 2.2 min. for DBA/1 mice and 35.4 min. for A/J mouse foursomes. A composite score composed of chase, attack, and fight indices (the CAF score) was found by the authors to be particularly useful as a summary statistic. The range of CAF scores for the fourteen strains was from 11.3 to 82.2; table 3.1 shows the specific CAF scores for five of the strains generally used by other researchers on aggression.

Noteworthy is the result that BALB/c animals have higher composite aggression scores than do C57BL/6 mice.

Southwick (1968) used the same foursome technique in assessing the effects of maternal environment on mouse aggressive

TABLE 3.1. *Composite aggression scores of five mouse strains.*

Strain	*CAF Score*
BALB/c	62.7
C57BL/6	49.7
DBA/2	40.8
C3H/J	27.1
A/He	11.3

SOURCE: From Southwick and Clark, *Communications in Behavioral Biology*, 1968, 49–59.

behavior. Particularly instructive are the results from cross fostering CFW and A mice. Three groups were observed within each strain: fostered animals were assigned to a female of the alternate strain within twenty-four hours of birth; in-fostered mice were transferred from their biological mother to another female of the same strain, also within twenty-four hours of birth; and normal control animals were handled in the same way, but returned to their own biological mothers. CAF scores for these groups are shown in table 3.2.

Two points emerge from this table. First, it is clear that maternal influence is strain dependent. Young A/J males reared by a female from the more aggressive CFW strain do show enhanced aggression scores, compared with their controls; CFW males reared by A/J mothers show no depression of aggressive behavior. Second, even though rearing by a CFW mother raises A/J aggressive behavior significantly, it remains well below the level of any of the CFW groups, no matter how they were reared.

TABLE 3.2. *Effect of maternal environment on aggressive behavior of two mouse strains.*

	Strain	
Group	*A/J*	*CFW*
Control	14.2	67.6
In-fostered	17.5	68.0
Cross fostered	26.6	65.1

SOURCE: From Southwick, *Communications in Behavioral Biology*, 1968, 129–32.

In an attempt to explore the relationship between sexuality and aggression in these mouse strains, Fredericson et al. (1955) introduced females into fighting chambers of highly trained fighters. This procedure greatly reduced the aggression of the C57BL mice, who left off the combat to investigate the female. In the case of BALB mice, the introduction of the female produced no effects, and vigorous combat continued. No clear-cut relationship between sexuality and aggressiveness was therefore demonstrable, but the results do once again demonstrate a genetic difference in social behavior and genotype dependence of the effect of an environmental variable on that behavior.

The most comprehensive approach to the study of the genetics of mouse aggression has been provided by the work of Lagerspetz (1964). This research utilized the technique of selective breeding rather than strain comparisons. In selective breeding, one begins with a genetically heterogeneous group of animals and mates together animals who display extreme levels of the trait under investigation. Depending upon the extent to which the phenotype of an animal selected to reproduce has a genetic basis (that is, depending upon the heritability of the trait), offspring of the mated animals with high manifestation of the trait should have higher average values than the average of the generation from which their parents were selected. Similarly, the offspring of animals selected to have low manifestation of the trait should have lower mean values than the mean of the population from which their parents were selected. The rate at which the selected lines diverge in fact constitutes a direct measure of the heritability of the trait in that population. Thus, a successful selective breeding program demonstrates conclusively that the trait under investigation has a heritable basis. Such a demonstration has been provided for a variety of behavioral traits including maze brightness and maze dullness in rats, high and low activity in rats, alcohol preference in mice, positive and negative geotaxis in fruit flies, and a variety of other behavioral characteristics.

In addition to providing a demonstration of the importance of genotype, a successful selective breeding program culminates in strains of animals from the same basic gene pool (the same foundation population) with highly different levels of the partic-

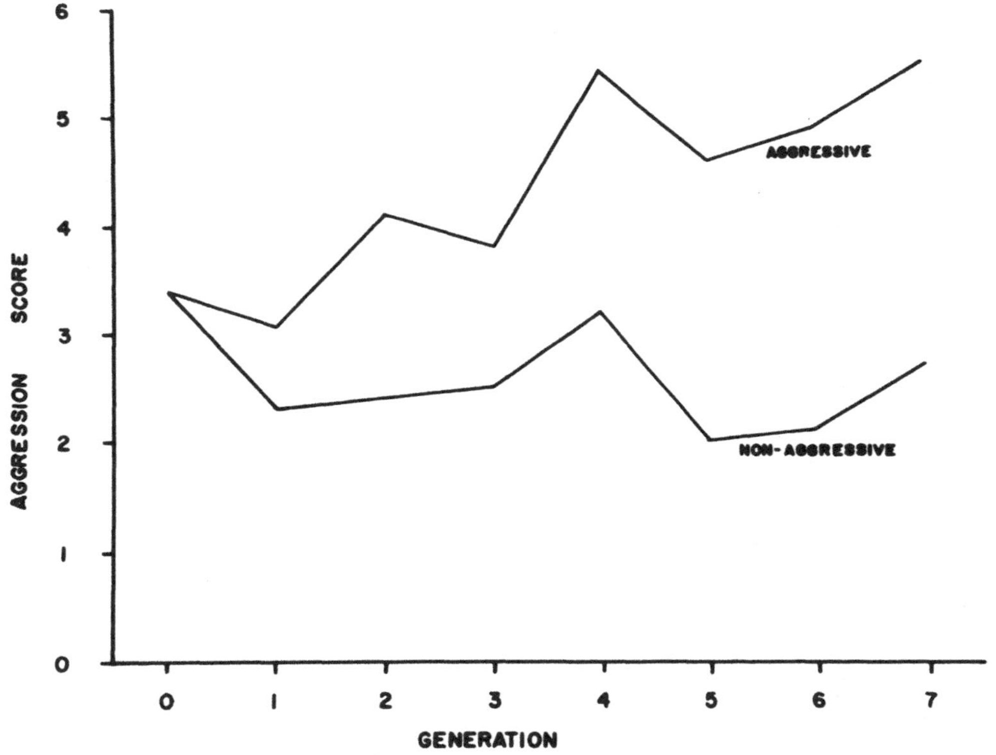

FIGURE 3.1. *Aggression scores of male mice in successive generations selectively bred for high and for low aggressiveness. Reprinted from K. Lagerspetz,* Studies on the aggressive behaviour of mice *(Helsinki: Soumalainen Tiedeakatemia, 1964).*

ular behavioral trait under investigation. These selected strains are therefore very useful for testing hypotheses about determinant systems and correlated characters. This general approach has been utilized by Lagerspetz in an experiment involving several generations of mice selectively bred for high and low aggressiveness. Figure 3.1 shows the mean aggressiveness scores utilizing the scale described earlier for seven generations of the aggressive and nonaggressive selected lines. The increasing divergence of the two lines is quite apparent. The somewhat erratic progress of the selection, particularly in the aggressive line, is a common feature of selection experiments, and presumably represents environmental changes that occur from generation to generation. Another way of examining the data, and one that typically gives rise to smoother results, is shown in figure 3.2, in which the difference between the upward and downward selected lines is plotted as a function of generation. In combination

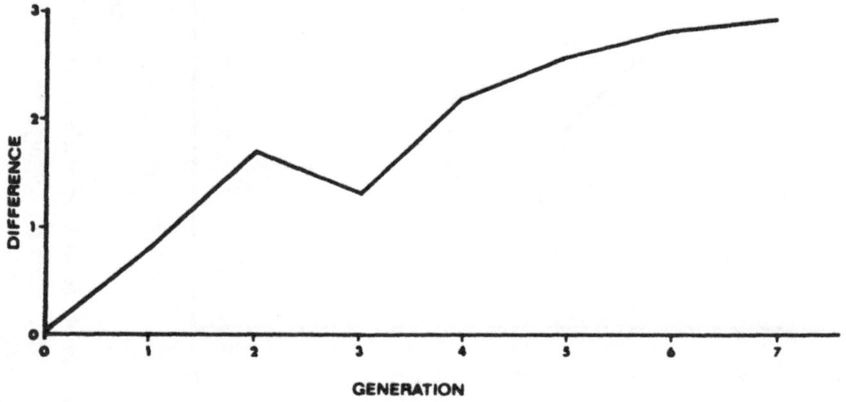

FIGURE 3.2. *Cumulative difference between high and low aggression selected lines over seven successive generations. Reprinted from K. Lagerspetz,* Studies on the aggressive behaviour of mice *(Helsinki: Soumalainen Tiedeakatemia, 1964).*

with the differences in aggressiveness among inbred strains, this success in selective breeding for aggressive behavior constitutes unassailable evidence of the importance of hereditary factors in determining individual differences in mouse aggressiveness.

Having generated these two lines, Lagerspetz was able to investigate a variety of hypotheses concerning interaction of genotype and environment and the correlation of other behavioral characters with the selected one. First, she investigated the effects of victories and defeats on the level of aggressiveness in mice. It was found that defeats reduced aggressiveness in animals of both aggressive and nonaggressive strains. The initial aggressiveness in animals from the aggressive strain could be enhanced by repeated victories, but victories did not have this effect on animals from the nonaggressive strain. Because they are frequently used as indices of emotionality in mice, scores on ambulation and defecation in an open field were obtained for animals of the aggressive and the nonaggressive strains. Aggressive animals defecated significantly less often and were more active in the open-field situation than were animals from the nonaggressive strain. In another measure of activity, a revolving wheel, animals from the aggressive strain were also more active. A somewhat superior maze-learning ability was demonstrated for the aggressive animals.

One of the more interesting experiments performed by Lagerspetz (1964) was directed to the question of the incentive value of aggressive behavior. Animals were tested in a two-compartment test chamber. A swinging door permitted movement from one chamber to the other, but not in the reverse direction. After two animals were placed in the same compartment for a standard period of time, they were then separated. The animal in one of the compartments was then in a position to enter the other compartment containing his erstwhile opponent. Briefly stated, the results indicated that when the first mouse had been victorious the latency to open the door into the opponent's chamber was very much lower than when the opponent had been victorious. An extension of this general approach was provided by investigating the willingness of animals to cross a grid floor whereby punishing electrical shocks were administered to their feet in order to make contact with a previous opponent. In general, animals from the aggressive strain were more willing to undergo this punishment than were animals from the nonaggressive strain. Furthermore, animals from the aggressive strain which had been exposed to a fight just prior to the experimental situation were very much quicker to cross the grid in order to reach their erstwhile opponent. The data from these two experiments strongly suggest that, once aggressive behavior has been initiated, the opportunity to continue or resume fighting has rewarding properties.

An exploration of possible physiological pathways through which the genetic differences between these strains are expressed has also been undertaken. Lagerspetz, Tirri, and Lagerspetz (1968) have reported that males of the aggressive strain have less serotonin in the forebrain, more noradrenaline in the brain stem, and higher testis weight than do males from the nonaggressive strain.

Which of the described differences between the aggressive and nonaggressive strains are fortuitous and which are indications of causal connections cannot be decided on the basis of strain investigations alone, but these observations serve the important function of generating further hypotheses.

Although this review has emphasized research on the genetics of aggression in the mouse, which has been most intensively studied in this regard, supportive evidence from other species can be cited. For example, breed differences in aggressiveness in dogs have been intensively studied by Scott (1958). As another example, selective breeding produced white leghorns with high and low levels of aggressiveness (Guhl, Craig, and Mueller 1960). In sum, these observations provide conclusive evidence that individual differences in aggressiveness within a number of species are influenced by genetic factors.

Social Dominance and the Genetic Composition of Populations

The experiments reviewed in the preceding section demonstrate that individual differences in aggressive behavior are due at least in part to gene differences. However, the converse is also true; that is, individual differences in aggressiveness may have effects on the genetic composition of populations.

Investigations of biochemical genetics of wild house mice (Selander 1970) and field and laboratory studies of their ecology and behavior (Anderson 1965; Crowcroft and Rowe 1963; Reimer and Petras 1967; Rowe and Redfern 1969; Young, Strecker, and Emlen 1950) all indicate that stable populations of house mice are subdivided into a mosaic pattern of small breeding units (demes), with little genetic interchange among them. For example, Reimer and Petras (1967) released mice into a cage that consisted of a series of nest boxes connected by runways. In each of four experiments, some with wild mice and some with laboratory stocks, the mice formed small breeding groups, each usually composed of one dominant male, several subordinate males, and several females. They concluded that formation of these breeding units was primarily due to male territoriality. Migration between breeding groups was rare and appeared possible only by females. When intruders were experimentally introduced, one at a time, 80 percent were dead within twelve hours. Resident females, as well as males, were involved in attacks upon the intruders.

Since the social behavior of house mice is apparently largely responsible for their population fine structure, this behavior may be an important factor in the evolutionary biology of the species. With small breeding units and little effective genetic interchange, chance factors (genetic drift) could play an important role in determining differences in gene frequencies among demes, at least at the local level. In addition, this population structure could facilitate evolutionary trial and error among local populations.

The extent to which this population structure may be important is largely a function of the effective population size, N_e:

$$N_e = \frac{4N_m N_f}{N_m + N_f},$$

where N_m and N_f are the number of males and females, respectively, that contribute to the gene pool of a population. From this expression, it may be seen that when the number of males is equal to one, N_e is less than four, regardless of N_f. Although the laboratory and field studies referred to above indicate that stable populations of house mice are subdivided into small breeding units, with little genetic exchange among demes, the actual effective population size could not be estimated from these studies since information about the reproductive success of individuals was not available. For example, until quite recently, the reproductive success of subordinate males was not clear. There have been theories that subordinate males contribute more (Crowcroft 1966), equally (Brown 1953), and less (Selander 1970) than do dominant males to the gene pool. Definitive results concerning the reproductive success of subordinate males have recently been obtained (DeFries and McClearn 1970).

Because of the paucity of information currently available regarding the genetics of social behavior, several experiments were undertaken in our laboratory.[1] In order to circumvent at least to some extent the artificiality of the twenty-minute-bout paradigm, standardized social living units were developed in which behavior could be observed over extended periods of time. Each such social living unit ("triad") is constructed from three standard mouse cages, interconnected by a Y-shaped plastic manifold. Adequate food, water, and bedding are available in each cage.

In the first experiment, three males, each from a different strain, were placed with three inbred BALB females in each of twenty-two triads. Combination of males was dictated solely by availability and by the possibility of ascertaining paternity of subsequent litters from their coat colors. Location of animals within the triad and behavioral observations were recorded three times daily. Males were examined daily over a two-week period for tail wounds and then discarded. Females were then isolated in individual cages and retained until resulting litters were old enough to be classified by coat color.

Within one or two days after introduction into the triad, one male was usually established as the clearly dominant animal. By

1. Institute for Behavorial Genetics, University of Colorado, Boulder, Colorado.

comparing the number of wounds on the tail with evaluations of dominance based upon observations of behavioral interactions, it appeared that a criterion of least number of tail wounds was an excellent index of social dominance. Fighting among females was rarely observed. Although the two subordinate males were usually found together in one cage (84 percent of observations), females were apparently free to come and go in the triad, including the cage of the subordinate males.

In this experiment, large strain differences in social dominance were observed. BALB/c and A males (related strains) were most frequently dominant, DBA/2 males were usually subordinate, and C57BL males tended to be intermediate. Even more striking, however, was the observed relationship between social dominance and reproductive success: Of sixty-one litters obtained in this experiment, fifty-six (92 percent) were sired by dominant males. This relationship was not due to the death of subordinate males, although death frequently occurred. Of the sixty-one litters obtained, only three were conceived after both subordinate males had been killed. Of the remaining fifty-eight litters, fifty-three (91 percent) were sired by dominant males.

In order to rule out the possibility that his relationship was due to the use of inbred females, the experiment was repeated with outbred (HS) females derived from an original cross of eight inbred strains (McClearn, Wilson, and Meredith 1970). Because of the greater difficulty of ascertaining paternity with these females, only those that were homozygous recessive for at least one of several coat-color loci (albino, brown, or dilute) were used. Two males, each from a different inbred strain, were placed with two or three females in each of twenty triads, combinations again being dictated by availability and by possible identification of paternity by coat color of pups. Strain differences consistent with those obtained in the first experiment were found. In addition, of the forty-two litters obtained in this experiment, forty (95 percent) were sired by dominant males.

In the third experiment, the generality of this relationship across male genotype was assessed. The F_1 males were paired with HS males in thirty-six triads and with inbred males in five triads. In one triad, neither male was found to have tail wounds, so this triad was excluded from further consideration. Females from the remaining forty triads subsequently produced a total of seventy-six litters, seventy (92 percent) of which were sired by dominant males. Of the remaining six litters, three were sired by subordinate males and three were of mixed paternity. It is interesting to note that the three mixed litters were produced by females from two triads in which very few tail wounds were found on either male, suggesting that the dominance hierarchy was not well established.

In more recent experiments (Kuse and DeFries unpublished) mice selected for open-field activity (DeFries, Wilson, and McClearn 1970) have been found to differ consistently in social dominance. In general, males from the low-active (high-defecation) lines have higher social-dominance scores than do controls (intermediate levels of activity and defecation), which in turn have higher scores than do males from lines selected for high open-field activity. In addition, presence of females in triads has been found to lead to increased aggression among males, thereby hastening the establishment of social-dominance hierarchies.

If the association between social dominance and reproductive success is as high in wild populations of mice as that observed in our laboratory stock, the effective population size within demes is quite small. If the dominant male within a deme sires 90 percent or more of the offspring, the effective population size will be less than four. Such a finding has important implications for the evolutionary biology of the species. This effective population size is sufficiently small that chance factors could play an important role in determining gene frequencies at the local level. In addition, the differential success of established demes in starting new breeding units could be an important force in evolution.

Christian (1970) has recently hypothesized that social behavior may be a major force in mammalian evolution. In stable populations, dominant animals will remain within their territory as long as the habitat is favorable. Therefore, animals that emigrate to less favorable habitats will usually have been subordinate. Although most such dispersing animals would not survive, rare genetic recombinations may sometimes occur which permit survival and reproduction in marginal habitats. In a territorial species, spatial separation restricting gene flow between the new colony and the old population could occur in the absence of geographic isolation. Thus, the genetic changes upon which natural selection operates would be found in socially subordinate animals. Although the validity of this hypothesis remains to be tested, it is interesting to speculate about the evolutionary significance of social dominance, especially in man.

That social behavior may have implications for the evolutionary biology of man has recently been shown by Neel (1970). Neel and his colleagues are currently studying intensively some of the most primitive indians of South America. Indians in these tribes live in small villages, and a marked genetic microdifferentiation has been observed between villages. These Indians are polygynous, the reward for male achievement being additional wives. In four villages studied in detail, a highly disproportionate number of grandchildren were born to a few headmen, greatly increasing the possibility of marriage between cousins in the villages. In addition, the four males with the most grandchildren were two father-son combinations.

According to Neel, Indian culture is much more egalitarian than our own; thus, leadership in an Indian community may more likely be based upon innate characteristics than it is in our culture. Although no data are yet available, Neel speculates that dominant males in a village may be more intelligent than subordinates, thereby providing a selective mechanism for higher intelligence. Thus, the population structure of mice may be rather similar to that of primitive populations of men.

Conclusions

Studies concerning the aggressive behavior of laboratory animals, principally the mouse, demonstrate conclusively that individual differences in aggression are influenced by genetic factors, a point that has been self-evident for many years to breeders of fighting bulls and game cocks. It has recently become clear, however, that the converse is also true, that is, individual differences in aggressive behavior may influence the genetic composition of populations. Dominant male mice contribute disproportionately to the gene pool of the next generation, resulting in an effective population size sufficiently small to have important implications for the evolutionary biology of house mice. Recent studies of primitive Indian tribes in South America suggest that a similar situation may once have been important for man.

References

Anderson, P. K. "The Role of Breeding Structure in Evolutionary Processes of *Mus musculus* Populations." In *Mutation in Populations,* edited by R. Honcariv, pp. 17–21. Prague: Academia, 1965.

Brown, R. Z. "Social Behavior, Reproduction, and Population Changes in the House Mouse (*Mus musculus* L.)." *Ecological Monographs* 23 (1953): 217–40.

Christian, J. J. "Social Subordination, Population Density, and Mammalian Evolution." *Science* 168 (1970): 84–90.

Crowcroft, P. *Mice All Over*. Chester Springs, Pa.: Dufour Editions, 1966.

Crowcroft, P., and Rowe, F. P. "Social Organization and Territorial Behavior in the Wild House Mouse (*Mus musculus* L.)." *Proceedings of the Zoological Society of London* 140 (1963): 517–31.

DeFries, J. C., and McClearn, G. E. "Social Dominance and Darwinian Fitness in the Laboratory Mouse." *American Naturalist* 104 (1970): 408–11.

DeFries, J. C.; Wilson, J. R.; and McClearn, G. E. "Open-Field Behavior in Mice: Selection Response and Situational Generality." *Behavior Genetics* 1 (1970): 195–211.

Falconer, D. S. *Introduction to Quantitative Genetics.* New York: Ronald Press, 1960.

Fredericson, E.; Story, A. W.; Gurney, N. L.; and Butterworth, K. "The Relationship between Heredity, Sex, and Aggression in Two Inbred Mouse Strains." *Journal of Genetic Psychology* 87 (1955): 121–30.

Ginsburg, B.; and Allee, W. C. "Some Effects of Conditioning on Social Dominance and Subordination in Inbred Strains of Mice." *Physiological Zoology* 15 (1942): 485–506.

Guhl, A. M.; Craig, J. V.; and Mueller, C. D. "Selective Breeding for Aggressiveness in Chickens." *Poultry Science* 39 (1960): 970–80.

Klein, T. W.; Howard, J.; and DeFries, J. C. "Agonistic Behavior in Mice: Strain Differences as a Function of Test Illumination." *Psychonomic Science* 19 (1970): 177–78.

Lagerspetz, K. *Studies on the Aggressive Behaviour of Mice.* Helsinki: Suomalainen Tiedeakatemia, 1964.

Lagerspetz, K. Y. H.; Tirri, R.; and Lagerspetz, X. M. J. "Neurochemical and Endocrinological Studies of Mice Selectively Bred for Aggressiveness." *Scandinavian Journal of Psychology* 9 (1968): 157–60.

McClearn, G. E.; Wilson, J. R.; and Meredith, W. "The Use of Isogenic and Heterogenic Mouse Stocks in Behavioral Research." In *Contributions to Behavior-genetic Analysis: The Mouse as a Prototype,* edited by G. Lindzey and D. D. Thiessen, pp. 3–22. New York: Appleton-Century-Crofts, 1970.

Neel, J. V. "Lessons from a "Primitive" People." *Science* 170 (1970): 815–22.

Reimer, J. D., and Petras, M. L. "Breeding Structure of the House Mouse, *Mus musculus,* in a Population Cage." *Journal of Mammalogy* 48 (1967): 88–89.

Rowe, F. P., and Redfern, R. "Aggressive Behaviour in Related and Unrelated Wild House Mice *(Mus musculus* L.)." *Annals of Applied Biology* 64 (1969): 425–31.

Scott, J. P. "Genetic Differences in the Social Behavior in Inbred Strains of Mice." *Journal of Heredity* 33 (1942): 11–15.

——. *Aggression.* Chicago: University of Chicago Press, 1958.

Selander, R. K. "Behavior and Genetic Variation in Natural Populations." *American Zoologist* 10 (1970): 53–66.

Southwick, C. H. "Effect of Maternal Environment on Aggressive Behavior of Inbred Mice." *Communications in Behavioral Biology* 1(A) (1968): 129–32.

Southwick, C. H., and Clark, L. H. "Interstrain Differences in Aggressive Behavior and Exploratory Activity of Inbred Mice." *Communications in Behavioral Biology* 1(A) 1968: 49–59.

Tellegen, A.; Horn, J. M.; and Legrand, R. G. "Opportunity for Aggression as a Reinforcer in Mice." *Psychonomic Science* 14 (1969): 104–5.

Young, H.; Strecker, R. L.; and Emlen, J. T., Jr. "Localization of Activity in Two Indoor Populations of House Mice, *Mus musculus.*" *Journal of Mammalogy* 31 (1950): 403–10.

Roger Ulrich received his bachelor's degree from North Central College, his M.A. from Bradley University, and his Ph.D. from Southern Illinois University. Dr. Ulrich has held faculty positions at Illinois Wesleyan University and Illinois State University, and he is currently research professor at Western Michigan University. Subsequent to his doctoral dissertation, "Reflexive Fighting in Response to Aversive Stimulation," Professor Ulrich has directed much of his research activity to the investigation of the pain-aggression hypothesis. In addition, he is interested in the applied behavioral analysis as it relates to education and the total human community. His three books reflect this interest in the applications of the experimental analysis of behavior. He has served on the editorial board of Journal of the Experimental Analysis of Behavior, Journal of Applied Behavior Analysis, *and* Behavior Modification Monographs. *He is a fellow in the American Association for the Advancement of Science.*

Sylvia Dulaney received her bachelor's degree from Western Michigan University and is currently on the faculty of Kalamazoo Valley Community College.

Marilyn Arnett received her bachelor's degree and M. A. from Western Michigan University and is currently teaching at Kalamazoo Valley Community College.

Kay Mueller received her bachelor's degree in English from Oakland University and after a history of free-lance writing became interested in pursuing advanced study in psychology. She is currently a graduate student at Western Michigan University.

4

An Experimental Analysis of Nonhuman and Human Aggression

ROGER ULRICH, SYLVIA DULANEY, MARILYN ARNETT, AND KAY MUELLER

Over the past fifty years, a scientific, experimental analysis of behavior has contributed extensively to psychology and the study of behavior. The methodology and conceptual framework developed have extended our ability to predict and control both nonhuman and human behavior. Analysis with nonhuman subjects has involved a standard experimental environment, fairly rigorous control of the animal's environment between experimental sessions, an objective measure of behavior that is more or less independent of topography, a treatment of behavior in terms of rate of response, and the fine-grained longitudinal study of the behavior of a few animals. The methodology has permitted the analysis of behavior, roughly in terms of operants and respondents. In the former case, responses are shaped and maintained by the stimuli that follow them, with the preceding stimulus serving a discriminative function. In the latter case, preceding events elicit physiologically predetermined responses.

In applying the experimental analysis of behavior to human organisms, two approaches have generally been taken. The first

This paper, and the human aggression research presented in it were funded through the National Institute of Mental Health (grant 5 R01 12,882-02), the Office of Naval Research (grant N00014-67-0421-0001).

puts the subject in the human analogue of the animal experimental chamber. There are visual and auditory isolation, response manipulanda, discriminative stimuli, and automatic recording equipment, just as there are in animal experiments. The human subjects are returned to the chamber for a number of experimental sessions, and records of their behavior are examined in terms of specific events occurring in the experimental environment. This approach is generally superior to averaging the one-session results of many subjects, since behavior can be analyzed in terms of specific environmental events, as opposed to more general "conditions." Results from studies of simple behaviors with little relation to the subjects' extraexperimental environments have been comparable to those obtained in nonhuman experiments (e.g., Holland 1958). However, results from studies of more complex behaviors typically show enormous variability among subjects (e.g., Cohen 1962). The experimenter has no control over the subject's extensive and complex history, nor has he control over the equally complex environment in which the subject lives between experimental sessions. Many human experiments try to circumvent the problem of individual variability by averaging results. However, as Sidman (1960) has pointed out, averaging only serves to obscure effects that could perhaps be traced more precisely to specific environmental events. Averaging and complex statistical treatments have their uses in large-scale actuarial studies; however, they are of little use in making a detailed account of the causes of behavior.

In a second approach, the experimental analysis of behavior has been applied to human subjects outside the laboratory. Such settings have ranged from mental hospitals, to schools, to prisons, to homes. Research in such settings typically singles out one of the subject's behaviors for study. No effort is made to isolate the subject in a rigorous experimental environment. Within the ordinary environment, the behavior is defined and a recording procedure is developed. During subsequent "samplings" of the subject's behavior, which may extend over days, weeks, or months, baseline rates are taken, experimental manipulations are introduced, and the results are recorded. The subject serves as his own control, either when a "reversal" is carried out by returning the subject to baseline conditions and measuring the result, or when another of the subject's behaviors is simultaneously measured but not subjected to experimental manipulation (the "multiple baseline" technique). Such studies normally do not yield the extremely detailed analyses produced by chamber-bound animal studies. However, their results can be striking and informative (Ullmann and Krasner 1965; Ulrich, Stachnik, and Mabry 1966, 1970). Again, the subject's behavior is only sampled at certain times; however, closer contact is usually maintained with the environment in which the subject lives between experimental sessions.

A newer, third approach to the analysis of human behavior attempts to deal more completely and objectively with the subjects' environmental conditions and behavior. Patterson and Cobb[1] have described techniques for coding numerous behavioral and environmental events and for analyzing the occurrence of many such events over time. Because of the amount of data collected and the complexities involved, computer analysis will probably be necessary. Perhaps in cases where human beings cannot successfully be brought to the laboratory, and laboratory can successfully be brought to them. In the meantime, the principal scientific source of information on behavior remains research with non human animals.

The Experimental Analysis of Aggression

The experimental analysis of behavior has significantly advanced our understanding of aggression. For centuries aggression has been the topic of verbal output, but it is only in the past ten years that a more complete understanding of the environmental causes of aggression has been achieved. Earlier studies had been done. For example, in 1939, O'Kelly and Steckle produced the first laboratory demonstration of the aggressive response to electric shock. In 1948 Miller published a classic study that seemed to condition aggression by reinforcing it with escape from shock. Probably later advances in the experimental analysis of behavior

1. See chap. 6 in this volume.

were necessary for such work to be properly appreciated and interpreted. Thus, when Ulrich and Azrin (1962) rediscovered the fact that antecedent shock will produce aggression apparently without any prior conditioning, the experimental techniques and conceptual framework were ready. The result has been an extensive and productive analysis of the nature and causes of aggression.

In some respects, the study of aggression departed from the traditions of the experimental analysis of behavior. Central to behavior analysis is the use of an arbitrary response that can be defined solely in terms of its relation to causative environmental stimuli. Aggression, on the other hand, is typically defined descriptively, in terms of behavior associated with injuring other organisms (Bandura and Walters 1963; Ulrich 1966). Other definitions (Scott 1970) exclude predatory aggression and refer to intraspecific aggression as "agnostic behavior." Since not all aggressive behaviors do immediate damage to other organisms, definitions sometimes include behaviors that reliably precede aggression. Some of these behaviors, such as intentions and feelings, are not observable. Sometimes the injury done is unobservable as well. Thus, we find research dealing with verbal aggression that may simply produce hurt feelings. Also, much human aggression is far removed from its injurious effects: Consider a shopper purchasing choice steaks in a supermarket as opposed to a wolf attacking livestock, or the industrial magnate who allows harmful chemicals to be dumped in rivers and lakes, thus killing thousands or millions of fish and wildlife and some human organisms as well.

Even in attempting to treat aggression on a far less complex scale, there have been problems in response definition. In initial experiments, human observers attempted to press microswitches for each "striking or biting" movement they observed (Ulrich and Azrin 1962). Although reliability among observers in one particular laboratory may be high, the chances of equal reliability among observers in different laboratories are unlikely to be as good. Other devices have been tried, such as restraining target animals in gadgets that closed a switch when they were struck (Azrin, Hutchinson, and Hake 1966). Finally, various inanimate "victims" of aggression were developed that could automatically record attacks on themselves (Azrin, Hutchinson, and Sallery 1964; Azrin, Rubin, and Hutchinson 1968). The device most commonly used at present is a rubber tube attached to a pneumaic switch that automatically records bites (Hutchinson, Azrin, and Hake 1966). Most squirrel monkeys will attack such a hose functionally in much the same way that they will attack each other, and in the way that a rat will attack a rat or a pigeon will attack a pigeon. Even so, there are problems. Some monkeys are "nibblers"; they bite the hose, but with insufficient force to close the switch. Nevertheless, the bite-hose apparatus has provided automatic, objective measurement of an aggressive response that makes it amenable to experimental analysis.

In another respect, aggression is also atypical of the responses usually studied in the experimental analysis of behavior. Most complex responses are studied in terms of operant conditioning; they are shaped and maintained by consequent, reinforcing stimuli. Most respondent behaviors, produced by preceding, eliciting stimuli, are relatively simple in terms of the musculature and neural mechanisms involved. Aggression, on the other hand, is an extremely complex response that can, nevertheless, be elicited in much the same way as an eye blink or a knee jerk is elicited. Because it is a behavioral oddity, as well as an observable emotion, aggression is an interesting topic for study (not to mention the topic's relevance to human survival).

RESPONDENT AND OPERANT ANALYSES OF AGGRESSION

Aggression has proved to be amenable to analysis both as a respondent and as an operant behavior. In addition to foot shock delivered through a floor grid, the range of stimuli that would elicit respondent aggression was explored and found to include heated floors (Ulrich and Azrin 1962), tail pinches (Azrin, Hake, and Hutchinson 1965), and morphine withdrawal from addicted rats (Boshka, Weisman, and Thor 1966; Davis and Khalsa 1971). Respondent aggression was also found to occur in a wide variety of animals, including rodents, reptiles, birds, and primates (Azrin 1967). This phenomenon persisted even when animals were paired with unlike species, such as rat paired with cat (Ulrich, Wolff, and Azrin 1964).

Aggressive responses can also be produced by antecedent

events other than physically painful ones. Environmental events that could be described as "psychologically painful" or "frustrating" have been found to produce aggression (Azrin 1967). These events include cessation of positive reinforcement, as in extinction-produced aggression (Azrin, Hutchinson and Hake 1966), and in difficult response requirements such as high-fixed-ratio schedules (Gentry 1968; Hutchinson, Azrin, and Hunt 1968), or some fixed-interval schedules (Flory 1969).

The aggressive response to aversive events can also be conditioned according to the classical, respondent paradigm. Classical, or Pavlovian, conditioning of aggression has been achieved by pairing a tone or buzzer with presentation of electric shock. After many such pairings, subjects will attack their partner (Creer, Hitzing, and Schaeffer 1966; Vernon and Ulrich 1966) or attack a target (Hutchinson, Renfrew, and Young 1971) upon presentation of the sound stimulus alone.

Even the organism's own behavior can become a conditioned stimulus for aggression. In recent experiments (Dulaney, Ulrich, and Kucera 1970) food-deprived squirrel monkeys were reinforced for lever pressing, and at the same time they were allowed continuous access to a rubber bite hose. After a stable rate of lever pressing for food was established, lever pressing was punished by electric tail shock. This shock, which was contingent on the animal's own lever pressing, in turn produced hose biting. Eventually, biting subsided when the monkey quit pressing the lever, thus receiving no shock, but also receiving no reinforcers. When punishment was discontinued, lever pressing gradually returned to its previous rate. However, biting still occurred and remained directly related to the subject's own lever pressing. In those early reversal sessions, when the subject pressed the lever, he bit the hose, even in the absence of shock. As the no-punishment, reversal phase was extended, biting behavior decreased, suggesting the possibility of extinction of classically conditioned pairings of shock with lever pressing. The organism's own behavior apparently had become a conditioned stimulus for aggression, and stimuli that originally were unrelated to shock or to hose biting came to produce aggression. These data tend to support punishment theories that suggest part of the punishment procedure's effectiveness lies in the fact that the punishment paradigm creates pairings between behavior and pain that may later cause the organism to avoid or escape its own behaviors (thus resulting in a suppression in rate of responses). Like other aversive stimuli, such conditioned aversive behaviors can apparently also produce aggression.

More general environmental conditions can probably also become conditioned aversive stimuli capable of producing aggression. When placed in a restraining chair for the first time, naïve squirrel monkeys will often bite a rubber hose in the chamber. After the initial strangeness of the situation has decreased (and escape attempts have been exhausted), biting behavior frequently decreases. But, after repeated exposure to a restraining chair and experimental chamber where shock has been delivered, some monkeys will continue to bite the hose during sessions long after shock has been discontinued, sometimes for periods of months (Hutchinson, Renfrew, and Young 1971). Perhaps human environments, such as schools or homes that have dispensed substantial amounts of aversive stimuli, can become capable, in themselves, of producing aggression.

Traditional techniques for the study of operant behavior have been applied to aggression. Miller's (1948) early attempt to negatively reinforce approximations to aggression by termination of electric foot shock has already been mentioned. Miller's results are, of course, clouded by the fact that shock alone, without termination, will produce respondent aggression.

Using positive reinforcing consequences, aggressive behavior has been shaped and maintained in a number of species. Reynolds, Catania, and Skinner (1963) produced pecking attack in pigeons by reinforcing them with grain. They also brought the aggressive behavior under stimulus control by reinforcing the pigeons for attack under one color of light and not under another. Ulrich et al. (1963) performed a similar experiment, using water to reinforce attack behavior in water-deprived rats. In both studies, reinforcer acquisition probably disrupted the aggressive response, and attack sequences would be interrupted as the animals stopped to eat or drink. To avoid this problem, Stachnik, Ulrich, and Mabry (1966) used intracranial stimulation to reinforce attack behavior in rats. With this procedure, the experimenters were able to shape rats to attack other rats and even to attack squirrel monkeys and cats.

INTERACTION BETWEEN RESPONDENT AND OPERANT AGGRESSION

Aggression maintained both by eliciting and by reinforcing stimuli can occur concurrently. Instances of respondent aggression were detectable in the above-mentioned experiments of the operant conditioning of aggression. Reynolds, Catania, and Skinner (1963) noted that fighting during reinforced periods carried over into periods where fighting was not reinforced; ordinarily, operant responses show a clear contrast between reinforced and nonreinforced periods. Ulrich et al. (1963) noted that their water-deprived rats fought more intensively when paired with other trained rats than when paired with naïve animals. This more intense fighting would continue even after water availability was signaled. Stachnik, Ulrich, and Mabry (1966) noted that unstimulated target animals would retaliate against attacks by animals reinforced with intracranial stimulation.

Other studies have deliberately set out to explore the relation between respondent and operant aggression (Azrin, Hutchinson, and Hake 1967; Ulrich 1967). Although various escape, avoidance, and attack parameters have been manipulated, with each variation changing the likelihood that attack or escape would be predominant, research to date seems to indicate that if organisms are allowed some effective (and not too difficult) means of escape from aversive stimulation this behavior will predominate over attack reactions. Qualifying this statement are, of course, complex interactions between events that usually determine the escape or avoidance performances and those that determine attack behaviors.

One recent experiment in our laboratory studied the effect on respondent aggression of teaching nonfighters to fight. As several other experimenters have reported, some squirrel monkeys will not attack each other (Azrin, Hutchinson, and Hake 1963) or will not bite a rubber hose (Azrin, Hutchinson, and McLaughlin 1965; Azrin, Hutchinson, and Sallery 1964) in response to shock. After a shock baseline demonstrated that certain monkeys in our colony would not attack (or in some cases even approach) the bite hose when shocked, subjects were food deprived, then shaped to bite the hose for food reinforcement. After a stable response rate for intermittent food reinforcement was attained, subjects' training was discontinued and they were returned to their original body weights so that they were relatively satiated. To insure the elimination of operant biting, subjects were reintroduced to the experimental environment where reinforcement for biting was discontinued (extinction procedure). After such training, monkeys would respond to shock by biting the hose. Although functionally the two biting responses are entirely different, their occurrence seems to be interrelated. Apparently acquiring the aggressive response under one set of motivational and stimulus conditions made it more probable under others. The operant aggressive response was acquired under food deprivation and was reinforced by food. The subsequent respondent aggression was produced by the antecedent shock and the intervening "aggression motivation" (Azrin, Hutchinson, and McLaughlin 1965). Nevertheless, acquisition of the aggressive response under one set of conditions seemed to cross over to the second set of conditions. This apparent ability of aggression to spread from one set of conditions to another should make us wary of generating aggressive behavior under any circumstances. Bandura and Walters (1963) have pointed out that an individual who has learned how to use a gun and what it can be used for will be more likely to use such a weapon for aggression than an individual who has not. The aggression displayed by a karate instructor when attacked will differ significantly from that of a ping-pong champion.

The Causes of Aggression: Results from Nonhuman Research

The experimental analysis of aggression has yielded data that exceed in extent and sophistication those reviewed above. Other studies of the relation between the stimulus and the aggressive response have been completed. Aggression elicited by shock has been used as a baseline for studying the effects of drugs (Hutchinson and Emley 1972), brain lesions and stimulation, and the relationship between aggressive and nonaggressive forms of behavior (Hutchinson, Renfrew, and Young 1971). Of more general interest is the possibility of relating aggression to adjunctive behavior as a class of responses (Falk 1972). However, even the earlier analyses of aggression were sufficient to reveal its two major causes: reinforcement and aversive stimuli.

It is not surprising that aggression, like any complex response, can be shaped and maintained by reinforcing consequences. Nor does it offend common sense to hold that painful and unpleasant events can cause aggression. What is perhaps surprising is the extent to which a wide variety of aversive events can, by themselves, produce complex responses that we call "aggression."

The account of aggression that has emerged from its experimental analysis is a parsimonious one. Intervening variables, such as anger, hostility, and even "frustration," can be eliminated. Such intervening variables, or "middle men," can can only add to the scientist's burden, since they in fact explain nothing and call themselves for an explanation (Skinner 1953). Nor must "aversive" and "reinforcing" stimuli be defined in terms of internal states such as pleasure and pain. Aversive stimuli are those events that an organism will work to avoid or escape. These same events, whether they are shock, termination of reinforcement, or high work requirements, can serve as antecedent causes of aggression. Reinforcing stimuli are events that the organism will work to acquire. These same stimuli are capable of reinforcing aggression, as they are capable of reinforcing almost any behavior. Species-specific visual and olfactory aggression-eliciting stimuli do exist. Aggression can also be analyzed in terms of hormone levels and in terms of brain function. However, aversive and reinforcing stimuli together probably account for the greater part of the aggression of most interest to the scientist concerned with its control.

The Control of Aggression: Results from Nonhuman Research

Once causes of aggression have been identified, the most obvious method of potential control is to eliminate those causes. If aggression is caused by foot shock, discontinuation of foot shock should eliminate much of the on-going aggression (although certain pairings between shock and environment may continue to produce some level of aggression for a while). If aggression is caused by reinforcement of an aggressive response, removal of reinforcement for that particular behavior should cause a decrease in its probability.

The ability to perform an aggressive response can be modified through some physiological manipulations, thus decreasing the probability of future aggression. Hooded rats who could not see, feel with their whiskers, or smell did not fight as much when shocked as did rats who were not disabled (Flory, Ulrich, and Wolff 1965). Other physiological and maturational variables can also alter the probability of aggression. Reduced androgen levels (castration) lowered the probability of aggressive reactions to foot shock in rats (Hutchinson, Ulrich, and Azrin 1965). The same investigators also found aggressive reactions to shock to be directly related to the rats' age when tested. Of course, physiological variables that alter the probability of aggression are not so readily manipulated outside the experimental environment, making their usefulness for social control rather limited.

Variables have been discovered which can be easily manipulated within nonexperimental environments and which also alter the probability of aggression. If an organism is in an aversive environment, but is allowed some effective means of escaping or avoiding the aversive events, the probability of aggression is decreased (Azrin, Hutchinson, and Hake 1967; Ulrich 1967). Evidence of this phenomenon is also reflected in folklore about the advisability of approaching caged, cornered, or hurt animals. If an organism is furnished with effective alternatives to aggression, attack may be averted. A citizen's right to grievance against governing bodies was created to avoid the possibility of attack or revolution.

After brief aversive stimulation, the probability of aggression decreases in direct relation to the time since termination of the aversive stimulus (Azrin et al. 1964). Further, if when briefly stimulated, there is no immediate object to attack, the probability of aggression once a target is available still decreases in direct relation to the time since termination of the aversive stimulus (Roediger and Stevens 1970). This type of procedure and its effects on behavior might be equated to "counting to ten" when angry. Therefore, if it were possible to reduce the number of attackable objects in the environment, aggression might also decrease. This method of averting aggressive reactions is often practiced by governments, which, after a tragedy such as Kent State, Jackson State, My Lai, or Attica, force the public to "count to ten" by withholding or misrepresenting facts until public outrage has diminished. The importance of an attackable object on the probability of aggression is also born out by evidence on the effects of crowding on aggression levels. As the number of organisms per unit space increases, the probability of aggression is also increased (Calhoun 1962; Ulrich and Azrin 1962).

Another potential control technique for some forms of aggression is extinction. Indeed, if aggressive behavior were maintained through operant positive reinforcement, extinction would in all likelihood decrease aggression. If aggression is maintained through operant negative reinforcement (escape or avoidance schedules), after which extinction is introduced and the subject's responses are no longer effective in postponing or terminating aversive stimulation, another form of aggression might well result, that is, aggression caused by inescapable aversive environments. In those cases where on-going aggression seems more related to antecedant event, such as painful stimulation, it is doubtful whether removal of positive consequences would have any predictable effect.

Other investigations have shown that extinction schedules themselves heighten aggression, as does Hutchinson, Azrin, and Hake's (1966) demonstration that squirrel monkeys will attack a rubber bite hose when placed on a stimulus-signaled extinction period. With these data, there might eventually be found some interaction between extinction procedures designed to decrease operant aggression and the fact that extinction schedules are aversive enough to sometimes produce aggression.

Many theoretical treatments of aggression imply that aggression levels automatically increase within organisms and that only inhibition prevents these levels from continuing to increase. If this were the case, schedules that failed to inhibit rising aggression would seem ineffective in controlling it. Lagerspetz (1971, pp. 7–8) has suggested that data on the effects of isolation on aggression might shed some light on the inhibition theories: "The spontaneous increase in aggressiveness which occurs in these animals [isolated mice] when no learning of aggression and practically no variation in external stimulation is present suggests that aggressiveness has a tendency to rise *if it is not suppressed.*" This type of information may tend to indicate that simple extinction of aggression may not be effective in keeping aggressive tendencies from "welling up." For example, Bandura and Walters (1963) suggest a similar situation in their work with children; where the adult experimenter makes no effort to discourage aggressive play, aggression will increase. It should be noted, however, that isolated environments are not neutral environments where the organism's *true* behavior patterns may develop freely. In fact, far from being neutral, isolated environments are more accurately categorized as aversive environments.

One method for the control of on-going aggression that has recently been subjected to experimental analysis is punishment. As researchers have pointed out, the use of punishment to suppress aggression is complicated by the fact that punishment involves the delivery of an aversive stimulus—something that has been proven to *increase* the likelihood of aggression. One of the first reports of an experimental procedure involving punishment of aggression involved punishment of the rather species-specific, instinctual display of Siamese fighting fish *(Betta splendens)* (Adler and Hogan 1963). More recent experimentation has involved the punishment of aggression produced by aversive events, which more readily allows for generalization among various species, and is directly related to variations in several potential independent variables. In the first of these experiments, Ulrich, Wolfe, and Dulaney (1969) used bite-contingent shock to suppress the attack of squirrel monkeys whose aggression has been produced by fixed-time presentation of scheduled shock. With this procedure, biting attack was suppressed to a near-zero level, but not without an initial facilitation of biting in two of the three subjects, and not without a reported observation of some other behavior (finger biting, face clawing, slumped postures for extended periods of time) during punishment conditions. In a similar experiment, Azrin (1970) found that the degree of suppression was directly related to the intensity of the punishing shock.

Both of the above experiments employed restrained squirrel monkeys and measured attack against a bite hose. Two other recent experiments have studied the punishment of aggression in paired-subject situations with rats. Baenninger and Grossman (1969) used tail pinches to produce aggression in partially restrained paired rats, after which they used electric shock to hind paws and then to forepaws to suppress subjects' biting attacks. While only biting attacks were explicitly punished, the frequency of expressions of dominance and of stereotyped fighting postures also decreased. The authors note: "This finding suggests an essential unity of the three aggressive behaviors measured in this experiment" (p. 1021). Roberts and Blase (1971) used electric foot shock to both produce and suppress aggression in unrestrained paired rats, and they also found that the degree of suppression was directly related to the intensity of the punishing stimulus. These authors reported some differences in the nature of the attacks, depending on whether aggression was punished. They noted that, although there were fewer fights in the experimental groups, there appeared to be more contacts and more attack movements. When a fight did occur, it seemed more vigorous than fights by controls, and it tended to last for a longer period of time. This effect was possibly due to the eliciting function of the punishing stimulus once a fight had begun.

In only the first of these experiments were individual data presented. Rate of biting attack within and between daily sessions was reported, as were changes in biting performance from minute to minute, showing sample biting performances in various phases for individual subjects. In the other three experiments data were averaged according to experimental group performance over sessions (Baenninger and Grossman 1969; Roberts and Blase 1971), or data were averaged according to individual performance across phases relative to individual baseline performance (Azrin 1970). This difference in individual data as opposed to averaged data is significant when some other issues regarding the use of punishment to suppress aggression are examined. Ulrich, Wolfe, and Dulaney (1969) reported some initial facilitation when punishment was introduced, which was observable in cumulative records taken from the first punishment session for two of the subjects. They also reported that observation of the subjects during experimental sessions indicated some other behaviors may have taken the place of hose biting during punishment conditions. Thus far, the possibility of such side effects has been only partially supported by Roberts and Blase, who mentioned differences in the attack responses to shock between rats who were punished for aggression and those who were not. Since they are critical to the control of aggression, these potential side effects require further experimentation and documentation.

Recent experiments within our laboratory have attempted to measure potential side effects from punishment of shock-induced aggression. By equipping a restraining chair with two bite hoses, it is possible to punish the biting of one of them and record nonpunished behavior resulting from punishment on the other. Thus far, data indicate that when a subject is punished for biting attack against one hose, biting on the other hose increases. In addition, some subjects continue to bit the hose that results in punishment for several minutes after the punishment schedule is first introduced, accumulating more bites on this hose than before punishment. Further, even after biting on the punished hose is suppressed to near zero, biting attacks on the nonpunished hose occur frequently. This behavior is very unstable, however, with subject's biting rates on the nonpunished hose fluctuating hundreds of bits from one session to the other, with no variation in number of shocks received (Dulaney et al., 1971). Thus far, such a phenomenon sheds little hope for the use of punishment to control aggression caused by aversive stimuli. To the extent that shock-induced aggression is also a technique for studying other, related forms of aggression, that is, aggression caused by other sorts of aversive events, data on the effectiveness of punishment of shock-induced aggression may have implications for these other aggressive reactions as well. This area, however, is relatively unexplored. Experimental designs employing other aversive events to produce aggression, such as extinction schedules, could reveal more general information on the effects of punishment on aggression.

The Laboratory Analysis of Human Aggression

Some attempts have been made to study human aggression in laboratory situations analogous to those used to analyze nonhuman aggression. Such studies feature a measurable, repeatable aggressive response, which usually involves delivering aversive stimulation to another organism. They retain the isolated experimental environment, repeated sessions using the same subjects under different experimental conditions, long-term, individual analysis of each subject's behavior, and analysis of aggressive responding in terms of rate. However, most of the problems that can be encountered in the laboratory analysis of human behavior are encountered, in force, in such studies. These examples illustrate both some of the results that can be achieved and some of the difficulties encountered.

Ulrich and Favell (1970) put children in a situation where they could acquire reinforcement for stacking bottle stoppers on a table. Completion of the task was sometimes interrupted by experimentally programmed table vibrations. The children were told that another child was in a similar situation in the next room and that presses on a button available to the subject shook the table of the other child. Aggression was measured as the rate of button pressing. As could have been predicted from animal research, those situations that were most aversive produced the greatest amount of aggressive behavior. The subjects pushed the button they thought would shake another child's table most often when experimentally programmed table vibrations caused the subject's stoppers to topple. Button pressing occurred, but at a lower rate, when the subject's stoppers toppled as a function of something other than table vibrations, such as when the child accidentally knocked them over. In both cases, the child was willing to shake the table of another child, even though the experimenters made no explicit connection between the subject's own table vibrations and the behavior of the "child" in the other room.

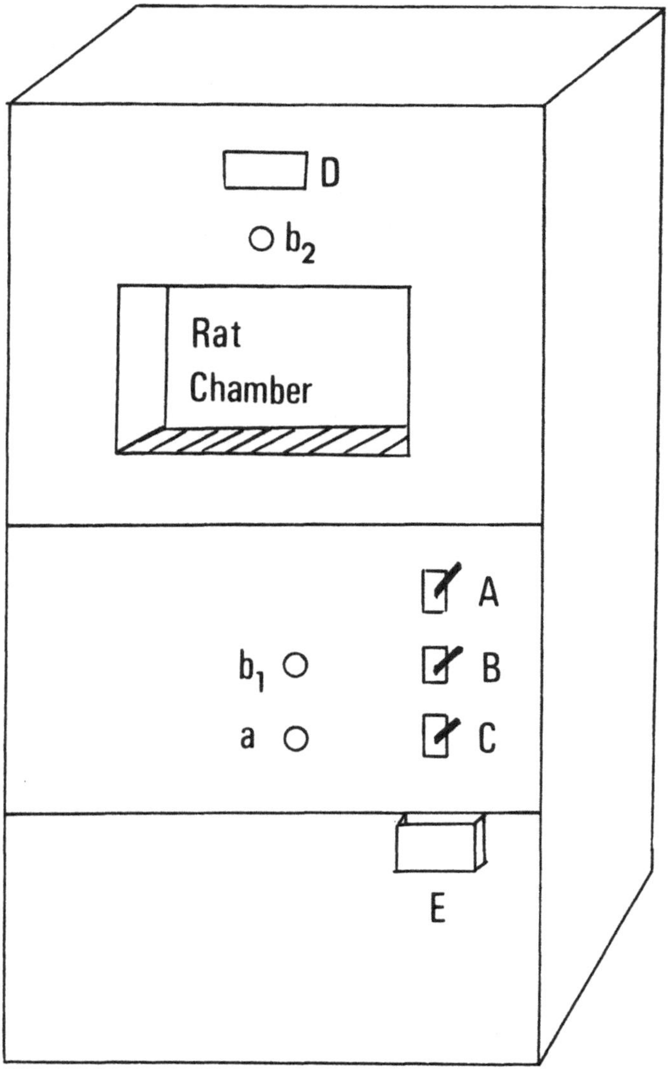

FIGURE 4.1. *Response console, measuring 2 × 2 × 7 feet high. A = reinforcer switch; B = avoidance switch; C = shock switch; D = counter; E = reinforcer container; a = discriminative stimulus for reinforcement period;* b_1 *= warning stimulus for avoidance;* b_2 *= red stimulus light. As necessary, during various experiments panels were interchangeable and removable.*

Kelly and Hake (1970) designed an experimental situation where aggression was defined as preference for a punching response over a button-pressing response. Teen-aged subjects pulled a knob for monetary positive reinforcement and concurrently avoided and escaped periodic presentations of a tone by either pressing a button or by punching a cushion. Either response was effective in terminating or postponing the tone. When placed on an extinction schedule were pulling the knob produced no monetary reinforcement, most of the subjects' rates of cushion punching increased. This increase was shown to be directly related to extinction itself rather than to an increase in the

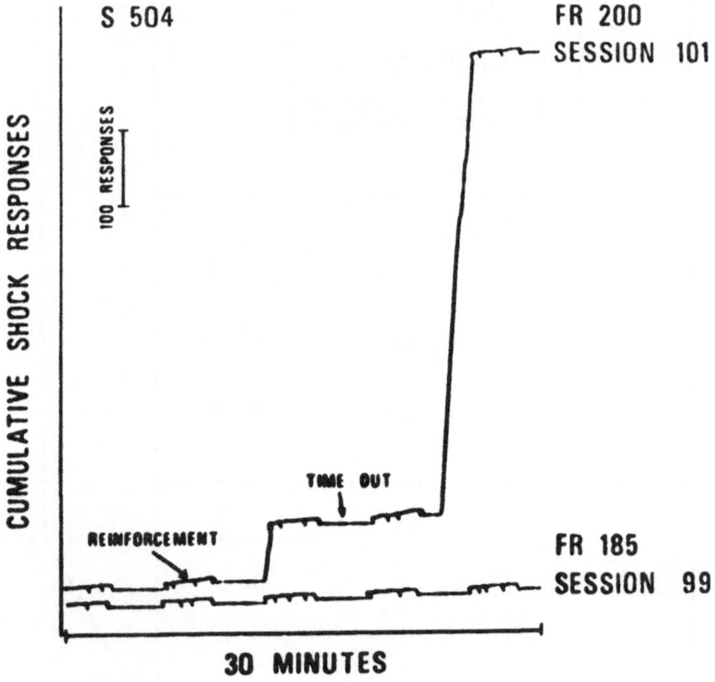

FIGURE 4.2. *Sample cumulative records of shock responding for S–504 under added cost contingencies for each time-out period. Subject 504 had to pay fifteen cents for each time-out that was not avoided. The two presented sessions (99 and 101) are the first sessions under the respective fixed-ratio requirement of FR–185 and FR–200. Time-out periods are indicated by downward deflections of the recording pen held into position for the duration of the time-out. Diagonal hash marks indicate the position of positive reinforcements for responses on switch A (the concurrent operant response).*

number of tone presentations. Also, when a nonaggressive alternative response was substituted for manipulation of the cushion, responding during extinction did not show the same increase. Thus, preference for punching the cushion appeared to be a function of extinction from positive reinforcement and to be unrelated to superstitious conditioning or to the possibility of preference over any previously nonpreferred response.

A series of experiments completed within our laboratory has yielded more information concerning another situation with aversive components sufficient to produce aggressive responding In these experiments, a complex schedule of reinforcement was in effect, and concurrently the subjects had to complete another response to avoid time-out (situations in which responses were not reinforced). The measure of aggression was the number of times (rate) that the subject would emit still another response to shock a rat caged in front of him. The basic apparatus is pictured in figure 4.1. Briefly, it consists of a sound-attenuated room, equipped with a chair for the subject and a response console with interchangeable front panels.

In one series of experiments,[2] college students were placed on concurrent schedules of positive reinforcement and positive reinforcement plus avoidance of time-out. Since time-out has been employed as an aversive stimulus for escape and avoidance conditioning, it is possible that unavoidable time-out may function as an aggression-producing event.

With this basic procedure, several incidences of schedule-related aggression were observed. For example, an addition of a cost contingency to time-out when avoidance criterion was missed was sufficient to produce an increase in rat shock (see fig. 4.2) for one subject (who had contingencies explained to him in advance). Prior to the manipulation of the cost contingency, the subject had a history of operating under the basic contingencies of the experiment, and it is doubtful whether the increase in rat shock was related to superstitious behavior.

With two other subjects and the one mentioned above, extinction of positive and negative reinforcement were manipulated.

2. Part of a master's thesis project conducted in the Behavior Research and Development Center by Brigette Symannek.

After a history of operating under the concurrent positive reinforcement/positive reinforcement plus avoidance of time-out, the apparatus was designed to malfunction. In extinction of positive-reinforcement conditions, the reinforcer dispenser was disconnected. In extinction of negative-reinforcement conditions, the avoidance lever was designed to break in the middle of the session, so that successful avoidance of time-out was no longer possible. In both cases, changes were blamed on recurring apparatus failure. Figure 4.3 shows cumulative records of rat-shock responses during two extinction-of-positive-reinforcement conditions. As can be seen, in both conditions of extinction the subject evidenced a greatly increased rate of rat shock. Since the subject knew the contingencies in effect, this behavior cannot be easily attributed to superstitious behavior. It should also be remembered that an increase in rate of rat shock produced no other effect but to limit the amount of time the subject could spend manipulating the reinforcement and avoidance levers. One other ex-

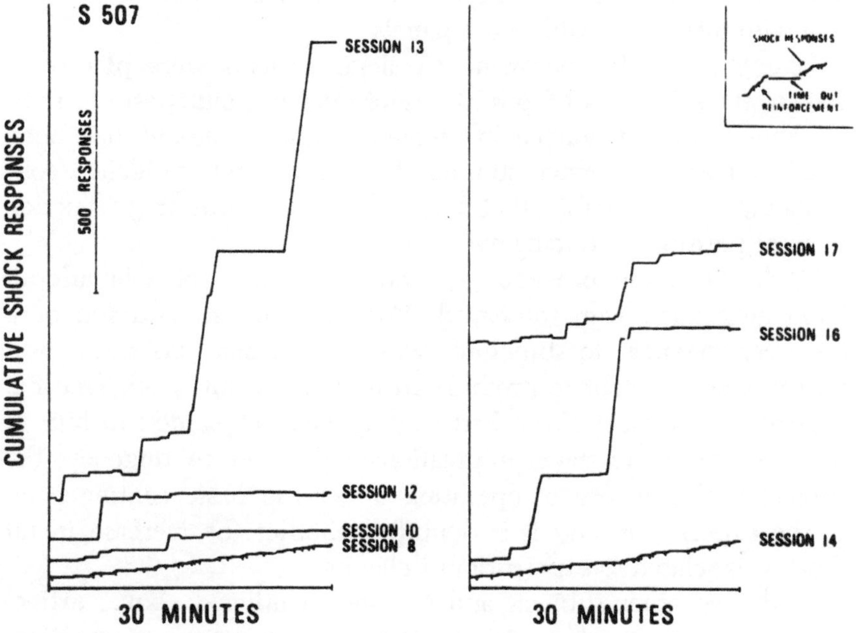

FIGURE 4.3. *Cumulative records of S–507's shock responding under positive reinforcement (sessions 8 and 14) and extinction (sessions 10, 12, 13, 14, 16, and 17) of responses for positive reinforcement.*

planation might be that, since the subject had less to do (no point in responding to procure reinforcement since the apparatus was broken), the subject simply shocked the rat for lack of something better to do. Were this the case, we should seriously reconsider whether shocking the rat was indeed aggression, or whether subjects responded simply for the novelty. Based on data from human and nonhuman aggression known to date, it would appear consistent with other findings to consider that rat shock was not just necessarily something to do.

Figure 4.4 *(top)* shows the performance of the other subject who was placed on extinction of positive reinforcement. The subject emitted a within-session increase in aggressive respond-

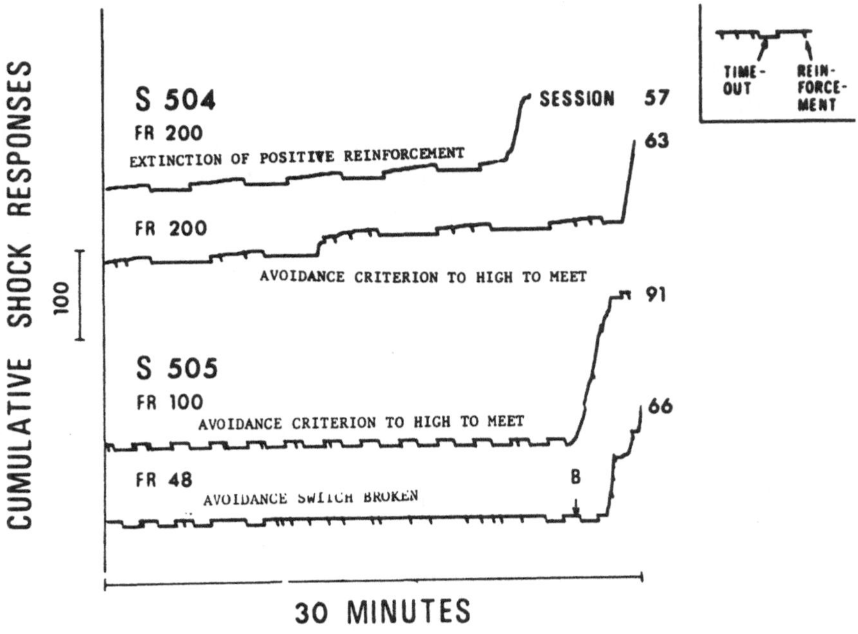

FIGURE 4.4. *Sample cumulative records illustrating within-session acceleration in shock responding for S–504 and S–505. In the upper portion of the figure, shock responding on switch A (for positive reinforcement) for S–504 during sessions 57 was subjected to extinction, and is compared with responding under FR–200 avoidance contingencies. In the bottom portion of the figure, S–505's shock responding during session 66, during which the avoidance switch broke (marked with arrow) is compared to responding under a too-high avoidance criterion (FR–100) in session 91.*

ing toward the end of the session, when the avoidance criterion was too high for him to meet or when he did not receive expected rewards (during extinction). Figure 4.4 *(bottom)* shows a similar within-session increase for another subject when he was on extinction-of-avoidance responding (the avoidance lever was programmed to break during the session), or when the avoidance criterion was too high to meet. The resulting pattern of behavior is equivalent to later sessions in which the avoidance criterion was too high for the subject to complete. It is interesting to note that rat shock occurred only at the onset of the next warning period, when the subject found he was unable to respond to the warning stimulus with the correct avoidance response. Later replications of the switch breakdown produced similar, though less dramatic effects with this subject. In all cases, however, rat shock did not occur until the subject found himself unable to avoid time-out.

Following similar lines of investigation, two naïve subjects were given instructions explaining the basic contingencies of another experiment. The procedure was a discrete trials avoidance of fixed amounts of money loss. A warning stimulus signaled to the subject when a warning period had begun. During the presence of the warning stimulus the subject had to emit a fixed number of responses in order to avoid losing five cents per trial. Money was given to the subject at the beginning of each session, and the subject then returned to the experimenter an amount equivalent to the number of times he was unable to complete the avoidance criterion. Although the number of avoidance responses necessary to avoid money loss varied, the subjects did receive the following explanation of the contingencies:

> All you have to be concerned with are these two switches, these two lights, and this counter. Your task will be to press this bottom button when the light near it is on. If you have pressed it enough times by the time it goes off, the red light will flash. If you do not press it enough times, the counter will count up one. That means that you owe me 5¢. For each count on the counter, you will owe me 5¢ and you will have to give back to me the amount you owe me at the end of the session. If the counter shows zero at the end of the session, you can keep all your money. Please do not manipulate the counter and stay in this room until I come to let you out.

Figure 4.5 *(top)* shows the relationship of ability to avoid money loss and frequency of rat-shock responses and *(bottom)* when shock responses occurred during trials. As can be seen, shock responses occurred for the most part in the last ten seconds of a trial and in the first ten seconds beginning each new trial—immediately after the counter recorded the loss of five cents.

The other subject did not shock the rat whether loss of five

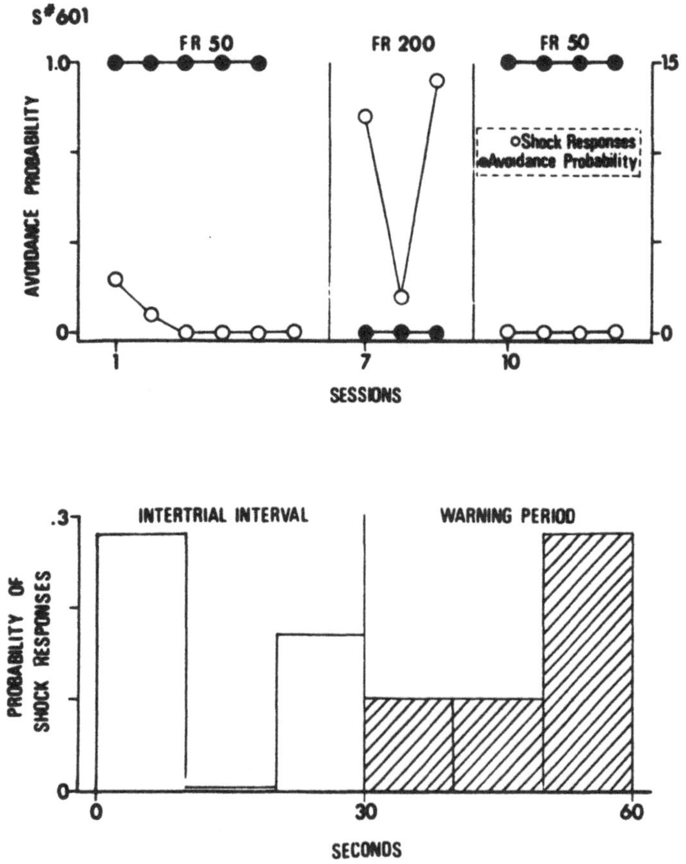

FIGURE 4.5. *Top, probability of avoidance of withdrawal of positive reinforcement responses and number of shock responses as a function of FR–50 and FR–200 avoidance for S–601. Bottom, probability distribution of temporal position of shock response probabilities for the three FR–200 (avoidance criterion) sessions. All three sessions were unsuccessful avoidance sessions.*

cents was caused by low or high avoidance criteria. When the amount of money he was paid was increased and the amount of Money he lost was also increased, some rat-shock responses did begin to occur after the counter signaled money loss. This subject, however, stopped participating in the experiment before adequate data could be collected.

Such experiments do indicate that it is possible to conduct an experimental analysis of human aggression which is comparable to that of nonhuman aggression and that similar variables seem to produce both. However, the data collected thus far in this laboratory have perhaps yielded more conclusions on the difficulties of human-aggression research than on its similarities to nonhuman experimentation.

First, in human-aggression research, the subject's history is difficult to control. Since the organisms are not raised from birth in the laboratory, any number of past events may affect performance. Past history becomes even more of a variable when attempting to study aggression, or the infliction of aversive stimulation on another organism (or responses associated with it). Some subjects may have attitudes on pressing a button for money, but all have attitudes on harming other organisms. Even if harm is not inflicted, but perhaps a task disrupted, human beings are social organisms, and they distinguish between those situations that typically are associated with social punishers and those that are not. Some examples will illustrate the problems created: In a series of experiments in our laboratory,[3] college males competed against each other for reinforcers and had the opportunity to deliver electric ankle shock to their opponent. Needless to say, *two* organisms interacting (for the first time) can create a wide variety of response patterns. For example, it turned out that the reason one of our subjects would not shock his opponent, even when he was losing or getting shock himself was because he had been a prisoner of war prior to the experiment and that experience had affected his willingness to deliver aversive stimulation to other humans. He would not shock his competitor.

Also, in relation to the effects of past histories, there seem to

3. Part of a master's thesis project conducted in the Behavior Research and Development Center by William Michael.

be several classifications of college males who will volunteer for "psychological experiments involving a small amount of electric shock," and which pay a lot of money. One may expect that this type of solicitation generates something less than a random population. The only objective statement that can be made is that, in general, they tend to be male students who do not have part-time jobs, but who need money.

The location of the experiment itself can give several clues to potential subjects, which may determine how much the individual knows about the nature of the research and whether he participates. Although our researchers never specified that they were engaged in aggression research, the Behavior Research and Development Center at Western Michigan University is well known on campus as a center for the study of aggression. In addition, Western has two faculty members who specialize in aggression research and at least five others who have published experiments in aggression. It is doubtful whether this type of subject bias is specific to Western Michigan University alone. It is also possible that students who volunteered for psychological research at the University of Wisconsin or Stanford University entered the experiment with preconceived notions on the nature of the experiment. If the experiment involves more than a one-trial affair, as do most of our experiments, the subject will eventually comment to a friend (who is a psychology major) about his current money-making project. The ensuing discussion will certainly change the subject's performance, even if only temporarily.

Besides not being able to control the subjects' past histories, the experimenter also has relatively little control over the subjects' current environments. In our experiments that involved competitors shocking each other, we took great pains to insure that the subjects did not meet or interact with each other in the laboratory. Halfway through one of our experiments we discovered (unknown to the subjects) that two of our competitors had met one day, found they had not only mutual friends, but mutual partners in a psychological experiment—each other. While their unknowing experimenters cleverly arranged for one to wait upstairs, and one to wait downstairs, and one to come fifteen minutes before the other, the subjects more cleverly arranged to ride to the lab together, where one waited outside for fifteen minutes before entering. After the experiment, one subject waited fifteen minutes for the other in their parked car. To add insult to injury, they arranged their "competition" so that each of them accumulated an approximately equal amount of reinforcers by the end of each session.

Since we only have the subjects for part of the day, it is difficult to control deprivation states from day to day. In an experiment where we were reinforcing (with money) subjects for shocking a rat during certain parts of a concurrent schedule, we encountered an avowed pacifist who refused to shock the rat. We found however that, when the rate of pay increased from five-cent reinforcers to fifty-cent ones, response rate increased immediately. But after two days, the subject's rate just as immediately declined to zero. Independent of our contingencies, the subject had gotten a part-time job. When deprivation states outside laboratory control changed, so did his behavior, including his return to pacifism. In fact, one might hypothesize that the major effect of increasing the value of the reinforcer on the probability of rat shock was to force the subject to look for reinforcers in a manner more in keeping with his beliefs. And, there is, of course, always the problem of subjects simply not returning for further experimental sessions, as a function of variables completely beyond laboratory control.

In addition to not having adequate control of deprivation states directly affecting the effectiveness of the reinforcers, other changes in deprivation outside the laboratory produce changes in behavior from day to day. When we quizzed our subjects on what caused them to shock or not shock the rat on a particular day, subjects more frequently gave such reasons as "I flunked my history test, and I'm just in a bad mood" than they gave reasons relating to obvious (or subtle) changes that we had programmed. Video tapes taken through a concealed camera confirmed one subject's analysis of a particularly low rate for one day: "I was out all night, and I kept falling asleep during the session."

Since the subjects are noncaptive, certain levels of stimulation (or deprivation) cannot be allowed. This sometimes creates whimsical attitudes in subjects regarding the experiment. Sleeping in the chamber is a good example. In many cases, the whimsical attitudes are justified. When an experimenter is forced to lie to a subject about an apparatus malfunction, or about the supposedly accidental presence of an aggressive cue in the environment, the subject is likely to be suspicious and set out to undermine the experiment. When shocks are given to subjects, the intensity must be carefully monitored. Usually the intensity employed is not sufficient to produce obvious aggressive reactions. Many of these problems could be averted by taking physiological measures to determine actual arousal levels, changes in blood pressure, heart rate, galvanic skin response, etc. But since nonhuman subjects also produce equally quantifiable physiological changes and are more under the control of the environment of the experimenter, nonhuman subjects seem to be preferable.

In addition to all the problems of data collection, whimsical attitudes, uncontrollable variables and histories, and less consistent data, experimental research in human aggression is no more easily extrapolated to control of behavior outside the laboratory than is experimentation with nonhuman subjects. There are, of course, situations that are peculiar to human beings. For example, the complexities in studying the effects of sibling rivalry, imitation, educational procedures, or media violence on aggression are questions that more appropriately fall under topics of human aggression. Although it may be possible to give other types of organisms histories sufficient to study these phenomena, or to retranslate these phenomena into more basic but still complex analyses of intricate, interlocking, concurrent schedules of reinforcement so that other organisms could be employed, this at the present time does not seem to be the most productive line of investigation. However, the human organism is a particularly difficult research animal, and reliance solely on human data for universal information about media, etc., may prove to be difficult, to say the least.

The Analysis of Human Aggression outside the Laboratory

Obviously, if we are to extrapolate the results of laboratory analyses of aggression to practical problems of human behavior, we are going to need data on human behavior as it exists in the everyday world. As already mentioned, "applied" behavior-modification studies frequently provide valuable analyses of human behavior. Unfortunately, such studies of human aggression are scarce. Aggression appears to be a relatively intractable problem for behavior modifiers, and the temptation has probably been to concentrate their efforts on behaviors they can reliably treat with success.

Most studies, of course, have concentrated of the reduction or elimination of aggression. Brown and Elliot (1965) reported success in decreasing the aggression of nursery-school children by ignoring aggressive behavior and reinforcing (with attention) incompatible responses. On the other hand, Ayllon and Michael (1959) tried a similar approach to a psychotic's behavior and found extreme variability in the behavior and apparent contrast effects in which the behavior would return to levels higher than baseline.

In some cases, punishment has apparently been successful in controlling aggression. Whaley and Tough (1968) eliminated severe self-destructive behavior in a retarded child by punishing it with electric shock. Time-out has been used to eliminate aggression in retarded females (Hamilton, Stevens, and Allen 1967).

Finally, there is some indication that simply creating behavioral alternatives can decrease aggression in some situations. One global behavior-modification program in an institution for the retarded produced an increase in a number of self-care and recreational behaviors. Simultaneously, the number of hours per month in which subjects had to be isolated as a result of aggressive episodes dropped from 2,400 to zero in eleven months (Thompson et al. 1970).

This information is scattered at best, and, for the most part, experimental controls have been far from rigorous. Numerous failures have probably gone unreported. Hopefully, techniques will be developed, in part as the result of laboratory work, that will make aggression a more popular behavior for modification. As anyone who works in education or mental health knows, the problems are certainly there. At present the state of the art is not far enough advanced to permit an effective attack on the applied level.

It is time for new directions in human-aggression research. Patterson and Cobb have described research techniques that can analyze the on-going relationship between an individual's aggressive behavior and the events in his environment. Such an analysis could yield information pertinent to the control of human aggression which cannot be obtained from laboratory studies of human and nonhuman subjects. It is certainly a research strategy worth exploring.

On still a grander scale, we can go on to apply what we do know about aggression to the institutions in our society. Our understanding of aggression is far from complete. However, we have identified two of its major causes: reinforcement and, especially, aversive stimuli. At the very least, we, as social scientists, can help in the design of environments that are less aversive, and, hence, less likely to cause aggression. We can urge the discontinuation of social practices that reinforce aggression. Perhaps, as we work, we can develop more complex strategies, such as teaching children nonaggressive ways to respond to aversive situations. We can discover if and when punishment is the best or only answer to aggression. We can develop ways of teaching people to analyze and control their own aggressive responses. Such "experimentation" will not yield data of laboratory quality. However, the results it does yield may be far more useful. In addition, each such "experiment" can represent a step toward the control of human aggression, which is probably the ultimate goal of every scientist who studies it.

References

Adler, N., and Hogan, J. A. "Classical Conditioning and Punishment of an Instinctive Response in *Betta splendens*." *Animal Behaviour* 11 (1963): 351–54.

Ayllon, T., and Michael, J. L. "The Psychiatric Nurse as a Behavioral Engineer." *Journal of the Experimental Analysis of Behavior* 2 (1959): 323–34.

Azrin, N. H. "Pain and Aggression." *Psychology Today* 1 (1967): 27–33.

——. "Punishment of Elicted Aggression." *Journal of the Experimental Analysis of Behavior* 14 (1970): 7–10.

Azrin, N. H.; Hake, D. F.; and Hutchinson, R. R. "Elicitation of Aggression by a Physical Blow." *Journal of the Experimental Analysis of Behavior* 8 (1965): 55–57.

Azrin, N. H.; Hutchinson, R. R.; and Hake, D. F. "Pain-induced Fighting in the Squirrel Monkey." *Journal of the Experimental Analysis of Behavior* 6 (1963): 620–21.

Azrin, N. H.; Hutchinson, R. R.; and Hake, D. F. "Extinction-induced Aggression." *Journal of the Experimental Analysis of Behavior* 9 (1966): 191–204.

Azrin, N. H.; Hutchinson, R. R.; and Hake D. F. "Attack, Avoidance and Escape Reactions to Aversive Shock." *Journal of the Experimental Analysis of Behavior* 10 (1967): 131–48.

Azrin, N. H.; Hutchinson, R. R.; and McLaughlin, R. "The Opportunity for Aggression as an Operant Reinforcer during Aversive Stimulation." *Journal of the Experimental Analysis of Behavior* 8 (1965): 171–80.

Azrin, N. H.; Hutchinson, R. R.; and Sallery, R. D. "Pain-Aggression toward Inanimate Objects." *Journal of the Experimental Analysis of Behavior* 7 (1964): 223–28.

Azrin, N. H.; Rubin, H.; and Hutchinson, R. R. "Biting Attack by Rats in Response to Aversive Shock." *Journal of the Experimental Analysis of Behavior* 11 (1968): 633–39.

Azrin, N. H.; Ulrich, R. E.; Hutchinson, R. R.; and Norman, D. G. "Effect of Shock Duration on Shock-induced Fighting." *Journal of the Experimental Analysis of Behavior* 7 (1964): 9–11.

Baenninger, R., and Grossman, J. C. "Some Effects of Punishment on Pain-elicited Aggression." *Journal of the Experimental Analysis of Behavior* 12 (1969): 1017–22.

Bandura, A., and Walters, R. "Aggression." In *National Society for the Study of Education, 62nd Yearbook*. Pt 1: *Child Psychology*, pp. 364–415. Chicago: National Society for the Study of Education, 1963.

Boshka, S. C.; Weisman, H. M.; and Thor, D. H. "A Technique for Inducing Aggression in Rats Utilizing Morphine Withdrawal." *Psychological Record* 16 (1966): 541–43.

Brown, P., and Elliot, R. "Control of Aggression in a Nursery School Class." *Journal of Experimental Child Psychology* 2 (1965): 103–7.

Calhoun, J. B. "Population Density and Social Pathology." *Scientific American* 206 (1962): 139–48.

Cohen, D. J. "Justin and His Peers: An Experimental Analysis of a Child's Social World." *Child Development* 33 (1962): 697–717.

Creer, T. L.; Hitzing, E. W.; and Schaeffer, R. W. "Classical Conditioning of Reflexive Fighting." *Psychonomic Science* 4 (1966): 89–90.

Davis, M., and Khalsa, J. "Some Determinants of Aggressive Behavior Induced by Morphine Withdrawal." *Psychonomic Science* 24 (1971): 13–14.

Dulaney, S. J.; Scherrer, J. J.; Ulrich, R. E.; and Jones, R. T. "Displacement of Shock-induced Aggression." Paper presented at Psychonomic Society Convention, St. Louis, 1971.

Dulaney, S. J.; Ulrich, R. E.; and Kucera, T. "Effects of Punishment of a Non-aggressive Response on Aggressive Behavior. Paper presented at Psychonomic Society Convention, San Antonio, 1970.

Falk, J. "The Nature and Determinants of Adjunctive Behavior." In *Schedule Effects: Drugs, Drinking and Aggression,* edited by R. Gilbert and J. Keehn. Toronto: University of Toronto Press, 1972.

Flory, R. K. "Attack Behavior as a Function of Minimum Inter-Food Interval." *Journal of the Experimental Analysis of Behavior* 12 (1969): 825–28.

Flory, R. K.; Ulrich, R. E.; and Wolff, P. C. "The Effects of Visual Impairment on Aggressive Behavior." *Psychological Record* 15 (1965): 185–90.

Gentry, W. "Fixed-Ratio Schedule-induced Aggression." *Journal of the Experimental Analysis of Behavior* 11 (1968): 813–17.

Hamilton, J.; Stephens, L.; and Allen, P. "Controlling Aggressive and Destructive Behavior in Severely Retarded Institutionalized Residents." *American Journal of Mental Deficiency* 7 (1967): 852–56.

Holland, J. G. "Human Vigilance." *Science* 28 (1958): 61–67.

Hutchinson, R. R.; Azrin, N. H.; and Hake, D. F. "An Automatic Method for the Study of Aggression in Squirrel Monkeys." *Journal of the Experimental Analysis of Behavior* 9 (1966): 233–37.

Hutchinson, R. R.; Azrin, N. H.; and Hunt, G. "Attack Produced by Intermittent Reinforcement of a Concurrent Operant Response." *Journal of the Experimental Analysis of Behavior* 11 (1968): 489–95.

Hutchinson, R. R., and Emley, G. "Schedule-dependent Factors Contributing to Schedule-induced Phenomena." In *Schedule Effects: Drugs, Drinking and Aggression,* edited by R. Gilbert and J. Keehn. Toronto: University of Toronto Press, 1972.

Hutchinson, R. R.; Renfrew, J.; and Young, G. A. "Effects of Long-Term Shock and Associated Stimuli on Aggressive and Manual Responses." *Journal of the Experimental Analysis of Behavior* 15 (1971): 141–66.

Hutchinson, R. R.; Ulrich, R. E.; and Azrin, N. H. "Effects of Age and Related Factors on the Pain-Aggression Reaction." *Journal of Comparative and Physiological Psychology* 59 (1965): 365–69.

Kelly, J., and Hake, D. F. "An Extinction-induced Increase in an Aggressive Response with Humans." *Journal of the Experimental Analysis of Behavior* 14 (1970): 153–64.

Lagerspetz, K. "Learning and Suppression of Aggressiveness in Animal

Experiments: A Reinterpretation." Report from the Institute of Psychology, no. 35. University of Turku, Finland, 1971.

Miller, N. E. "Theory and Experiment Relating Psychoanalytic Displacement to Stimulus-Response Generalization." *Journal of Abnormal and Social Psychology* 43 (1948): 155–78.

O'Kelley, L. E., and Steckle, L. C. "A Note on Long-enduring Emotional Responses in the Rat." *Journal of Psychology* 8 (1939): 125–31.

Reynolds, G. S.; Catania, A. C.; and Skinner, B. F. "Conditioned and and Unconditioned Aggression in Pigeons." *Journal of the Experimental Analysis of Behavior* 1 (1963): 73–74.

Roberts, C., and Blase, K. "Elicitation and Punishment of Intraspecies Aggression by the Same Stimulus." *Journal of the Experimental Analysis of Behavior* 15 (1971): 193–96.

Roediger, M., and Stevens, M. "The effects of Delayed Presentation of the Object of Aggression on Pain-induced Fighting." *Psychonomic Science* 21 (1970): 55–56.

Scott, J. P. "Biology and Human Aggression." *American Journal of Orthopsychiatry* 40 (1970): 568–76.

Sidman, M. *Tactics of Scientific Research.* New York: Basic Books, 1960.

Skinner, B. F. *Science and Human Behavior.* New York: Macmillan Co., 1953.

Stachnik, T. J.; Ulrich, R. E.; and Mabry, J. H. Reinforcement of Intra- and Inter-Species Aggression with Intracranial Stimulation." *American Zoologist* 6 (1966): 663–68.

Thompson, R.; Grabowski, J.; Errickson, E.; and Johnson, R. "Development and Maintenance of a Behavior Modification Program for Institutionalized Profoundly Retarded Adult Males." *Psychological Aspects of Disability* 17 (1970): 117–24.

Ullman, L. P., and Krasner, L. V. *Case Studies in Behavior Modification.* New York: Holt, Rinehart & Winston, 1965.

Ulrich, R. E. "Pain as a Cause of Aggression." *American Zoologist* 6 (1966): 643–62.

Ulrich, R. E. "Interaction between Reflexive Fighting and Cooperative Escape." *Journal of the Experimental Analysis of Behavior* 10 (1967): 311–17.

Ulrich, R. E., and Azrin, N. H. "Reflexive Fighting in Response to Aversive Stimulation." *Journal of the Experimental Analysis of Behavior* 5 (1962): 511–20.

Ulrich, R. E., and Favell, J. E. "Human Aggression." In *Behavior Modification in Clinical Psychology,* edited by C. Neuringer and J. Michael, pp. 105–32. New York: Appleton-Century-Crofts, 1970.

Ulrich, R. E.; Johnston, H.; Richardson, J.; and Wolff, P. C. "The Operant Conditioning of Fighting Behavior in Rats." *Psychological Record* 13 (1963): 465–70.

Ulrich, R. E.; Stachnik, T. J.; and Mabry, J. H., eds. *Control of Human Behavior*. Vol. 1: *Expanding the Behavioral Laboratory*. Glenview Ill.: Scott, Foresman & Co., 1966.

——. *Control of Human Behavior*. Vol. 2: *From Cure to Prevention*. Glenview, Ill.: Scott, Foresman & Co., 1970.

Ulrich, R. E.; Wolfe, M.; and Dulaney, S. J. "Punishment of Shock-induced Aggression." *Journal of the Experimental Analysis of Behavior* 12 (1969): 1009–15.

Ulrich, R. E.; Wolff, P. C.; and Azrin, N. H. "Shock as an Elicitor of Intra- and Inter-Species Fighting Behavior." *Animal Behaviour* 12 (1964): 14–15.

Vernon, W., and Ulrich, R. E. "Classical Conditioning of Pain-elicited Aggression." *Science* 152 (1966): 668–69.

Whaley, D. L., and Tough, J. *Treatment of a Self-injuring Mongoloid with Shock-induced Suppression and Avoidance*. Michigan Department of Mental Health Research Bulletin. Publ. by Mich. Dept. of Mental Health, Lansing, 1968. 33–35.

Leonard Berkowitz received his bachelor's degree from New York University and his Ph.D. from the University of Michigan. After four years as a research psychologist with the Human Resources Research Center, he joined the faculty of the University of Wisconsin, where he is currently the Vilas Research Professor in Psychology. In 1970–71 he was a fellow at the Center for Advanced Study in the Behavioral Sciences. Professor Berkowitz has been engaged in research on aggressive behavior and his book Aggression: A Social Psychological Analysis *is well known. He has served as a consulting editor for* Journal of Experimental Social Psychology *and* Journal of Experimental Research in Personality, *as an associated editor of* Journal of Personality and Social Psychology, *and as editor for* Advances in Experimental Social Psychology. *In 1971–72 he was president of the Division of Personality and Social Psychology of the American Psychological Association.*

5

Words and Symbols as Stimuli to Aggressive Responses

LEONARD BERKOWITZ

We all know that direct attacks and insults can instigate aggressive reactions. Researchers have also shown that pain, task frustrations, and instrumental learning can also lead to aggressive behavior. Aggression can result, in other words, if the individual has been exposed to a painful or definitely unpleasant experience or has learned that he can satisfy certain desires by attacking other people. Aggression has other causes as well, however, and I will try to show that verbal and/or symbolic stimuli can also produce aggressive responses because of their semantic significance. Simply put, my thesis is that, because of their aggressive meaning, these stimuli can elicit impulsive aggressive responses from those persons who are set to act aggressively.

I find it convenient to view this process as an outcome of classical rather than operant conditioning. Since this interpretation is bound to upset some people, let me explain what these concepts mean to me.

For Skinner, of course, the operant is a voluntary response that acts upon the environment to generate consequences; the behavior is emitted—that is, comes about voluntarily or spontaneously—upon the appearance of a signal, the discriminative stimulus. The discriminative stimulus does not elicit the response. It only "sets the occasion" for the action, generally by informing

The author's research reported here was supported by grants from the National Institute of Mental Health.

the organism of the probable appearance of a reinforcement if the response is made. Virtually every act besides simple reflexes—that is, all behavior of interest to social psychology—is operant behavior, according to Skinner. However, with Staats (1968, p. 35), I suspect this approach has been unduly one-sided and has neglected the operation of classical conditioning in social behavior. My misgivings, such as they are, center around the idea, implicit in the operant formulation, that practically all human conduct is voluntarily directed toward the attainment of some anticipated reward. We might want to believe this for self-glorifying as well as theoretical reasons. But I would like to suggest that this is only part of the picture, although probably the largest part. Some actions, and also certain aspects of other behaviors, could come about automatically, involuntarily, because they are elicited by particular stimuli. These responses, or components of a complex response, are not governed to any important extent by anticipated rewards and, moreover, can be of considerable interest to social psychology and even the "man on the street."

To highlight the issue at hand, let us consider my extension of the Staats and Staats (1958) language-conditioning experiment. In that study the experimenters trained subjects to have either positive or negative attitudes toward certain names by pairing these names with either pleasant or unpleasant words in a classicial conditioning paradigm. Berkowitz and Knurek (1969) asked if these acquired attitudes would influence behavior toward a person bearing the name having the conditioned emotional value.

Following the Staatses' procedure, undergraduate men were trained to have a negative attitude toward a particular name, either Ed or George, and were then either insulted or treated in a neutral fashion by the trainer. At the completion of this phase of the investigation, each subject went into another room, supposedly for another experiment with a new researcher, where he engaged in a brief discussion with two fellow students. The two men were introduced as "Ed" and "George" so that one of them had the critical name. These poeple, of course, were the experimenter's accomplices, but neither of them knew the condition to which the subject had been assigned.

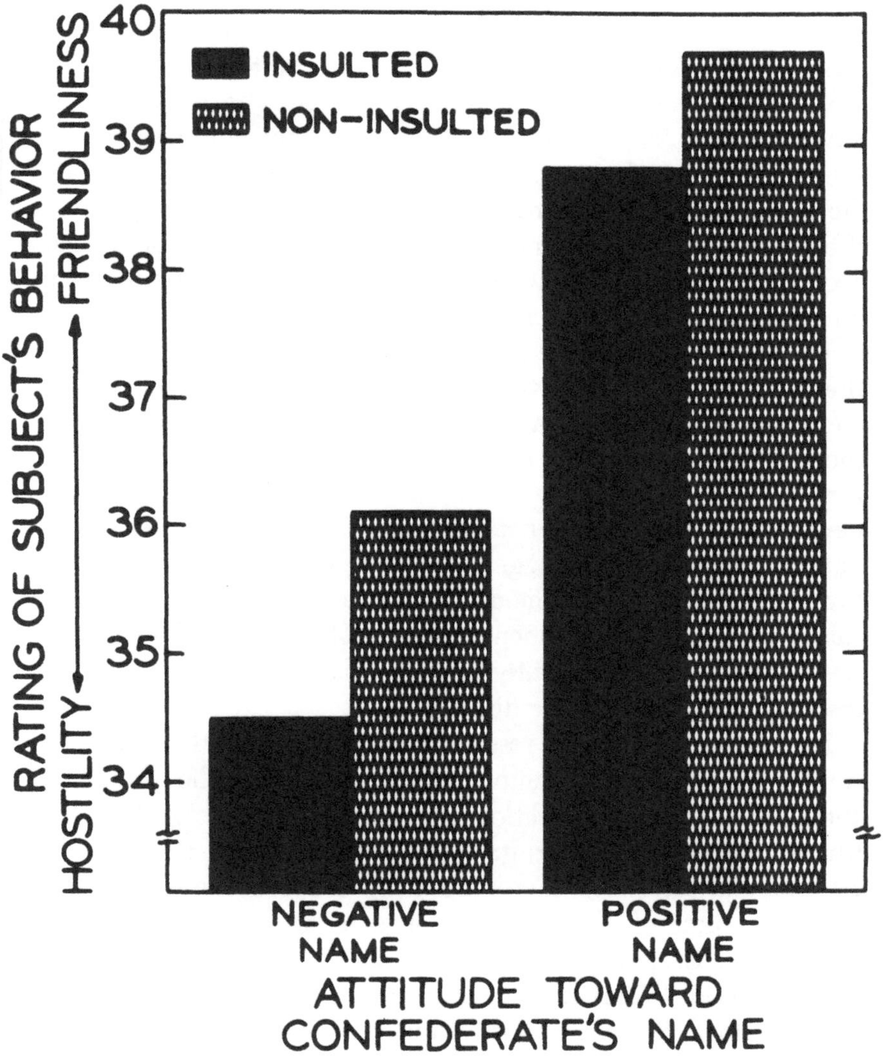

FIGURE 5.1. *Confederates' mean rating of subject's behavior toward them (after Berkowitz and Knurek, 1969).*

Two different measures indicated that the acquired negative feeling had carried over from the conditioned name to the person bearing that label. First, each subject evaluated his two partners' contributions to their discussion. For the nonangered subjects the accomplice having the disliked name was rated less favorably than the partner with the neutral name, but the difference was not significant. There was the expected reliable difference, however, in the case of the angry men, as if the anger had facilitated the expression of the learned hostility toward the person carrying the "bad" name. More important for our present purposes, each accomplice also rated how friendly the subject had been toward him in the discussion. The results are shown in figure 5.1.

The confederates had detected the subject's attitude toward them even though they were unaware of the experimental treatment given him. The accomplice bearing the disliked name thought that the subject had been more unfriendly toward him than did the accomplice with the neutral name. Although the experimental variables did not interact to a significant degree, the data in the table also suggest the men were particularly hostile toward the negatively named confederate after they had been insulted by the first experimenter. The hostility aroused in the earlier encounter had evidently been displaced somewhat onto the discussion partner with the disliked name.

In talking about this research, I have noted that many instances of racial and ethnic prejudice could be the product of this kind of classical conditioning. People may develop hostile attitudes toward particular groups merely because their parents, friends, and associates have repeatedly coupled unpleasant words with the sight of these groups or even the utterance of their names. Many psychologists of various theoretical persuasions have objected to this kind of interpretation, however. They have claimed that Staats's (1958) subjects did not respond automatically to the names to which they were supposed to be conditioned but, instead, had consciously grasped the experimenter's purpose, or the rule he presumably was following, and then cooperated with the experimenter by adhering to this rule. Staats (1969) has effectively countered these arguments. Among other things, he has pointed to several studies in which the classical conditioning of attitudes occurred although it was extremely unlikely that the subjects had been aware of the conditioning rule. The Berkowitz and Knurek experiment provides yet another demonstration of this involuntary carry-over effect.

In addition to demonstrating the generalization of a negatively conditioned attitude, the Berkowitz-Knurek (1969) experiment had tried to show that persons having certain stimulus properties are particularly likely to be the "scapegoat" victims of "displaced hostility" following anger arousal: persons having characteristics the angry individual had previously learned to dislike. Having acquired aversive stimulus characteristics, these individuals can presumably evoke the aggressive responses that the provoked person is disposed to make. Although the results in this first study were not as clear-cut as we would have wished, a later experiment by the same investigators (unpublished) yielded somewhat better evidence.

Each male subject first worked together with a fellow student (actually the experimenter's confederate) for a cash prize, and was either *(a)* successful in his assigned task, *(b)* thwarted by his partner's ineptitude, or *(c)* could not do the assignment satisfactorily and was insulted by the confederate. The subject then participated in a supposedly different study in which he was to evaluate two applicants for the position of dormitory counselor. By a "coincidence" (that was not very surprising to the subjects), one of the job candidates had the same first name as the subject's previous partner.

TABLE 5.1. *Mean number of bad personal qualities attributed to each counselor candidate*

Candidate's Name-mediated Connection with First-Phase Partner	*First-Phase Experience* frustrated	insulted	successful
Same name	4.1_b	1.3_a	2.1_a
Different name	1.8_a	1.2_a	1.3_a

NOTE: Cells having different subscripts are significantly different at the .05 level.

SOURCE: Adapted from Berkowitz and Knurek (unpublished).

This name influenced the judgments expressed by the thwarted subjects. As table 5.1 indicates, very few unfavorable personality traits were attributed to both job applicants, and the candidates' names did not affect these evaluations if the subjects had been insulted by their first-phase partner. This other person apparently was so clearly different from the job candidates in being unusually obnoxious that the insulted subjects did not generalize from him to the applicant carrying the same name. However, the generalization did occur when the previous emotion-arousing partner had not been so distinctly unique; the frustrated men attributed reliably more bad qualities to the crucial applicant bearing the same name as the thwarting confederate than to the neutrally named applicant. The job candidate's name-mediated association with the prior frustrater caused him to evoke hostile reactions from the aroused men—providing the frustrater and target were not clearly different in other respects.

An experiment by Ervin (1964) also illustrates the automatic operation of language-mediated associations. French men and women residing in Washington, D.C., who were fluent in English, composed stories in response to thematic-apperception-test (TAT) pictures, once in French and once in English. (Needless to say, the order of the French and English requirements were counterbalanced.) A content analysis of the stories showed that the language spoken had elicited somewhat different ideas. As Ervin had predicted, the subjects expressed more ideas related to autonomy and withdrawal when they spoke in French; and also, as she had expected, they had a higher frequency of themes dealing with aggression against their peers in the French language. The language itself seemed to carry with it a chain of associations facilitating certain ideas, particularly about independence and aggression.

The ideas and feelings involuntarily evoked by words can also affect behavior. This phenomenon was demonstrated in a recent field experiment carried out by Jacqueline Macaulay and me. Women shoppers were interviewed one at a time about the topic of helpfulness: how helpful they would be in various situations and how helpful other people would be. Approximately half of the women were rewarded with the interviewer's approval, but the nature of the remarks given this approval varied, depending upon the experimental condition. In one group the interviewer smiled and praised the respondent every time she expressed a helpful idea—that is, when she was in favor of aiding other persons in need. For the other group, by contrast, the interviewer rewarded remarks advocating distrust and noninvolvement with other people. The remaining subjects were either not rewarded at all during the interview or were in a noninterviewed control condition. Shortly afterward, a young male college student approached the women and asked if he could borrow forty cents for a bus ticket to a nearby community, explaining that he had lost his wallet. The subjects did not connect this request with the preceding interview. We found, nevertheless, that the nature of the ideas rewarded during the interview had affected the respondents' willingness to aid the college student. Where only about half of the women in the nonrewarded and noninterviewed groups donated the money, 65 percent of the respondents gave the student the requested money if helpful statements had been rewarded, but only 41 percent did so if selfish notions had been praised. This difference is sharpened even further if we exclude those cases in which the interviewer believed she had failed to reward the appropriate ideas (generally because they had been too infrequent). The donation rate in the reward-helpfulness group went up only to 66 percent, but dropped to a very low 28 percent when selfish ideas had been rewarded. The experimentally evoked and reinforced ideas facilitated behavior consistent with these ideas. Other data suggest that the reward manipulation had also affected the respondents' mood. Over all, they were judged to be in a pleasant mood if the interviewer had approved help-related statements, and in a pretty bad mood if cynical, selfish ideas were rewarded. These feelings could have influenced their reactions to the student in need.

Automatic Reactions to the Meaning of Words

The words we use evoke associated ideas and feelings, especially if the verbal responses are rewarded. These associations comprise the words' meanings. Many words have aggressive connotations and thus carry with them associated ideas and feelings that can facilitate aggressive behavior.

Whatever else is involved here, a broad variety of aggressive occurrences and reactions are tied together semantically as "aggression." Lang, Geer, and Hnatiow (1963), among others, have demonstrated the existence of such a dimension of hostile meaning. In their study, galvanic skin responses that had previously been conditioned to words having a highly hostile meaning were also evoked by other highly hostile words, but not by words lacking this connotation.

Similarly, several experiments have shown that the reinforcement of one kind of aggressive response increases the likelihood of other types of aggressive reactions as well. To sample just a few of these studies, Loew (1967) reinforced a group of college students whenever they spoke a hostile word aloud, and he showed that these students later administered more intense electric shocks to other persons engaged in a learning task (as punishment for supposed errors) than did other subjects reinforced for speaking nonaggressive words. Geen and Pigg (1970) reversed this sequence in a recent investigation. After their college men were given verbal approval for administering shocks to a fictitious learner, the subjects had a higher frequency of aggressive word associations on a later word-association task than did a nonreinforced control group.

It would seem that the first responses made by the subjects (whether verbal or electrical aggression) had elicited other aggressive-response tendencies as well, so that at least some of these were also strenghened by the reinforcement. But as the classical conditioning model requires, the heightened tendency is the probability of making a particular class of responses (aggressive ones in this case) *to a particular class of stimuli* (stimuli associated with aggression). Geen has provided evidence on this point. In his study with Pigg, the reinforced men gave more aggressive word associations only to words having an aggressive meaning and not to nonaggressive words. A later study (Geen and Stonner 1971) also demonstrates the elicting role of aggressive cues: The subjects were first either reinforced or not reinforced by the experimenter for giving electric shocks to another person. Then, following this training, the subjects were to shock the other person again each time a word was flashed on the screen. Some of the words had aggressive connotations (e.g., "murder"), while the others did not (e.g., "travel"). Although the experimenter did not say anything about the nature of these words, the men reinforced for aggression gave significantly more intense punishment to the supposed learner only in response to the aggressive words. The reinforcement had strengthened a tendency to react aggressively to aggressive cues. Probably because of this kind of reinforcement history, when hyperaggressive people act violently, they usually do so in reaction to stimuli that for them are associated with aggression.

Language-elicited responses strengthen similar or compatible reactions, but can interfere with semantically opposed reaction tendencies. We have already seen this in my previously mentioned experiment with Macaulay. There, women were more likely to be helpful to a college student if their help-related statements had previously been rewarded, and they were less inclined to render assistance if their selfish, noninvolvement ideas had been approved earlier. These latter notions were incompatible with helping and, when spoken and reinforced, had dampened the women's willingness to give aid. Parke, Ewall, and Slaby (1972) demonstrated a similar phenomenon in the case of aggression. Using a procedure similar to the one employed by Loew (1967), they required each male college student in their study to speak one word out of the three presented to him. His choice of a particular kind of word was given verbal approval. In one condition aggressive words were rewarded, while help-related words were reinforced in another group, and neutral words clearly differentiated from either of the other categories were rewarded in the third condition. These conditions did not differ in the number of trials to the criterion or in the number of errors made during learning. At the completion of the training phase, each subject served as a "trainer" in a supposed learning study and had to shock a fellow student each time that person made a mistake on the learning task. The "trainer" was informed when each mistake occurred but could vary the intensity of the shocks he administered. Parke and his students found that the earlier word usage affected the intensity of the punishment the subjects inflicted upon the "learner" in this task. The three conditions differed significantly, with the men rewarded for speaking aggressive words showing the strongest aggression and the group approved for using help-related words being the least punitive. In this study, as in the field experiment, then, the rewarded usage of particular words subsequently facilitated behavior consistent with the meaning of these words and inhibited semantically opposite actions.

Parke has offered several observations that are relevant here. For one thing, he noted that these findings were consistent with other research results also showing that aggression could be minimized by rewarding responses incompatible with aggression. Brown and Elliot (1965) had lessened the aggression displayed by nursery-school children by reinforcing cooperative behavior. Parke wondered if the effect described were dependent upon reinforced verbalizations. The experimenter's approval could have directed the subject's attention to the particular word category and might have helped to lower inhibitions against semantically similar behavior, but otherwise might not have been necessary.

Finally, Parke also indicated that we can be affected by the words of other persons as well as by our own. In a later experiment he and his associates found that subjects who merely observed a model being reinforced for aggressive verbalizations later increased their level of physical aggression. The model's aggressive words evidently evoked aggression-facilitating reactions within the observers. We have now come to the consequences of witnessed aggression.

Aggression in the Mass Media

Some mass-media effects can also be understood as classically conditioned responses. Up until now I have suggested that the words we use can serve as stimuli to evoke aggression-facilitating reactions. But as Parke's last-mentioned results indicate, we can also encounter these stimuli visually and orally. They can be introduced by the printed page, the movie or television screen, or even by nearby objects.

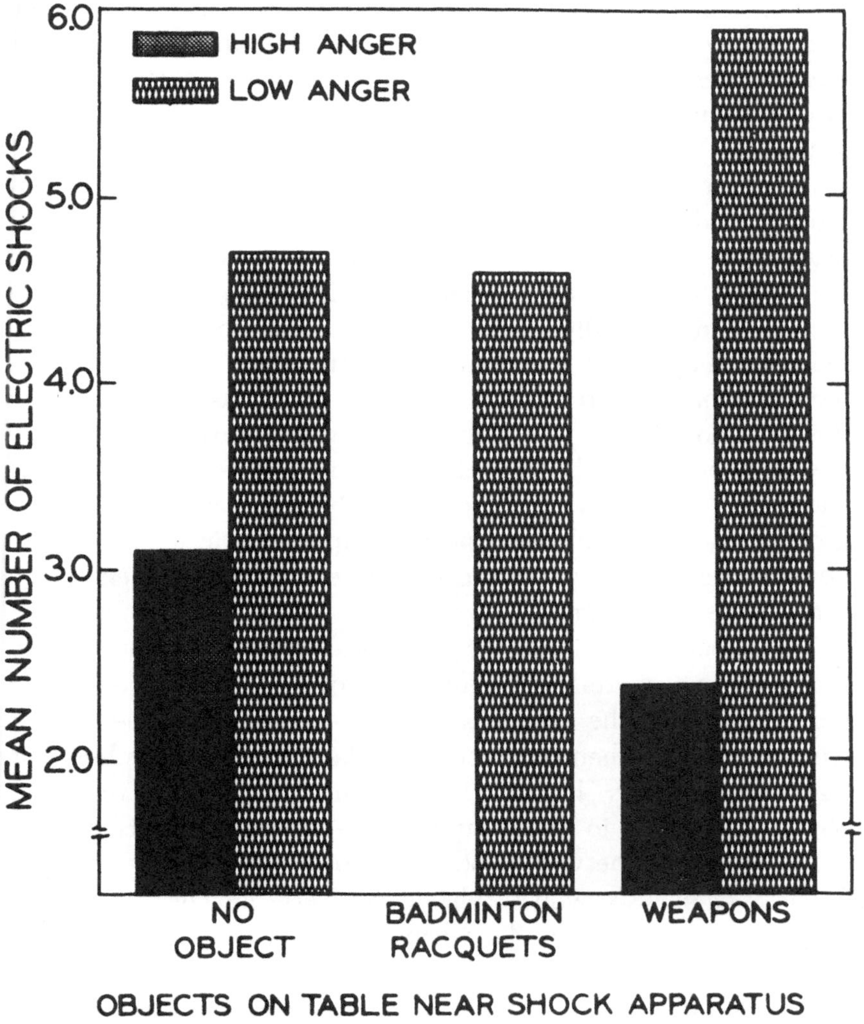

FIGURE 5.2. *Mean number of electric shocks given in weapons and no-weapons conditions (after Berkowitz and LePage, 1967).*

Weapons are a good example of stimuli having a fairly clear aggressive meaning. For many people in our society, these objects are closely associated with aggression. Assuming that the weapons do not produce inhibitions that are stronger than the evoked aggressive reactions (as would be the case, e.g., if the weapons were labeled as morally bad), the mere presence of these aggressive objects should lead to stronger attacks upon an available target than would occur if only a neutral object were nearby.

An experiment by Berkowitz and LePage (1967) yielded confirming evidence. Half of the male-undergraduate subjects were made to be angry with the experimenter's confederate, while the other men had a neutral encounter with them. After this, the subjects had a socially sanctioned opportunity to attack the confederate; they could give him from one to ten shocks as their judgment of his performance on an assigned task. For some of the men, however, a rifle and revolver were nearby (supposedly having been left in the room by a previous experimenter), while badminton racquets were close to the shock apparatus in another group, and nothing else was near the apparatus in a third condition. Figure 5.2 shows the mean number of shocks given to the confederate in each group.

The hypothesis guiding the study was supported: the strongly provoked men were more aggressive towards their tormentor in the presence of the weapons than when nonaggressive objects were nearby or when only the shock key was on the table. The aggressive objects had elicited implicit aggressive reactions, which then added to the strength of the aroused subjects' attacks.

Let me take issue with another interpretation of these findings. Some psychologists, who I believe are overly attached to operant theorizing, contend that the weapons served only as discriminative rather than as conditioned stimuli. They prefer to believe that these objects only informed the subjects that aggression was permissible and that they did not otherwise elicit aggressive responses. Contrary to this view, however, it seems to me there is ample reason to think aggressive reactions were evoked. Some of the findings previously discussed are consistent with my argument, and I will present other evidence later; but some results obtained by Page and Scheidt (1971) are also pertinent. They repeated the essential features of the Berkowitz and LePage (1967) study with two populations: naïve students who had never been in a psychology experiment before and experienced subjects. Each subject was angry with the confederate. The weapons effect was obtained with the experienced subjects, but, equally interesting, the naïve men were *less* aggressive in the presence of the weapons than when nothing was near the shock apparatus.

Assuming with the investigators that the naïve subjects had a high level of evaluation apprehension, I suggest (on the basis of these results and of very similar patterns obtained in other studies) that the weapons *had* evoked implicit aggressive reactions in these anxious people. However, they apparently thought the experimenter would evaluate them harshly if they attacked the confederate strongly and, therefore, leaned over backwards to avoid displaying intense aggression. Clark (1952) had obtained the same kind of "denial" reaction when men were sexually aroused in a nonpermissive setting. Relatively strong but socially disapproved responses (aggression or sex) were presumably elicited in these instances and then were suppressed because the subjects feared that the open behavior would be punished in one way or another. Why, otherwise, did the subjects show an *unusually low* level of this behavior (below that exhibited by a nonstimulated group) in response to stimuli that ordinarily evoke these reactions?

There is more direct evidence in an investigation of comic-book violence. In essential agreement with the psychiatrist Frederick Wertham, I thought that aggressive scenes portrayed in comic books would stimulate aggressive ideas in the readers. An unpublished experiment by Parker, West and myself showed this was the case. Third-, fourth-, and fifty-grade school children were asked to select words completing a series of incomplete sentences both before and after they read a particular comic book. The youngsters given a war comic book to read *(Adventures of the Green Berets)* were much more likely to exhibit an increased usage of aggressive words in finishing these sentences than the control children required to read a neutral comic book *(Gidget).* For example, if the subjects had to complete a sentence such as "I want to ____ the book" and could choose between "read" and "tear," the children who had read the war comics were more apt to select "tear."

These aggressive ideas and images evoked by violent scenes are probably usually too weak and short-lived to influence the behavior of most viewers. Under some conditions, however, these implicit reactions might lead to fairly open attacks upon an available target, even by people who ordinarily have strong inhibitions against direct aggression. This is shown in an experiment in which college girls listened to a humorous tape recording (Berkowitz 1970*a*). The co-eds were required to rate another girl's suitability for a job as dormitory counselor after they had heard a brief excerpt from a comedian's routine. Half of the subjects listened to a nonaggressive comedian (George Carlin), while the other girls heard the very hostile comedian Don Rickles in a very aggressive routine. As table 4.4 demonstrates, the female undergraduates were much more critical of the job applicant after hearing the aggressive humor than after listening to the neutral humor. Moreover, and contrary to some recent studies purporting to demonstrate the supposedly beneficial effects of aggressive humor, there was no evidence of a cathartic reduction of hostility in the aggressive-humor condition; Don Rickles's comic routine led to heightened hostility whether or not the job applicant had previously provoked the subjects. In both cases, as can also be seen in table 5.2, the hostile jokes had stimulated aggressive reactions in the listeners, which then caused them to evaluate the job applicant less favorably.

PERCEIVED AGGRESSIVENESS OF CONTACT SPORTS

An external stimulus obviously does not have "meaning" in itself; the meaning is imparted to the stimulus by the perceiver. To recite a truism, where one person might regard an event as an aggressive encounter, someone else could view the same scene as a nonaggressive situation. This implicit labeling could determine whether a witnessed occurrence will evoke aggressive reactions. Football is often called an aggressive sport, but not everyone thinks of it this way. Those persons who define the game as "aggression" should be most likely to attack someone after seeing a gridiron contest. Berkowitz and Alioto, (in press) recently carried out an experimental test of this reasoning.

As is customary in our research, each male subject was first provoked by his partner, the experimenter's confederate, and was then shown a brief film. The subjert watched either our standard boxing movie or an equally long film of a professional football game. A tape-recorded voice provided a brief introduction to the contest, supposedly so that the subject would have a better understanding of what he saw. In half of the cases, for each type of movie the voice indicated that the contest winner (either the boxer or the football team) had wanted to hurt the opponent because of some earlier insults. In other words, the winner in the filmed encounter was intentionally aggressive toward the opponent. The remaining subjects were told that the participants were professional contestants, unemotionally engaged in their business, and did not have any particular feelings toward their opponent, thus defining the contest as essentially nonaggressive in nature. At the end of the movie the confederate went into a separate cubicle where he could not be seen, and the subject was given four opportunities to shock him.

Several aggression measures yielded the predicted significant effect for the perceived aggressiveness of the contact sport, as shown in table 5.3. Thus, the first time the shocks were given,

TABLE 5.2. *Aggression measures yielding significant differences between agressive and neutral humor conditions*

Measure: Number of Adjectives Attributed to Job Applicant	*Insulting Job Applicant*		*Noninsulting Job Applicant*	
	aggressive humor	*neutral humor*	*aggressive humor*	*neutral humor*
Moderate Hostile	5.4_a	4.2_b	0.8_c	0.6_c
Friendly	1.4_a	1.8_a	9.4_b	12.2_c
Questionnaire Evaluation	79.7_a	75.2_a	43.6_b	34.9_b*

NOTE: Cells having different subscripts are significantly different by Duncan test at the .05 level. On the final questionnaire evaluation, the higher the score, the greater the expressed hostility toward the job applicant.

* This mean is different from 43.60 at the .06 level.

SOURCE: Adapted from Berkowitz, 1970.

but *not* on the other shock trials, the men who had been induced to think of the filmed contest as an aggressive competition gave their partner reliably more shocks than did the subjects who had been led to define the encounter as nonaggressive. The former subjects also gave the accomplice significantly longer shocks over the four trials and, on the final questionnaire, indicated a reliably weaker desire to serve with him again in another experiment. All in all, the movie had an aggression-enhancing effect when it had an aggressive meaning for the subjects.

Since other investigators have obtained essentially comparable findings, these results should not be particularly surprising. In the important research by Lazarus and his colleagues (e.g., Lazarus and Alfert 1964), for example, subjects watched a movie showing a primitive subincision ceremony after having been given a particular orientation to the scene. While one group watched the movie showing the hazardous operation without any prior introduction, so that the subjects were highly aware of the danger and pain they were witnessing, the men in another condition were told about the positive aspects of the ceremony (the native boys were joyful at being initiated into manhood), and the possible pain was minimized. Following the language of my own

TABLE 5.3. *Aggression measures showing significant main effect of perceived aggressiveness of film*

Interpretation of Filmed Contest	*Filmed Contact Sport*				
	Prize Fight		*Football*		
	aggressive	*nonaggressive*	*aggressive*	*nonaggressive*	*p-Value for Main Effect*
Numbers of shocks,* trial 1	2.6	2.3	2.8	2.1	.036
Total duration of shocks, all trials (sec.)	4.0	2.4	4.0	2.2	.001
Want to serve with partner again†	11.3	7.7	10.9	10.3	.012

* Not more than five shocks nor less than one could be given on any trial.
† The higher the score, the *less* S wanted to serve with partner again in another experiment.
SOURCE: Adapted from Berkowitz and Alioto (in press).

research, I would say that this latter introduction gave a certain kind of meaning to the observed event: it was understood as a happy and untraumatic occurrence. Since, in the latter case, the movie was not a strongly aversive stimulus, the subjects seeing it became much less aroused physiologically than did the control subjects not given this "positive meaning" orientation. In this research, as in my own study, the viewers reacted to the scene in terms of the meaning they had imparted to it.

JUDGING THE PROPRIETY OF THE OBSERVED AGGRESSION

We have just seen that the observer cannot be viewed as merely a passive recipient of the stimuli presented to him. He imparts meaning to these stimuli, sometimes classifying the witnessed event as "aggressive" and sometimes as "nonaggressive." He may also judge any observed violence he sees as "good" or "bad," "moral" or "immoral," "justified" or "unjustified." Five separate experiments employing college students have demonstrated that this interpretation of the propriety of the witnessed aggression can influence the observer's own aggressive behavior immediately after the movie.

In four of these studies (Berkowitz 1965; Berkowitz, Corwin, and Heironimus 1963; Berkowitz and Geen 1967; Berkowitz and Rawlings 1963) the "Champion" prize-fight scene was introduced to deliberately provoke students in one of two ways: by varying a supposed summary of the plot, the fight's loser (the main character in the movie) was portrayed either in a favorable or relatively unfavorable manner, so that the beating he received was generally regarded as either unjustified or justified aggression. Immediately, afterward, when the men had an opportunity to attack their tormentor, they displayed weaker aggression toward him after seeing the film victim get the less justified beating than following the more justified injury to the movie character.

CHARACTERISTICS OF THE AVAILABLE TARGET

The general line of reasoning I have advanced here also suggests that aggressive reactions can be governed by the available target as well as by the events portrayed on the screen. For example, in considering the consequences of filmed violence, I have proposed that the aggressive responses elicited by the movie or television program are often relatively weak and do not show up in overt behavior unless the viewer happens to encounter someone associated with the witnessed violence (cf. Berkowitz 1962).

A series of experiments conducted in our Wisconsin laboratory has been guided by this kind of analysis. What we have found is that a target person tends to draw the strongest attacks if he is associated with the victim of the witnessed aggression.

Typically in these studies, the subject, a male college student, was first either angered or treated in a neutral fashion by the experimenter's accomplice. Under a pretext appropriate to the ostensible purpose of the study, the subject was then shown a brief film, either a prize-fight scene or an exciting but nonaggressive film of a track race between the first two men to run the mile in less than four minutes. About seven minutes later, at the conclusion of the film, the subject was given an opportunity to administer shocks to the other person (the confederate) as a judgment of this person's performance on a task that had been assigned to him.

In the first experimental test of the effects of the target's stimulus properties (Berkowitz 1965), the confederate's degree of association with the aggressive prize-fight film was manipulated by means of the role he occupied when he was introduced to the subject. Since the crucial scene was a prize fight, the accomplice had been introduced in half of the cases as a "college boxer." For the other subjects, those for whom the confederate was to have a low association with the aggressive movie, he had been introduced as a "speech major." In accord with prediction, the target person received the strongest attacks when he had provoked the subjects, they had seen the boxing film, and he had been identified as a college boxer. (By the way, I doubt that this label had informed the subjects that it would be safe to attack the target person.)

In yet another study (Geen and Berkowitz 1966), the association with the aggressive film made use of the names employed in the film story. Kirk Douglas played the part of a boxer called "Midge Kelly," so the confederate was at times introduced as "Bob Kelly." The character who punished him severely was called "Dunne," and in a second condition the confederate was introduced as "Bob Dunne." In a third group, the confederate was introduced as "Bob Riley," a name not used in the film scene. Finally, as a fourth test of the name-mediated associations, one group of subjects shown the prize-fight scene was told that the confederate's name was "Kirk Anderson." All of the subjects were angered by the confederate before seeing the film.

Again, our reasoning was upheld, as can be seen in figure 5.3. The greatest number of shocks was given by the angered subjects who had seen the aggressive film *to the confederate who was associated with this film* by means of his name, either "Kelly" or "Kirk." We can even see indications of a generalizaton gradient based on the "Irishness" of the confederate's name. The men witnessing the prize fight attacked the confederate somewhat more frequently when his name was "Riley" than when it was "Dunne." Furthermore, if this generalization gradient is a reliable phenomenon, we might even conclude that the important association is with the victim of the observed aggression; the available target's likelihood of being attacked is a direct function of his association with the observed victim.

THE OBSERVER'S ANGER OR AROUSAL LEVEL

Our Wisconsin research has generally obtained significant effects only when the subjects have been angered before seeing the movie. Other findings indicate, however, that this anger is not absolutely necessary if media violence is to produce aggressive consequences; the anger facilitates the aggressive reaction but is not necessary. Many different kinds of emotional arousal can also have this effect. In one demonstration of this phenomenon, Geen and I (1967) have reported that task frustrations can increase subjects' responsiveness to the aggressive stimuli in their environment.

Other sources of heightened arousal have the same consequences—again, if clearly defined aggressive stimuli are present. Geen and O'Neal (1969) found that men who heard a loud but not painful "white noise" after seeing the prize-fight film attacked their partner more strongly than did other subjects who had not watched the fight or who had not heard the sound. The

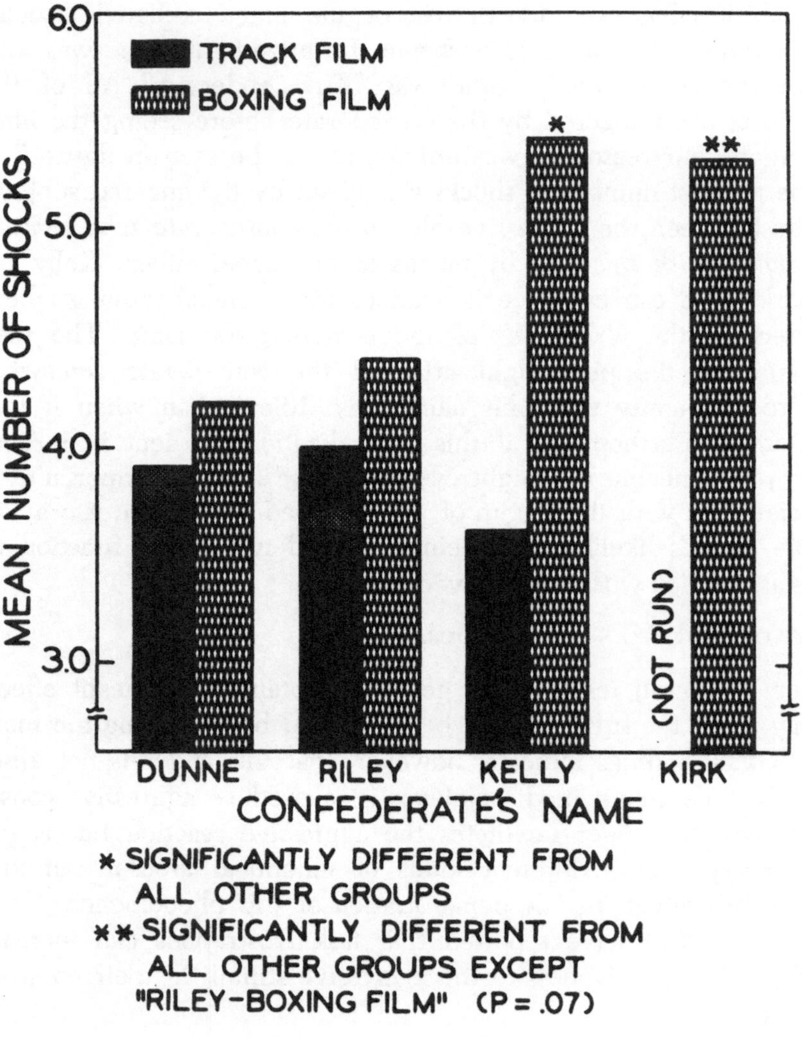

FIGURE 5.3. *Mean number of shocks given to confederate (after Geen and Berkowitz, 1966).*

excitation resulting from this noise had evidently strengthened the aggressive reactions stimulated by the aggressive movie.

Similarly, when Tannenbaum and Zillman (personal communication) showed a brief sex film to one group of men who had been provoked by a partner, these sexually aroused subjects gave him stronger electric shock punishment than did similarly angered but nonsexually aroused men in the control group. The sexual arousal had evidently helped "energize" the aggresive responses elicited by the provocation and the opportunity to attack the partner. In a later variation on this study, these researchers obtained results consistent with the previously cited Berkowitz and LePage (1967) experiment. The strongest electric attacks on the tormentor were given by men who watched the sex film and at the same time heard a tape recording of the woman character's thoughts about killing her lover. In this case, the viewers' sexual arousal apparently also strengthened the aggressive responses elicited by the aggressive tape recording. This kind of phenomenon, in which sexual arousal functions like other arousal sources to facilitate aggressive responses to aggressive cues, could contribute to the apparent connection between sexual and aggressive motivation posited by some writers.

APPETITIVE EFFECTS

The witnessed aggression can also create a general arousal. One must not forget that observed violence is often exciting, and this diffuse excitement can also energize the dominant response tendencies. Thus, Tannenbaum (personal communication) recently found that subjects gave stronger *rewards* to a person they previously had been induced to like after viewing the prize-fight film than after seeing a neutral and less exciting movie. These people were inclined to reward the other person and, because of the experimental requirements, were also set to do so. The arousal generated by the exciting aggressive scene facilitated the occurrence of the positive reactions the subjects were predisposed to display.

I have been arguing, however, that observed violence also has specific effects that often facilitate any aggressive responses the viewer is set to perform. Indeed, the witnessed aggression may also have appetitive consequences in which there is a specific preference for further aggression-associated stimuli. This possibility is consistent with Staats's (1968) classical conditioning analysis of human motivation. Staats maintained that, through classical conditioning, particular environmental stimuli are capable of evoking emotional reactions and can also function as reinforcing and discriminative stimuli. For many people in our society aggressive scenes can do all of these things if they do not produce strong anxiety or digust. Moreover, the observed aggression may also elicit aggression-related anticipatory goal responses; the scene could cause the viewer to remember some of the gratifications he had obtained through his own aggression, especially if the witnessed event is not anxiety provoking. As a result, the observer will want to encounter more aggressive events until satiation sets in. His appetite for viewing still more aggression has been heightened.

Lovaas (1961) provided a nice demonstration of this phenomenon. Nursery-school children were given an opportunity to activate either an aggressive or nonaggressive toy after watching either an aggressive or neutral cartoon movie. Bar presses put both toys in motion, with the aggressive toy showing one doll hitting another with a stick and the other toy being an attractive but neutral mechanical affair. The two films were equally arousing, apparently, since both led to about the same number of bar presses. However, the aggressive cartoon had increased the youngsters' taste for still more aggression. The children who had watched the aggressive movie had a highly selective preference to see the aggressive toy in operation.

Essentially comparable findings were obtained in an experiment by myself and Alioto (1971, unpublished). Our male University students were shown one of our standard films, either the brief prize-fight scene or the equally long and equally arousing movie of a track race, following which they indicated their attitudes toward various kinds of movies and television programs that had previously been classified as either aggressive or nonaggressive. Only 10 percent of the men seeing the boxing film expressed a greater preference for the nonaggressive over the aggressive programs. By contrast, after seeing the neutral film a reliably greater 37 percent preferred the nonviolent content over the aggressive movies and programs.

The experiment was continued: Half of the people in each film group listened to one of the two tape-recorded comic routines used in my aggressive-humor study, either the nonaggressive one or the hostile routine by Don Rickles, after which they rated their enjoyment of this humor. The previous film did not affect the subjects' attitude toward the neutral comic routine to any substantial extent, but did significantly influence their liking for the hostile routine. Thus, when we dichotomized the sample into those having high or low liking for the aggressive humor, 71 percent of the men expressing the strongest enjoyment were in the group that had seen the fight movie earlier. In comparison, only 31 percent of the subjects not caring for the hostile humor were in this aggressive-movie group. All in all, then, the earlier brief exposure to the violent scene had increased the students' preference for aggressive entertainment in general and their enjoyment of the hostile humor in particular.

SEXUAL REACTIONS TO EROTIC STIMULI

Sexual movies have not received as much systematic research attention as have aggressive films, at least until recently. Consequently, we cannot make the same kinds of detailed statements about erotic stimuli. Nevertheless, it appears that sexual responses can be elicited by sexual stimuli just as aggressive reactions can be evoked by stimuli having aggressive meaning. One of the experiments sponsored by the Pornography Commission produced interesting data along these lines.

Mann, Sidman and Starr (1970) recruited middle-class and middle-aged married couples through newspaper and supermarket ads for a study on "marital behavior." All of them had been married for at least ten years. The subjects first filled out questionnaires reporting their sexual activities every day for a month and then were assigned to one of three major conditions. One group saw seven erotic films in four weekly sessions; a second group condition viewed nonerotic movies during these periods; and the control group did not see any films at all. Finally, at the completion of this movie phase, the subjects again reported their daily sexual behavior for a month.

These daily reports and a final questionnaire administered at the end of the third month indicated that, with one major exception, the sex movies had not produced any sustained changes in behavior or attitude. This exception had to do with attitudes toward erotic films; in general, the individuals seeing the stag movies become somewhat more favorable to these films and less opposed to their legal exhibition. Otherwise, the subjects reported the same kinds and same level of sexual activity they had carried out before the experiment began. No new habits were acquired and few inhibitions were lost. The erotic films did have an important effect, however. As my classical conditioning model suggests, these movies had evoked relatively short-lived sexual reactions (sex-related ideas and feelings), which facilitated sexual behavior *temporarily*. The couples in the erotic-film condition were much more likely than before to have sexual intercourse on the film-viewing nights, while this change did not occur with any particular frequency in the other groups. The couples seeing the stag movies were significantly more active sexually than the others, but only on the night they had returned home from the movies. In sum, there's little reason to think that the erotic movies had lessened the subjects' inhibitions against sex, and good reason to believe the sex scenes had stimulated sexual reactions.

Clinical Implications

My argument has fairly obvious implications for psychotherapy, and certainly questions some of the expressive-treatment methods used by dynamically oriented therapists. In these conventional procedures the patient is usually urged to reveal his feelings, as if benefits would be derived mainly from the sheer expression of emotion. But do these benefits actually occur? Theory and research suggest that expressive treatments need not have socially desirable consequences, at least in the case of aggression.

I have criticized the energy model of motivation underlying some of the expressive therapies in other papers (Berkowitz 1970*b*, 1972) and shall not repeat my objections to the orthodox hostility-catharsis notion here; there simply is very little empirical support for the contention that people will "drain" a supposedly pent-up aggressive drive by attacking just anyone available or by displaying their hostile feelings. The outcome might be just the opposite: a greater rather than lesser likelihood of subsequent aggression. In considering these consequences, it is necessary to distinguish between long- and short-term effects.

OVERCOMING FRUSTRATION OF AGGRESSION

One can readily conceive of some immediate benefits that might be derived from aggressive behavior: A would-be aggressor is not frustrated if he can attack his intended victim. An angry person usually wants to hurt the individual who had provoked him and is frustrated at not being able to do so, especially if he had been thinking of injuring this person.

As an illustration, in one of my experiments (Berkowitz 1964, 1966), the subjects were insulted by the experimenter's confederate, and half of the men were led to think that they would have an opportunity to attack this person by means of electric shocks. After receiving suitable explanations, however, only half of the subjects expecting to shock the confederate were permitted to do so, while half of those who had not anticipated this aggressive opportunity were required to shock the confederate. In sum, we had two groups that expected to be able to attack the anger instigator, but only one of them was able to fulfill the expectation. There were also two groups that did not have this aggressive anticipation, with one of them then being required to attack the tormentor. In addition, a noninsulted control condition had been led to expect the opportunity to administer shocks and was able to give them.

Once these experimental variations were established, all subjects were required to shock the confederate, supposedly as their final evaluation of him. The results show that the angry men had been frustrated if they had not been able to shock their tormentor as they had expected to do. Although the provoked men, as a whole, administered reliably more shocks to the confederate than did the subjects of the nonangered control group when they had their final aggressive opportunity, the greatest punishment was given by the individuals who had previously thought they would be able to get even with the anger instigator and then could not satisfy their aggressive expectation. These angry subjects had been anticipating some of the rewards to be derived from the punishment they would inflict on the man who had insulted them, and then were frustrated when they were suddenly prevented from realizing these rewards.

What is suggested, then, is that the failure to hurt an intended victim as one had wanted and expected to do may be a "frustrative nonreward." This frustration could temporarily heighten the strength of the ongoing, although implicit, aggressive reactions in the manner of any other frustration drive. But, in addition, since frustrations are aversive, the thwarted individual might experience unpleasant feelings of tension. These feelings could conceivably be lessened by later direct or indirect attacks upon the anger instigator. For example, in talking to the therapist about how he had been ill-treated, the patient might believe he had hurt his tormentor. He now has done what he had wanted to do earlier, if only indirectly; his frustration is lessened, and he feels better. Worchel (1957) has reported some supporting evidence. Angry college students given an opportunity to complain to an authority about the person who had insulted them subsequently performed better on an assigned digit-symbol task than did similarly provoked subjects who had not been provided with this chance to attack their insulter. These latter people were presumably frustrated by their inability to aggress, and the resulting tension apparently interfered with effective performance.

REINFORCEMENT OF AGGRESSION

Even if individuals do feel better at times when they hurt someone who has attacked them, and may even become less inclined to injure their tormentor again in the near future (because they had reached their goal), the long-run consequence could be very different. Learning that the intended victim has been hurt, or seeing him submit, generally reinforces the aggressive behavior (Patterson, Littman, and Brinker 1967). As a result, although there may be a short-term diminution of aggression, this behavior has become more likely over an extended period.

Aggression can be reinforced by social approval even without signs of pain or submission from the intended victim. Walters and Brown (1963) demonstrated that when children were suitably rewarded by an adult for punching a Bobo doll, much as a therapist might reward a child's play aggression, the youngsters were subsequently more likely to behave aggressively in an interpersonal setting. The reinforcement effect can also generalize across a variety of responses, as long as they have the same meaning to the rewarded person. We saw earlier, as an example, that adults rewarded for using words having aggressive connotations were subsequently more prone to administer severe electriral punishment to another individual (Loew 1967; Parke, Ewall, and Slaley 1972). Psychotherapists might reward their patients' hostile expressions in a very comparable manner, and as a result, unless other behavior patterns are also strengthened, these people could well be more apt to act aggressively outside the therapy room.

THOUGHTS AND AGGRESSION

Other mechanisms can also produce an enhanced probability of further aggression. In accord with the theory of cognitive dissonance, several experiments have shown that people who voluntarily attack someone else often seek to justify their behavior by expressing still more hostility toward him afterward. They strive to act in a consistently hostile manner when their initial behavior departs from the values they hold for themselves and they want to preserve a favorable self-image (see, e.g., Brock and Pallak 1969). The atmosphere of candor and honesty ideally developed in psychotherapy could well minimize this type of self-justifying, consistent aggression, but the traditional treatment procedures also make the patients highly conscious of any anger they may feel. They are encouraged to think about and verbalize their emotional feelings as well as to talk about their inclinations and desires. Cognitively oriented research indicates that these verbalizations might increase the chances of aggressive behavior. Schachter's (1964) well-known cognitive theory of emotion maintains that emotionally aroused persons are inclined to act in accord with their conception of their emotional state. They will be disposed to behave aggressively if they think they are angry —and also believe that a particular attack on someone is warranted in the given situation (also see Berkowitz and Turner 1971). Thinking about one's anger may also have other effects. Because of the associations they have, these thoughts could cause people to remember the particular aversive events that had provoked them, and perhaps other unpleasant experiences as well. They also think of the people they want to hurt, their frustraters, and these images also elicit aggressive reactions. Recalling and reliving their anger, these people have stirred themselves up still more.

Such a possibility is suggested by another recent Wisconsin experiment (Berkowitz and Turner 1971). College men were made to be moderately angry and where then hooked up to physiological apparatus, supposedly akin to a lie detector, which would reveal how angry they "really" were. Most of the subjects were instructed to think of the person who had insulted them and were then given false information about their anger level. A control group of similarly angered men were not required to think of the anger instigator and received no feedback about their anger level. Immediately afterward, when all of the subjects had an opportunity to shock their tormentor, the individuals who had just been made highly aware of their anger and of the person who had provoked them behaved more punitively toward him than did the subjects in the control condition. Their rated anger level was also stronger than that reported by the control subjects. By thinking about the man who had insulted them and their feelings toward him, the former subjects had apparently restimulated aggression-facilitating reactions that otherwise would have died down with the passage of time. In the same vein, Feshbach (1971) has noted that anger can be aroused by having people recall earlier events which had provoked them. The thoughts and brief description of these frustrating incidents can rekindle the emotions previously lit by those situations. For at least a brief while, then, the person remembering these incidents is more, not less, likely to show open aggression.

This memory of the torment and insults previously suffered may do some people good under certain conditions. I suspect that many individuals are "brooders" who frequently recall the injuries inflicted on them so that they often stir themselves up. If they have also learned to be anxious about their aggressive inclinations, their brooding could generate considerable tension. The open recall of these earlier frustrations in the permissive psychotherapy setting might be beneficial through weakening the anxiety reactions to their own anger and by promoting a new and more constructive understanding of their past and current situations. Nonetheless, it is the anxiety extinction and the cognitive reorganization that have helped rather than a supposed drainage of pent-up emotions. These beneficial consequences conceivably could be achieved in other ways as well, and probably should be, because the free expression of aggression may have other, unfortunate outcomes. Whether we perform the responses ourselves or see other people carry them out, expressed aggression in word or deed could evoke further aggressive responses in many situations.

References

Berkowitz, L. *Aggression: A Social Psychological Analysis.* New York: McGraw-Hill Book Co., 1962.

——. "Aggressive Cues in Aggressive Behavior and Hostility Catharsis." *Psychological Review* 71 (1964): 104–22.

——. "Some Aspects of Observed Aggression." *Journal of Personality and Social Psychology* 2 (1965): 359–69.

——. "On Not Being Able to Aggress." *British Journal of Social and Clinical Psychology* 5 (1966): 130–39.

——. "Aggressive Humor as a Stimulus to Aggressive Responses." *Journal of Personality and Social Psychology* 16 (1970): 710–17. *(a)*

——. "Experimental Investigations of Hostility Catharsis." *Journal of Consulting and Clinical Psychology* 35 (1970): 1–7. *(b)*

Berkowitz, L. "Two Cultures of Violence." Presidential Address to Division of Social and Personality Psychology, APA meetings, Honolulu, Sept. 1972.

Berkowitz, L., and Alioto, J. T. "The Meaning of an Observed Event as a Determinant of its Aggressive Consequences." *Journal of Personality and Social Psychology,* in press.

Berkowitz, L.; Corwin, R.; and Heironimus, M. "Film Violence and Subsequent Aggressive Tendencies." *Public Opinion Quarterly* 27 (1963): 217–29.

Berkowitz, L., and Geen, R. G. "Stimulus Qualities of the Target of Aggression: A Further Study." *Journal of Personality and Social Psychology* 5 (1967): 364–68.

Berkowitz, L., and Knurek, D. A. "Label-mediated Hostility Generalization." *Journal of Personality and Social Psychology* 13 (1969): 200–6.

Berkowitz, L., and LePage, A. "Weapons as Aggression-eliciting Stimuli." *Journal of Personality and Social Psychology* 7 (1967): 202–7.

Berkowitz, L., and Rawlings, Edna. "Effects of Film Violence on Inhibitions against Subsequent Aggression." *Journal of Abnormal and Social Psychology* 66 (1963): 405–12.

Berkowitz, L., and Turner, C. "Perceived Anger Level, Instigating Agent and Aggression." In *Cognitive Alteration of Feeling States*, edited by H. London. Chicago: Aldine Publishing Co., 1971.

Brock, T. C., and Pallak, M. S. "The Consequences of Choosing to be Aggressive." In *The Cognitive Control of Motivation*, edited by P. G. Zimbardo. Glenview, Ill.: Scott, Foresman, 1969.

Brown, P., and Elliot, R. "Control of Aggression in a Nursery School Class." *Journal of Experimental Child Psychology* 2 (1965): 103–7.

Clark, R. A. "The Effects of Sexual Motivation on Fantasy." *Journal of Experimental Psychology* 44 (1952): 391–99.

Ervin, Susan M. "Language and TAT Content in Bilinguals." *Journal of Abnormal and Social Psychology* 68 (1964): 500–507.

Feshbach, S. "Dynamics and Morality of Violence and Aggression: Some Psychological Considerations." *American Psychologist* 26 (1971): 281–92.

Geen, R. G., and Berkowitz, L. "Name-mediated Aggressive Cue Properties." *Journal of Personality* 34 (1966): 456–65.

——. "Some Conditions Facilitating the Occurrence of Aggression After the Observation of Violence." *Journal of Personality* 35 (1967): 666–76.

Geen, R. G., and O'Neal, E. C. "Activation of Cue-elicited Aggression by General Arousal." *Journal of Personality and Social Psychology* 11 (1969): 289–92.

Geen, R. G., and Pigg, R. "Acquisition of an Aggressive Response and Its Generalization to Verbal Behavior." *Journal of Personality and Social Psychology* 15 (1970): 165–70.

Geen, R. G., and Stonner, D. "Effects of Aggressiveness Habit Strength on Behavior in the Presence of Aggression-related Stimuli." *Journal of Personality and Social Psychology* 17 (1971): 149–53.

Lang, P. J.; Geer, J.; and Hnatiow, M. "Semantic Generalization of Conditioned Autonomic Responses." *Journal of Experimental Psychology* 65 (1963): 552–58.

Lazarus, R. S., and Alfert, Elizabeth. "Short-circuiting of Threat by Experimentally Altering Cognitive Appraisal." *Journal of Abnormal and Social Psychology* 69 (1964): 195–205.

Loew, C. A. "Acquisition of a Hostile Attitude and its Relation to Aggressive Behavior." *Journal of Personality and Social Psychology* 5 (1967): 335–41.

Lovaas, O. I. "Effect of Exposure to Symbolic Aggression on Aggressive Behavior." *Child Development* 32 (1961): 37–44.

Mann, J.; Sidman, J.; and Starr, S. "Effects of Erotic Films on Sexual Behavior of Married Couples." Paper presented at meeting of American Psychological Association, Miami, Florida, September 1970.

Page, M. M. and Scheidt, R. J. "The Elusive Weapons Effect: Demand Awareness, Evaluation Apprehension, and Slightly Sophisticated Subjects." *Journal of Personality and Social Psychology* 20 (1971): 304–18.

Parke, R. D.; Ewall, W.; and Slaby, R. G. "Hostile and Helpful Verbalizations as Regulators of Nonverbal Aggression. *Journal of Personality and Social Psychology* 23 (1972): 243–48.

Patterson, G. R.; Littman, R. A.; and Bricker, W. *Assertive Behavior in Children: A Step Toward a Theory of Aggression. Monographs of Society for Research in Child Development,* 32, no. 5 (1967): 1–43.

Schacter, S. "The Interaction of Cognitive and Physiological Determinants of Emotional State." In *Advances in Experimental Social Psychology,* edited by L. Berkowitz. New York: Academic Press, 1964.

Staats, A. W. "Social Behaviorism and Human Motivation: Principles of the Attitude-Reinforcer-Discriminative System." In *Psychological Foundations of Attitudes,* edited by A. G. Greenwald, T. C. Brock, and T. M. Ostrom, pp. 33–66. New York: Academic Press, 1968.

——. "Experimental Demand Characteristics and the Classical Conditioning of Attitudes." *Journal of Personality and Social Psychology* 11 (1969): 187–92.

Staats, A. W., and Staats, Carolyn. "Attitudes Established by Classical Conditioning. *Journal of Abnormal and Social Psychology* 57 (1958): 37–40.

Walters, R. H., and Brown, M. "Studies of Reinforcement of Aggression. III. Transfer of responses to an interpersonal situation." *Child Development* 34 (1963): 563–71.

Worchel, P. "Catharsis and the Relief of Hostility." *Journal of Abnormal and Social Psychology* 55 (1957): 238–43.

Gerald R. Patterson received his bachelor's degree and M.A. in psychology at the University of Oregon, and his Ph.D. from the University of Minnesota. He has held faculty positions at the Psychiatric Institute of the University of Nebraska Medical School, the Department of Psychology of the University of Oregon, and the School of Education of the University of Oregon. Dr. Patterson is currently research associate at the Oregon Research Institute. He is a recipient of a Research Scientist Development Award and a Career Development Award from NIMH. He has served as a consulting editor to both Child Development *and* Journal of Applied Behavioral Analysis. *In 1971–72 he was president of the Association for the Advancement of Behavior Therapy. Dr. Patterson's research interests in social learning theory, behavior modification, aggression, and marital conflict are reflected in both his articles and his recent books:* Living with Children: New Methods for Parents and Teachers *(with M. E. Gullian) and* Families: Applications of Social Learning to Family Life.

The late Joseph P. Cobb received his bachelor's degree from Harvard University and his Ph.D. from the University of Oregon. After receiving his Ph.D. degree he held a faculty position in the College of Education, University of Oregon and was a research associate, Oregon Research Institute. In addition, Dr. Cobb was a research associate, Center at Oregon for Research in the Behavioral Education of the Handicapped. In situ behavioral analyses, and research in human aggressive behavior are reflected in his very productive career.

6

Stimulus Control for Classes of Noxious Behaviors

G. R. PATTERSON AND J. A. COBB

Analysis of Stimulus Control

This chapter explores some of the stimuli that control the occurrence of noxious behaviors exhibited by boys in their homes. We assumed that the controlling stimuli consisted in large part of behaviors exhibited by other family members as they interacted with the child. Certain agents and certain agent behaviors presumably function as stimuli for setting the occasion for a wide range of noxious responses. In keeping with an earlier formulation (Patterson and Cobb 1971), we also hypothesized that the effective antecedent stimuli for many of these responses would have aversive, or unpleasant, characteristics.

As a basis for exploring these functional relationships, an analysis was made of the sequential dependencies found in interaction patterns for families of both problem and nonproblem

This research was supported by grants MH 10822 and R01-MH-15985 and a career development award to the senior author, MH 40,518, from the National Institute of Mental Health, U.S. Public Health Service. Many of the ideas presented here were shaped as a result of continuous interchanges with our colleagues Vern Devine, Hy Hops, S. Johnson, R. Jones, and Roberta Ray. We wish particularly to thank J. Reid for his energetic critique of an earlier draft of the paper. His ability to question favored phrases and assumptions resulted in improvements in our attempts to communicate these ideas. We are also indebted to Mark Layman, programmer, for his high level of professional competence in translating these complexities into computer language. His programs may be obtained at Oregon Research Institute, Eugene.

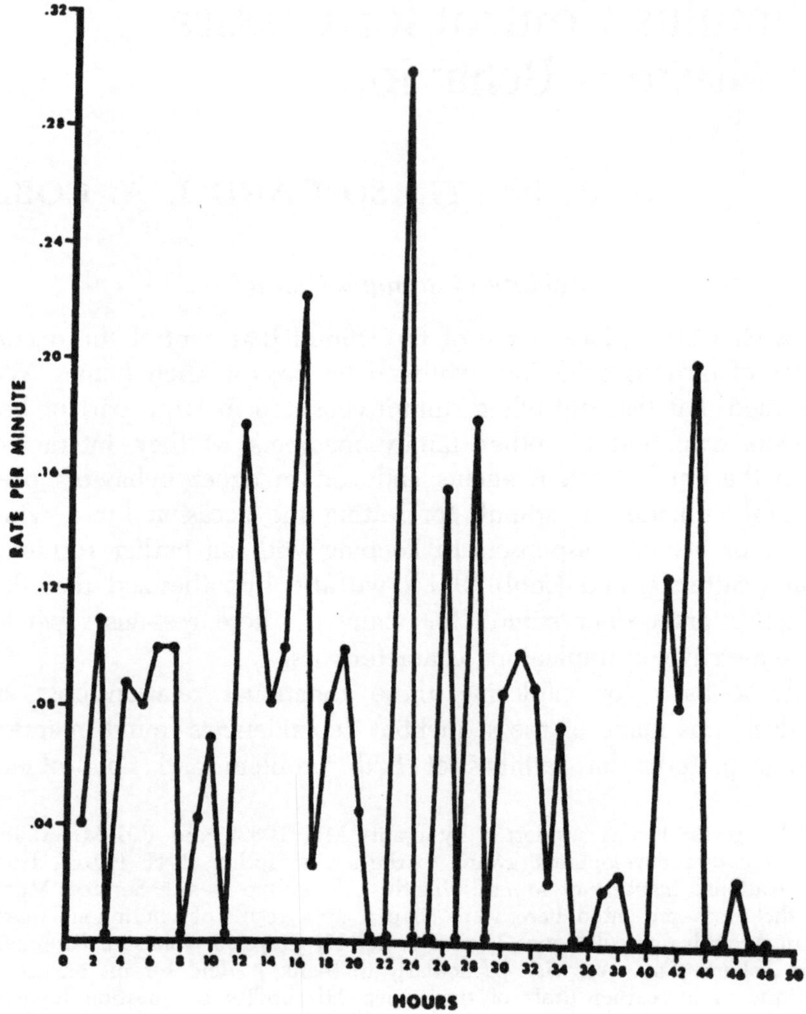

FIGURE 6.1. *Variations in rate per minute of hitting.*

boys. Presumably, the stimuli that controlled noxious responses would be similar in both samples.

We were also interested in exploring the possibility that classes of noxious responses might exist in which class members were controlled by similar social stimuli. The existence of such classes would have implications both for intervention strategies designed to alter the occurrence of noxious responses and for theories of social behavior. The present report details such a strategy and the date generated by such a search. (See p. 194 for a glossary of terms used in this report.)

A Strategy for Constructing a "Theory" of Aggression

The data establishing an empirical basis for understanding the stimuli that control some noxious behaviors do not, of course, constitute a "theory" of aggression. However, the procedures and data presented here are viewed as a necessary first step toward constructing such a theory. Because a general set of notions about how to proceed in such a task directed the design for the present study, it seems reasonable to begin by outlining these assumptions.

In making field observations of behaviors, one fact becomes immediately clear: for a given subject, there are enormous variations in the rate with which a given response occurs, even when one observes the same subject in the "same" general setting over time. For example, three to four hours of observation data were obtained in the home on each of twelve days, sampling the Hitting behaviors of a seven-year-old problem child. Figure 6.1 summarizes the variations in rate over the forty-eight hours of observations.

The differences in rate ranged from one Hit every three minutes to as little as one event every 100 minutes. In the present context, the function of a theory of aggressive behavior would be to account for such variations.

It was assumed that the differences in rates were determined primarily by variations in the density with which the controlling stimuli occur. While this hypothesis was not explored in the present report, the general model has been tested by Hops (1971).

He showed that variations in rates of social interaction could be accounted for by covariations in the density with which two sets of controlling stimuli were presented. Extensive samplings of social-interaction rates were made for two preschool subjects. The multiple *R*'s summarizing the amount of variance accounted for was .50 for one boy and .59 for the other.

Variations in rate of a response, then, were not considered errors of measurement. Rather, variations in rate are the *sine qua non* for a functional analysis. They constitute the dependent variables to be explained. Specifically, it was hypothesized that response rates varied as a function of the interaction among four variables: (1) The rate of response, R_j, will be high in settings in which relevant controlling stimuli are presented in high densities. Stimuli whose presence increases the probability of the occurrence of a response have been labeled "facilitating stimuli." Those events associated with a reduced probability of occurrence for the response have been labeled "inhibitory stimuli." (2) The rate of R_j also varies as some unspecified function of the density with which facilitating stimuli for competing concurrent operants are presented. (3) The rates of R_j can be suppressed by intense punishment. It is therefore hypothesized here that the rate may be temporarily decelerated during intervals or settings in which high-amplitude punishment is made contingent upon R_j. (4) The rate of R_j could be accelerated if intense punishment were made contingent upon the competing concurrent operants.

It is assumed that moment-by-moment fluctuations in rate of responding are not determined by corresponding fluctuations in schedules of positive reinforcement. Previous efforts to empirically establish such correspondence have not been very successful. Only inconsistent relations were found between rates of behavior and positive reinforcement or punishment schedules for disruptive classroom behaviors (Ebner 1967) and for aggressive behaviors in the nursery school (Patterson, Littman, and Bricker 1967).

One may think of a set of correlations from data collected over time for a single child. Each correlation would specify the covariation between variations in rate of response R_j, on the one hand, and the density with which controlling stimuli occurred during the same time intervals. Other correlations might specify the contribution made by stimuli that control concurrent operants, or stimuli that dentoe punishment for R_j.

A table of such correlations would describe the available information about stimulus control for that R_j and for that particular subject. One means for summarizing and organizing this information would be to view the contribution of each controlling variable as a standard partial-regression coefficient. The magnitude and the level of significance of the standard partial-regression coefficients would attest to the contribution of each variable in predicting the aggressive behavior of that child. The magnitude of the resulting multiple-correlation coefficient would indicate the level of development of a "theory of aggression" developed for that R_j and for that child.

While such an analysis might detail the degree of understanding of determinants for a single response and a single child, it would be of little interest unless it could be demonstrated that the findings were generalizable. Generalizability could consist of several different things. To be of even minimal interest, one should demonstrate that the general pattern of determinants would also apply to a comparable sampling of the same subject's behavior at some later point in time. A completely idiographic theory for response R_j might contain a different set of determinants at different points in time or significant variations in the magnitude of the standard partial-regression coefficients for the same set of variables. It is assumed that such analyses will demonstrate stable patterns of determinants over time.

Demonstrating that the determinants and/or their weightings hold across other responses for that same subject would further enhance the utility of such a research strategy. For example, if it could be demonstrated that daily variations in rate of Hitting *and* Teasing covaried with changes in density for the same set of stimuli, then one might choose to label such emerging relations as the "beginnings" of a theory about the behavior of that subject.

As theories of personality are usually conceived, one would hope to be able to generalize findings for a single subject to other subjects. It is assumed, for example, that within our culture the Hitting behavior of younger boys is in fact controlled by similar sets of agents and similar sets of agent behaviors. Furthermore, it is assumed that classes of R_j's will be identified which are under comparable stimulus control, and these classes will obtain across subjects.

In the context of this tactic for generating a "theory" of aggressive behaviors, the current report provides data relevant only to the one or two steps in such a strategy. The data identify the stimuli controlling a number of noxious behaviors exhibited by boys. An attempt was also made to identify classes of R_j's which hold across subjects. Later studies will explore the use of multiple-regression equations to describe the degree to which these variables account for daily variations in noxious responses.

ANALYSIS OF SEQUENTIAL DEPENDENCIES

In the present report the analysis of sequential dependencies obtained from in situ observations provided a basis for identifying the stimuli which controlled the occurrence of boys' noxious behaviors. The first problem encountered in following such a tactic lay in the measurement of these events. Data collection and available models of analysis require the sampling of categorical data. In point of fact, some on-going social behaviors seem more continuous than discrete. Much of the social environment seems not to be arranged in neatly defined S's and *R*'s, or any other obvious discrete categories. Even such "simple" responses as the lever press have neither readily definable beginnings nor endings. Most complex social behaviors seem to have even less readily identifiable boundaries.

The strategy adopted in the research reported here was to sample the behavior of the target subject at some point in time and to then classify the event as one of twenty-nine possible categories. Then the observer went on to sample the behavior of persons with whom the subject was interacting. Alternating in this fashion made it possible to "categorize" events, some of which were relatively continuous in nature.

Each investigator must construct categories to fit the hypothesis he wishes to test and make his own intuitive guesses as to to the most appropriate intervals to use in sampling these categories. This obviously becomes a high-risk enterprise, in that if inappropriate categories were selected, or the events were sampled on the wrong time intervals, then one would have data that would be reliable but irrelevant for the hypotheses being tested.

The current code system generates sequential samplings of events arranged along a time line. For such data it was sufficient to use only simple statements that described the fact that one event preceded, or followed, another. It was assumed that most social behaviors were in some measure under the control of immediately impinging social behaviors exhibited by other persons. In the present analysis, it was assumed that much of the control was exerted by stimuli that occurred just a few seconds prior to the occurrence of the response. Similarly, it was assumed that events that immediately followed a response partially determined whether the response would recur in the next adjacent time interval. In effect, such a functional analysis attempted to account for perturbations in on-going social interactions. The "predictions" made were concerned only with behaviors occurring in the immediately prior, or following, time interval.

For example, in figure 6.2 the immediate antecedent at t_1 for the response Brother Hit was X_2. An analysis of a large number of Brother Hit events might indicate that the antecedent event is often X_2. If the conditional probability, $p(\text{Hit}/X_2)$, is significantly higher than $p(\text{Hit/all non-}X_2)$, this would suggest that X_2 has some "control" over the occurrence of that response. If the presence of the stimulus is associated with an increased probability that the response will follow it, it is a facilitating stimulus (S^F). Such an analysis might also identify other X's as inhibitory stimuli (S^Is), in that the probability of Broth-

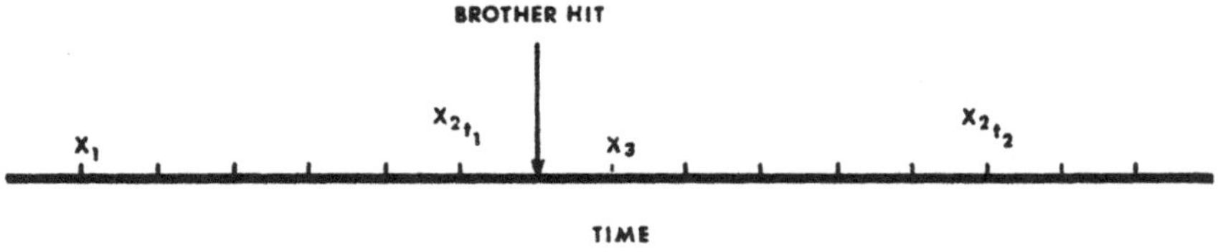

FIGURE 6.2. *The analyses of adjacent events.*

er Hit is significantly reduced. The X_2 could have statas as a controlling stimulus if either type of conditional probability value, S^F or S^I, was significant.

While the present report focuses upon the control exerted by immediately preceding social stimuli, it is also possible to analyze events occurring earlier in time for their possible impact in controlling the target event. For example, in figure 6.2, X_1 and X_2 may have some unique joint function as controlling stimuli for the target response which is greater than would be predicted from information from either event in isolation. Such a configural analysis would, of course, require large amounts of data. However, such a functional analysis would be of great interest in that it would effectively identify the background "themes" which obviously interact with immediately impinging social stimuli in controlling behavior. In the present report the analysis will focus on stimuli occurring in the immediately prior three-second interval. Later analyses will search for greater complexities to be found in larger time units or in complex interactions, effects for agents, agents' behaviors, and settings.

In some sense, information about S^F's contributes an increment to the efficacy of moment-by-moment predictions in that they specify which response(s) is likely to be introduced into the immediately following time interval. Knowledge of events that *follow* a response would also provide significant contributions to predictability. Consequences are simply events which follow responses. They may increase the probability that the immediately prior response will recur in the next time interval. When they are significant, such arrangements were labeled "accelerators," a term that was contributed to the literature by O. Lindsley. Similarly, those consequences associated with significant decreases in probabilities of recurrence were labeled "decelerators."

Previous analyses of sequential dependencies (Patterson and Cobb 1971, p. 108) showed that there were indeed consequences to be found for target events such as Talk and Hit which reliably altered the probabilities of their recurrence. For example, the p(Talk) was .5. The p(Talk) given that the previous

Talk had been consequated by Yell was only .32. Yell, then, was a significant decelerating consequence for Talk.

Evidently there are many different classes of stimuli that may serve to disrupt or decelerate on-going behaviors. For example, it was noted in the previous study that Praise or Caress also decelerated the response Talk. The conditional probability values for Talk, given its immediately prior consequation by these events were .36 and .22, respectively. We hypothesize that these consequences served as powerful facilitating stimuli, which produced responses other than Talk. In this case the mechanism for deceleration was assumed to be response interference.

A sequential mode of analysis could also be used to analyze positive and negative reinforcement effects. While a reinforcing event may function as an accelerator or decelerator, a necessary and sufficient condition for the use of the term *reinforcement* would require alteration of response probabilities at a more distant point in time. This would require an analysis of a large segment of the time line, including the S^F (X_2) at time 1, the response, the consequence (X_3), and a later presentation of the same S^F (X_2) at t_2, to the same subject. The prediction would be that a positive reinforcer would increase the probability of the target response's recurrence, given the presentation of the controlling stimulus (X_2) (at some later point in time (t_2). Similarly, the effect of events thought to be punishing could be investigated by determining the impact of such events upon the occasion of future presentation of the stimuli that controlled the punished response. While no such analysis was attempted in the present report, a preliminary analysis of the reinforcers for Hit was carried out in the paper by Patterson and Cobb (1971, p. 123).

RESPONSE CLASSES

The term *class* as used here, refers to two characteristics, both deemed conditions for use of the term. First, a functional relationship must exist between some environmental event and a behavior. A predictable correlation between the presentation of a stimulus (S^F) and the occurrence of the response that it controls would be a case in point. To the extent that the occurrence of one stimulus serves as a basis for making significant predictions about several responses, it may be said a response class exists.[1] Given that the stimulus is Little Sister Teases, and the knowledge that this event is likely to be followed by either a Yell *or* a Hit by older brother, the implication would be that *both* responses are under the control of the same stimulus. Therefore, they are members of the same "class of responses." It was assumed that there are, in fact, such classes of response. One of the major concerns of the present report was the search for such classes among a variety of aggressive-like responses exhibited by boys.

AGGRESSIVE BEHAVIORS

Buss (1961) and others have defined an aggressive response as one that delivers pain to another person. As viewed here, the term *aggression* would apply to only a few restricted aspects of pain-control processes. It is assumed that the aggregate of responses typically labeled "aggressive" have no characteristics that are uniquely different from other painful stimuli exchanged in social interaction. In the present report, responses were investigated which sampled all of the readily observable child behaviors that seemed to fit, a priori, the usual definitions of aggressive behavior: Hit, Tease, Yell, Humiliate, Disapproval, and Destructive. In addition, other behaviors were included which, while they might be thought to be aversive, might not ordinarily be considered aggressive: Command Negative, Dependency, High Rate, Ignore, Negativism, Noncomply, and Whine.

As outlined previously (Patterson and Cobb 1971), there seemed to be two general processes for producing aggressive behaviors, each characterized by distinct controlling stimuli and ac-

1. In this sense one might analyze organization by defining the network of responses controlled by a single stimulus or the network of stimuli controlling a single response. It is apparent that if one is making *postdictions,* then the latter provides information to a *range* of antecedent events. However, if one is making predictions about *following* events, then the former increases the range of possibilities. The operational definition about organization varies, then, as a function of whether one is making pre- or postdictions.

companying reinforcers. The two processes, positive and negative reinforcers, have been previously noted by writers such as Buss (1961). For any given aggressive response, the acquisition and maintenance contingencies actually provided in situ by the social environment probably represent a mixture of these two processes.

Positive reinforcement. In the positive-reinforcement process, the victims may be carefully *delineated* by the culture as being "natural targets." They can be selected for a variety of characteristics, ranging from differences in size, skin color, dress, or religion to geographic location. The aggressor subgroup provides programmed training for the young boys, shaping attitudes, values, and a variety of acceptable aggressive skills. The "machismo culture" provides an excellent description of such a training program (Lewis 1965; Toch 1969)—as do the programs characterizing most militaristic cultures, which emphasize competition and aggressive body-contact sports. High orders of skills produce immediate social reinforcers from the peer group and status and prizes from society. In a militaristic society, adults routinely receive advanced training in skills necessary to inflict pain or death; the effectiveness of such training is reflected in the casualty statistics.

Scapegoating and warfare represent examples of "organized violence" condoned by society. Most of the young people in the group receive careful training in delineating the relevant discriminative stimuli for attacks; similarly, the positive consequences for performance are immediately available. However, it is also true that some of the aggressive behavior in these situations may also be controlled by negative reinforcement.

There is another sense in which positive reinforcement may play an important role in understanding aggression. Patterson, Littman, and Bricker (1967) and Patterson and Reid (1970) described the process by which a "skilled" aggressor inflicted pain and the victim provided what seemed to be a positive reinforcer. The latter consisted of the victim's giving up the territory, his toy, or crying. When any of these positive consequences occurred, the attack terminated. The aggressor was presumably reinforced by occupying the vacated territory, possessing the toy, or perhaps by the victim's crying. An analysis of several thousand aggressive incidents among nursery-school children showed that such consequences increased the probability of similar attacks in the future upon the same victim by the aggressor (Patterson, Littman, and Bricker 1967).[2]

It is not known how important this reinforcement process is for the maintenance of aggressive behavior. Persons who presumably find pain reactions in victims to be reinforcing have been described in fiction by Wilson's *A Clockwork Orange* (1962), in Toch's clinical studies, *Violent Men* (1969), and in textbooks on aggression (Berkowitz 1962). However, such individuals seem to be the exception rather than the rule. Scott and Fredericson (1951) noted that pain reactions in victims seemed to be an S^D for attacks for trained fighting mice. Also, Hartmann (1965) demonstrated that films of victims' pain reactions served as eliciting stimuli for increases in attacking behavior in a laboratory-analogue situation.

Negative reinforcement. In the negative-reinforcement process, that response is strengthened which is followed by the termination of an aversive stimulus. This process occurs in social interaction when one or more members introduces an aversive stimulus. For example, a child may present an aversive stimulus, such as Whine, and terminate it only when the mother complies with his request. This increases the likelihood that in the future Whine will be followed by mother's compliance. In some set-

2. Our recent investigations suggest that Accelerator and Reinforcer events may or may not represent similar processes. In fact, the most reasonable position is to assume that they are related only under special conditions and to carry out separate analyses to detect their presence. To the extent that the processes are orthogonal, the data in the 1967 monograph (Patterson, Littman, and Bricker) may have been confounded. At that time the writers assumed that a reinforcer would increase the probability of a response's recurrence, and this effect was similar whether the time intervals were immediately adjacent or distant future. Some of the recurring attacks occurred in the immediate setting (Acceleration) and others included attacks recurring the following day (possible reinforcement effect). While the victims' behavior increased the likelihood of attacks, the arrangement did not produce a clear test of victims' behavior as *positive reinforcers.*

tings, *both* members of the dyad may use aversive stimuli to control each other's behavior. The network of assumptions describing these interchanges has been labeled as the "coercion process" (Patterson and Cobb 1971; Patterson and Reid 1970), and they constitute the main focus for dealing with aggression in the present report.

It is our belief that pain-control techniques are a ubiquitous feature of many of the socializing processes found in our society. For example, base-rate data from the present report showed that young boys were more likely to provide insult or humiliating remarks to another family member rather than praise, affection, or approval. Data for boys from nonproblem families showed a mean of 3.1 Approval in contrast to a mean of 11.3 Disapprovals. While the boys exhibited 1.7 Physical Positive responses, they displayed 1.9 Physical Negative responses. Observations studied in the homes of nonproblem children showed that significant proportions of parents' reactions to child behaviors were aversive (Shaw 1971; Wahl 1971). Often it seems that it is the person who lacks the requisite social skills to produce social reinforcers who resorts to the use of aversive stimuli to control the behavior of the other person.

It is also assumed that individuals who are labeled as "deviant" would tend to be characterized as dispensing higher rates of aversive stimuli. Presumably, members of problem families would exhibit higher rates of aversive interactions than would members of nonproblem families.

Pain is a powerful means of controlling social behaviors. The appropriate behavior of the "victim" terminates the presentation of the aversive stimulus. The "aggressor" presents the aversive stimulus repeatedly until the appropriate victim response is produced. The negative-reinforcement process in the hands of an adult or child skilled in the presentation of aversive stimuli can be a powerful device to use in shaping his immediate social environment. The details of this shaping process are outlined in the section which follows.

In order to clarify the following discussion, it is necessary to define the terminology used. Functional relations that evoke aversive events are labeled differently from aversive events that evoke responses. *Aversive stimulus* is an antecedent event that is aversive. *Noxious response* refers to a functional relation in which the aversive event follows some other event. The term *aggressive* will be replaced by references to these two terms.

COERCION PROCESS

The characterization of a behavioral event as aversive or noxious is central to a proper delineation of the coercion process. It must be said at the outset that in our own work this definitional problem has not, as yet, been adequately resolved.

Aversive stimuli. The post hoc analyses of the data reported by Patterson and Cobb (1971) suggested that many of the stimuli-controlling Hit seemed aversive. The problem lay in defining the process by which these, or any other, stimuli might be labeled "aversive." One step which has been suggested, but not as yet tried, would be to have parents or children scale the various stimuli in terms of their "aversiveness." Such data, however, would provide only a weak definition and would have to be supplemented by additional operational definitions. There are several means by which a functional analysis could be used; to date, two stuch studies have been completed.

Laboratory studies have demonstrated that various arrangements of aversive stimuli produce reliable changes in behavior. Making an aversive stimulus contingent upon the occurrence of a response will often suppress the rate of occurrence of that response (Church 1963). Responses that terminate the presentation of adversive stimuli are usually strengthened (LoLordo 1969). Presumably, stimuli that may be shown to suppress response rates or whose termination is reinforcing could be said to be aversive.

The study by Patterson and Cobb (1971) investigated, among other things, the occurrence of 56, 632 episodes in which one of the family members exhibited a talk. Given the first occurrence of Talk, the probability was .52 that the same person would emit it again in the immediately following time interval. Given that the first Talk was consequated by Hit, the conditional probability of Talk recurring was .09. The *t*-test of the difference between these two proportions was 10.01 ($p < .001$). Clearly, the consequence Hit decelerated the response Talk. In the a priori list of thirteen noxious responses serving as the focus for the present report, all but two were shown to have a significant effect in suppressing the recurrence of Talk. The two exceptions, Destructive and Humiliate, occurred at such low rates that, while suppression was produced, the effects were not statistically significant.

Given that *only* aversive stimuli could decelerate or suppress on-going behavior, then this functional analysis would be a sufficient means for identifying aversive stimuli. However, as noted earlier in the discussion, it is also the case that S^Fs setting the occasion for concurrent competing operants could *also* serve to decelerate a response such as Talk. Therefore, the characteristic of serving as a decelerator for prosocial responses is thought of as a necessary, but not sufficient, condition to warrant the label "aversive."

The second required characteristic, the negative reinforcement function, could be defined by an analysis of sequential dependencies in which the effect of a reinforcing arrangement could be detected by the alterations in the probability of the R_j, given the presentation of the same S^F at some future time. However, such an analysis would require large amounts of data collected on the same individual for long periods of time. Our current mode of data collection (five minutes per S) does not lend itself to such a mode of analysis. Pending changes in our data collection, laboratory tests could be devised to test each stimulus thought to be aversive. The fact that the aversive status may vary as a function of the age of the subjects involved makes this a formidable task indeed.

To explore the feasibility of such a laboratory analysis for this problem, one behavioral event that had previously been identified as a decelerator for Talk was selected. Given that Talk occurred and was consequated by Ignore, the conditional probability was .33 that Talk would recur (Patterson and Cobb 1971, p. 108). The *t*-test for the difference between this value and the base-rate figure for recurrence of Talk was 8.81 ($p < .001$).

Atkinson (1971) devised a laboratory situation and applied a reversal design to demonstrate the stimulus control exerted by Mother-Ignore over the behavior of her own preschool child. The same procedures were later used to test the negative-reinforcement hypothesis. In the second study (Devine 1971) young children and their mothers participated first in a baseline period, during which time the mother and child played. During the first experimental period the mother was programmed to ignore all initiations from the child. In one group, only a prosocial response by the child would be followed by a removal of this arrangement. In the other group, only a coercive behavior by the child would result in the mother's terminating her Ignore behaviors. The analysis showed that whichever behavior produced the termination of the Mother-Ignore arrangement was strengthened. In effect, Mother-Ignore constituted a powerful aversive stimulus; its removal was reinforcing. It should be noted, however, that the mother not only terminated Ignore, but she also provided a positive reinforcer when she again attended to her child's behavior. While this dual strengthening probably characterizes in situ reinforcement for many coercive behaviors, it also means that the study did not clearly identify the effect as negative reinforcement.

While the negative-reinforcement characteristic is deemed a necessary and sufficient condition for status as an aversive stimulus, it must be said that, at this juncture, there are no behavioral events in the code system which have earned unequivocal status as aversive stimuli.

Some coercive patterns. In a coercive interchange, the behavior of one or both parties is controlled by aversive stimuli. Assuming that S_1 presented an aversive stimulus to S_2, one might raise questions as to the antecedents for the behavior of S_1. Where does the *first* aversive stimulus in the interchange come from? There is little data from the observations of human behavior which bear upon this point. There are, however, investigations employing animal subjects which provide suggestive evidence to the effect that one or more of the most likely antecedents for S_1's noxious behavior might have been something unpleasant introduced from a source external to the dyad.

Scott (1958), for example, noted that pain was a "primary stimulus" for aggression among many species of animals. Laboratory studies cited by Flory, Ulrich, and Wolff (1965) noted that electric shock and other painful events elicited aggressive behavior. Ulrich and Azrin (1962) and their colleagues carried out an impressive series of laboratory studies demonstrating the effect of electric shock upon paired animals, including rats, hamsters, cats (Ulrich, Wolff, and Azrin 1964) and monkeys (Azrin, Hutchinson, and Hake 1963). This group of investigators also carried out parametric studies investigating such variables as frequency (Ulrich and Azrin 1962) and duration of shock (Azrin et al. 1964), together with the effects of age, social isolation, and castration upon reflexive aggression (Hutchinson, Ulrich, and Azrin 1965).

Several investigators have demonstrated in laboratory analogue settings that if an outsider insults a subject, it will increase the intensity of his attacks upon a "victim" (Berkowitz 1971; Buss 1966*a*, 1966*b;* Hokanson and Eddman 1966; Hartmann 1965; Hokanson, Willus, and Koropsak 1968).

The question concerning the antecedent for the first aversive stimulus introduced into dyadic interaction was not answered directly by any of these laboratory studies. The classic analysis of interactions of adolescent boys by Raush (1965) showed that in 8 percent of the interactions among "normals" and aversive stimulus was introduced following friendly interactions. However, when observing disturbed boys, the aversive stimulus was introduced "unexpectedly" 45 percent of the time. In either case, the immediately preceding antecedent behavior was a friendly act. It may be that an analysis of antecedents occurring a moment or ten minutes prior to the aversive stimulus would show that in the majority of cases an aversive stimulus of some kind had been presented to the subject, who then introduced the first aversive stimulus in an on-going dyadic interaction.

Given that one subject has introduced an aversive stimulus into the interaction, the odds become very great that the other subject will reciprocate. Raush (1965) noted that, for both disturbed and nondisturbed adolescent boys, the odds were about .75 that an unfriendly act would be followed by an unfriendly act. Self-report data for adolescent subjects suggested a linear relation between the intensity of the attack and the amplitude of the response they reported they would make to it (Graham et al. 1951).

Patterson and Cobb (1971) analyzed 117,033 interaction episodes among family members to determine that the base rate, *p*(Hit), for all members was .002. However, given that the younger sister had just Teased, the conditional probability was .020 that a Hit would follow. Similarly, the probability of a Hit following younger sister Hitting was .323. When one individual introduces an aversive stimulus to the interaction, the odds increase heavily that the other individual will reciprocate in kind. Reid (1967) investigated the equity of such exchanges among members of families with problem children. He showed that the family member who received the highest rates of aversive stimuli also dispensed the highest rates. The median correlation was .65 for rankings of "giving" and "receiving." Pain produces pain.

Escalation. It was hypothesized that in interchanges where painful stimuli are exchanged there is an escalation process which may be characterized by either or both of two kinds of variables. On the one hand, there is an increase in the probability of aversive events recurring. The more extended the chain, the greater the increase in probability values. Second, there may be an increase in the intensity of the stimuli being delivered until one or both members terminate the interaction.

It was, in fact, the apparent escalation in these two characteristics which first led us to use the term *coercive* when describing the noxious behaviors of preschool children (Patterson, Littman, and Bricker 1967). The observation of preschool interchanges suggested that the skilled coercer would increase the amplitude of his blows or shoves until the victim conceded. The "escalation hypotheses" were not a necessary derivation from either social learning theory or from the escape-avoidance literature. Rather, they were a simple description of what seemed to occur rather often in interchanges.

It was our impression that high-amplitude behaviors were

more likely to occur in the longer sequences of aversive interchanges. Each event unit in the exchange led each member to dispense ever-increasing intensities of pain to the other. Presumably, the final result might be the chains leading to homicide or physical assault described by Toch (1969). For example, in their review, Shah and Weber (1968) noted that 28 percent of all homicides involved killing within families. It was hypothesized by the present writers that these extremes were reached after extended exchanges of aversive stimuli.

Kopfstein (1971) and Patterson and Cobb (1971) showed that aversive consequences for noxious responses *accelerated* the likelihood of recurrence of these noxious responses. While these same aversive consequences suppressed the probability of recurrence for Talk, they functioned as *facilitating stimuli* for recurrence of *noxious responses* (Patterson and Cobb, 1971, p. 120). Data from the same study supported the hypothesis about an increase in probability values for noxious responses given extended exchanges. The analysis of the sequential dependencies among family members produced the following conditional probability values:

Young Sisters Tease → $_p$(Hit/Tease as antecedent) = .067

Victim consequates Hit with a Hit → $_p$(Hit/Previous Hit consequated by Hit) = .44

$_p$(Hit) = .003

The dramatic increase in magnitude of the conditional probabilities for Hit was suggestive evidence for one aspect of the pain-escalation hypotheses.

Further investigations of this type are required in order to fully explicate the escalation hypotheses. Analyses are planned for the coming year to determine the condition under which such chained sequences occur and to define the manner in which conditional probability values for noxious responses vary as a function of these sequenced matrices. As it now stands, the two escalation hypotheses remain relatively untested heuristic devices for describing a process we believe to be found frequently in interchanges among families of problem children.

GENERALIZATION OF COERCION PROCESS

It was assumed that the same coercion process previously ascribed to families of aggressive boys would also describe those occurrence of noxious responses found in families of matched nonproblem children. This is to say only that aversive stimuli presented to "normal" boys tend to increase the likelihood that the boys will exhibit a noxious response. Such a finding has already been reported (Raush 1965) for a small group of normal adolescent boys interacting within an institutional setting.

This hypothesis suggests that, given a high density of presentation of aversive stimuli, boys are likely to respond with high rates of noxious responses. This being the case, then families of aggressive and nonaggressive boys would tend to differ in the rates of noxious responses and the densities for their controlling stimuli. This is in keeping with our general notion that the coercive process is to be found in many social interchanges among problem and nonproblem individuals alike.

HYPOTHESES TO BE TESTED

Observation data were collected in the homes of thirty-two families of problem boys and twenty-six families of nonproblem boys. The fifty-eight families included fifty-three boys in the problem-family sample and forty-five in the nonproblem-family group. Each family was observed in the home, for six to ten hours for the nonproblem families and for a minimum of twelve hours in the problem families.

For this analysis, thirteen behavior events were identified, a priori, as noxious responses. These included Command Negative, Dependency, Destructive, Disapproval, High Rate, Humiliate, Ignore, Negativism, Noncomply, Physical Negative, Tease, Whine, and Yell. The list was compiled largely on the basis of the seeming aversive quality of the responses. It seemed to us that if classes of aggressive-like responses existed, they would be comprised in large part of some combination of these thirteen responses. The present analysis focused first upon identifying the antecedent stimuli that had significant control over the occurrence of each of these thirteen aversive behaviors.

The conditional probability of noxious response R_j, given antecedent stimulus X_i, was calculated across agents for each of the twenty-nine behavioral events coded by our observational system. The $p(R_j/X_i)$ values were then compared with the corrected base-rate values for the target response in order to determine whether the antecedent stimulus served to significantly inhibit or facilitate its occurrence.

1. It was hypothesized that significant facilitating (S^F) and inhibiting (S^I) stimuli would be identified by this process.

2. It was predicted that the stimuli identified as significant S^F's for the noxious responses would be drawn primarily from the a priori list of aversive stimuli. The inhibitory stimuli (S^I's), on the othr hand, would more likely consist of stimuli which appear, a priori, to be "reinforcing."

3. It was hypothesized that the network of antecedents found significant for the thirteen noxious behaviors for the boys from problem families would be similar to those identified for boys from the nonproblem families.

4. It was hypothesized that some of the thirteen target behaviors would be under the control of similar stimuli. Antecedent behavioral stimuli would be analyzed to determine the proportion of the base-rate probability for each noxious response accounted for by antecedent events common to both. A significant amount of overlap found among some of the thirteen events would constitute a "class" of responses. Presumably, several such classes would be found among the noxious responses.

Procedures

SAMPLE

The sample consisted of fifty-eight families, thirty-two of which had been referred to the Social Learning Project by community agents because one or more of the children had displayed high rates of aggressive behavior.[3] The identified problem children were boys between the ages of three and fourteen years, approximately one-fourth of whom had been diagnosed as minimally brain damaged. None of the parents, or children, had been diagnosed as psychotic or severely retarded. Only those families were accepted which consisted of three or more persons living within a twenty-minute drive of the laboratory; it was not required that the father be living in the home.

The parents were informed prior to the intake interview that the "fee" required for the treatment they would receive would consist of a number of observation sessions in the home prior to, during, and following treatment.

Twenty-six "nonproblem" families were obtained by advertising in the local newspaper and by contacts with the welfare department. The large number of volunteers were screened by telephone to select only those who provided a close match to one of the problem families. The families in the two samples were matched on the following variables: father's presence or absence, number of children in family, age of mother, age of identified problem child, and occupation of parents. None of the parents or children in the nonproblem-family sample were currently receiving psychiatric treatment; several of them did report, however, that they had previously received professional assistance. The families were informed that a series of six to ten observation sessions would be needed. They were to receive a minimum of $1.50 per hour for the sessions and $20.00–$30.00 if they completed the whole series.

There were eighty-six children in the nonproblem families and

3. The treatment procedures developed for these families and the data describing the outcome were presented in several reports. The intervention procedures describing the training procedures for the families were described in Patterson, Cobb, and Ray (Forthcoming). The replication study for these procedures was detailed in the report by Patterson (1971). Some of the families required that a second set of intervention procedures be developed to handle out-of-control behaviors occurring in the classroom. These procedures and the observation data describing performance during baseline, intervention, and follow-up were presented in the report by Patterson, Cobb, and Ray (1971).

102 in the families of problem children. The median number of children per family was 3.0 for both kinds of families. Data used to test the hypotheses outlined in the present report were provided by boys between the ages of three and fourteen. Fifty-three boys in the families of problem children met this requirement, and forty-nine boys in nonproblem families. The distributions by age for these two samples are summarized in table 6.1 below.

The data showed the distributions to be very similar. The median age was 7.0 years for both samples.

As noted in the clinical literature, there seemed to be a disproportionate number of problem families in which the fathers were absent from the home. In the present report, the figures of 71 percent father present for the nonproblem families and 68 percent for the problem families attest to the care with which the two samples were matched on this variable. It was our general impression that, for the problem families, the father-absent homes produced higher rates of aggressive child behavior than did father-present homes.

The distributions of mothers' ages are summarized in table 6.2.

By and large, the parents of the problem families were in their early thirties. The median age of the mothers was thirty-three years for both samples. While the age distributions were comparable, there was a slight skew at the upper age levels for the sample of problem families.

Table 6.3 summarizes the information relative to occupation

TABLE 6.1 *Distribution of boys' ages for the two samples, in percentages*

Age (years)	*Nonproblem Families (%)*	*Problem Families (%)*
3–5	13	11
6–8	35	42
9–11	29	23
12–14	16	15
15+	07	09
Median age	7 years	7 years

TABLE 6.2. *Distribution of mothers' ages for the two samples, in percentages*

Age of Mothers (years)	*Nonproblem Families (%)*	*Problem Families (%)*
26–30	34.6	34.4
31–35	50.0	46.9
36–40	15.3	9.4
40+	0	9.4
Median age	33	33

class for the samples. Both groups showed a disproportionate emphasis on the lower-middle and lower classes, which is probably not representative of the local community at large. There were some disparities in the matching for occupational class, in that the nonproblem group tended to oversample the upper and middle classes. The data for adjoining classes were grouped to form four occupational classes. The χ^2 value of 5.29 (df = 3) showed the differences in distribution to be nonsignificant.

OBSERVATION

A minimum of six to ten observation sessions were conducted in the homes.[4] In the case of the problem families, an additional twenty-six sessions were obtained during and following intervention. Baseline data for the problem families and all of the data for the nonproblem families were collected on consecutive weekdays, usually between 4:00 P.M. and 7:00 P.M. The members of the family were required to remain either in the kitchen or an ajoining room, with the television set turned off. No outgoing phone calls were made, and no visitors were present.

4. At the inception of the project, an arbitrary decision was made to use ten observation sessions as a baseline measure of both experimental and control families. After several years of data collection, an analysis was made to determine the minimum amounts of data sufficient for a stable estimate of behavioral events. The analysis described in the report by Patterson and Cobb (1971) and in Patterson, Cobb, and Ray (forthcoming) showed that three sessions provided estimates that were minimally reliable for most of the code categories. Following completion of these analyses, the decision was made to collect baseline data for six days for both samples of families.

TABLE 6.3. *Distributions of parent occupations, in percentages**

Parent Occupation	*Nonproblem Families* (%)	*Problem Families* (%)
I. Major professional or large business	11.5	6.3
II. Lesser professional or business	26.9	6.3
III. Administrative, or small business	7.7	6.3
IV. Clerical	23.1	37.5
V. Skilled laborers	7.7	9.4
VI. Semi-skilled laborers	11.5	18.8
VII. Unskilled laborers	0	6.3
Mothers on welfare	11.5	9.4
Median occupational class	IV	IV

* The system described by Hollingshead and Redlich (1958) was used to classify the parent occupations.

Each observer was equipped with a clipboard that contained a built-in interval-timing device. At thirty-second intervals the observer received both a visual (light) and an auditory stimulus (via earphone). On those occasions when reliability data were being collected by two or more observers, the timing devices were synchronized. Family members were observed in random order.

The target's behavior was coded, as were the consequences provided by others for their behavior. This yielded a continuous account for each family member for a five-minute period. After each member had been the target, the whole series was repeated once during that session.

After extensive field observations in the homes of both deviant and nondeviant children, the first coding system was developed in 1966. It was designed to test some specific hypotheses based upon social learning principles and is therefore not an omnibus system. Currently, it consists of twenty-nine categories that describe various behavioral events: Approval, Attention, Command, Command Negative, Comply, Cry, Dependency, Destructiveness, Disapproval, High Rate (hyperactive), Hit, Humiliate, Ignore, Indulge, Laugh, Negativism, Noncomply, Normative, No Response, Play, Physical Positive, Receive, Self-stimulation, Talk, Tease, Touch, Whine, Work, and Yell. A manual providing operational definitions for these categories, together with the rules for their use, has been deposited with the National Auxiliary Publications Service.[5]

Observer training and reliability. The observers were intelligent, mature women, who, for the most part, had already met the usual obligations of education and/or motherhood. Each required approximately twenty hours of training in the use of the code system, which involved practice sessions viewing videotapes of family interaction. Then they went into the homes with the experienced observers until their agreement with the observer reached 75 percent. All five observers participated in biweekly sessions in which they viewed videotapes and coded the interactions. During these sessions there were discussions about any disagreements arising from their data.

To calculate reliability, the observation protocols from two observers were compared unit by unit for each thirty-second interval. Errors in identifying the behavioral event, the persons involved, or the sequence of events were identified for each thirty-second interval. The overall percentage agreement was calculated by summing the events observed for all family members in a session for both observers. This sum was divided into the total number of events (behavioral events, persons, and sequences) for which they were in agreement. Observers' data were compared in the field regularly; the mean percentage of agreement figures among five observers were as follows: 83, 81, 85, 81, and 85 percent.

To compensate for the "observer drift phenomenon" noted by Reid (1970) and Thomas, Loomis, and Arrington (1933), biweekly training sessions were held in which videotapes of family interaction were coded. The group compared their observations, discussed discrepancies, and reran the tapes until *all* observers agreed.

5. To obtain, order document No. 01234 from ASIS National Auxiliary Publications Service, c/o Microfiche Publications, 305 E. 46th St. New York, New York 10017. Remit $2.00 for microfilm or $5.30 for photocopies. Make checks payable to Microfiche Publications. Videotapes of family interaction, together with scoring keys, may be obtained by contacting Oregon Research Institute, P.O. Box 3196, Eugene, Oregon 97403.

The problem of observer bias has been noted by Kass and O'Leary (1970), Scott, Burton, and Radke-Yarrow (1967), Rapp (cited by Rosenthal 1966), and Rosenthal (1966). They have shown that assumptions held by observers may lead to distortions in the data. To counteract this effect, a "calibrating observer" who was unaware of which families were being treated and which were control was added to the staff. Each observer coded in a home with the calibrating observer once a month. The analysis of these data by Skindrud (1970) showed that, for the small sample used, there was no significant bias.

Data sampling. In a previous report (Patterson, Cobb, and Ray, in press), data for twelve families were analyzed separately for mothers, deviant children, and oldest siblings in order to determine the stability of the estimates for each code category. In that analysis an effort was made to determine whether individuals would maintain their ordinal rankings for any given code category when sampled at different points in time. The reliability correlations were calculated for estimates based upon the first five and the last five sessions. The analysis was analogous to test-retest reliability, or split-half reliability for each of the twenty-nine code categories. The median correlation for the response categories was .71; the median for the consequence categories was .60. Two code categories were identified as unreliable (Self-stimulation and Work). These findings exclude those categories whose frequency was less than one event per hour (Dependency, Destructiveness, High Rate, Humiliate, Physical Positive, and Whine). The analysis showed that three to five sessions were sufficient to establish a rather stable estimate of the individuals' rates for a number of the code categories.

Individuals' rankings for any given code category were relatively stable over time. However, the mean levels for the codes could vary even though the rankings for individuals were stable. As a preliminary test, the mean level for twelve mothers, fathers, deviant children, and siblings were analyzed for each code category across ten sessions. The analysis of variance (ANOVA) for repeated measures for the ten baseline sessions produced a total of 116 F-values, of which only two were significant at the 0.5

level (Patterson and Cobb 1971). These analyses suggested that there were no systematic changes in mean level over ten baseline sessions.

Because of the small samples, the foregoing test for changes in mean level would be sensitive only to large magnitude changes. As a more powerful test, the data for seventeen problem children

TABLE 6.4. *Changes in mean rate across baseline sessions*

	Observation Session							
Code Category	1	2	3	5	7	9	10	*F-Value*
Approval	0.036	0.032	0.023	0.010	0.010	0.023	0.010	1.17
Attend	1.510	1.142	1.632	1.710	1.371	1.297	1.581	1.34
Command	0.026	0.023	0.036	0.029	0.052	0.026	0.032	0.37
Command Negative	0.010	0.003	0.003	0.007	0.007	0.007	0.000	0.42
Comply	0.136	0.136	0.139	0.132	0.152	0.136	0.113	0.20
Cry	0.010	0.000	0.013	0.007	0.003	0.003	0.000	0.89
Disapproval	0.165	0.061	0.113	0.113	0.113	0.087	0.132	1.05
Dependency	0.007	0.023	0.003	0.000	0.019	0.007	0.003	0.59
Destructiveness	0.013	0.007	0.029	0.029	0.003	0.019	0.013	0.69
High Rate	0.016	0.016	0.016	0.045	0.039	0.013	0.023	0.60
Humiliate	0.010	0.003	0.000	0.023	0.019	0.023	0.013	0.86
Ignore	0.010	0.016	0.010	0.003	0.000	0.013	0.013	1.09
Laugh	0.068	0.068	0.097	0.155	0.077	0.052	0.161	1.44
Noncomply	0.042	0.032	0.045	0.071	0.065	0.016	0.029	1.05
Negativism	0.097	0.103	0.103	0.087	0.058	0.184	0.100	0.56
Normative	3.132	3.848	3.123	3.226	3.074	3.145	2.781	0.87
No Response	0.068	0.068	0.065	0.019	0.058	0.036	0.052	1.33
Play	1.661	1.526	1.607	1.252	1.800	2.219	2.090	0.80
Physical Negative	0.010	0.029	0.029	0.061	0.023	0.042	0.010	0.92
Physical Positive	0.007	0.003	0.139	0.016	0.007	0.048	0.061	0.76
Receive	0.084	0.055	0.039	0.036	0.032	0.052	0.042	1.37
Self-stimulation	0.142	0.126	0.190	0.300	0.158	0.365	0.132	1.21
Talk	2.094	1.742	1.823	2.142	2.623	1.807	2.129	2.47
Tease	0.074	0.019	0.045	0.026	0.029	0.032	0.071	1.15
Touch	0.023	0.026	0.029	0.029	0.032	0.042	0.032	0.17
Whine	0.032	0.019	0.090	0.058	0.007	0.123	0.007	1.64
Work	0.739	0.910	0.903	0.794	0.736	0.642	0.729	0.17
Yell	0.065	0.023	0.058	0.039	0.058	0.039	0.042	0.48

and fourteen boys matched for age from nonproblem families were analyzed. Each of the code categories was subjected to an ANOVA for repeated measures for sessions 1, 2, 3, 5, 7, 9, and 10.[6] The mean rate per minute estimated for each session and the F-values are presented in table 6.4 below.

None of the changes in mean level for the categories was significant. It must be concluded that the observation data were moderately stable for most code categories in terms of rankings among individual subjects and for mean rates across time.

Observer effect. Parents often reported that the observers did not see the family as it "really was." Some parents reported that the children acted worse when the observers were present, others reported that the children, and they themselves, were better behaved when the observers were present. Within the present context, the presence of the observer in the home was viewed as a significant social stimulus that probably had some effects upon family interaction. The question, however, concerned the magnitude and the duration of these effects.

Comments from family members and general subjective impressions suggested to our observers that roughly half of the families were distorting their interactions in some manner. Most of the distortion is probably biased toward social desirability. After making extensive observations in homes, Littman, Pierce-Jones, and Stern (1957) and Schalock (1958) commented that there seemed to be some distortions in family interactions as a function of their presence in the home.

Both writers also noted that some families seemed characterized by increased variability during the early sessions. A carefully conducted study by Paul (1964) tested Schalock's hypothesis that observers' presence produced increased variability in mother-child interactions. While the outcome did not support that hypothesis, the other features of the analysis showed that there

6. During a period of a year and a half, fathers were requested to absent themselves from the home while the observers collected data during sessions 4, 6, and 8. These manipulations were introduced by D. Shaw for an investigation of the effects of fathers' presence or absence on rates of observed deviant child behavior.

were a number of changes in rates of behavior suggesting some type of habituation-to-observer effect. For example, the following behaviors increased over sessions: seek recognition, statement of action, rejection as a person, and physical restraint. The following decreased: information by demonstration and permissiveness with qualification. The general trend in these and other categories was for mothers to become more restrictive. In interviews at the end of the session the mothers all reported that they were very much aware of the observer's presence.

In a study by Harris (1969) and an earlier analysis of the data by Patterson and Harris (1968), mothers were trained to use the coding system, after which they collected data in their own homes. A control group of mothers collected data for a series of ten sessions. A second control group of outside observers collected data for the entire period. In the experimental group the mothers observed for the first five sessions, and "outside" observers came in to observe for the last five (in which the mothers were absent). The analyses of rate of social interaction showed no significant main effects between groups or across trials (Harris 1969). Similarly, no significant effects were found for a comparable analysis of deviant behaviors (Patterson and Harris 1968). This suggested that the effects of observer presence were not of such a high magnitude that they can be detected with small samples of subjects.

Harris (1969) provided some support for Schalock's variability hypothesis. It was assumed that one effect of the observers' presence might be reflected in alterations in the "predictability" of subjects' behavior from one point in time to another. The individuals' social interaction rates for time 1 and time 2 showed much higher correlations when the mothers observed than when outside observers observed (Harris 1969). While it may be simply that mothers were more reliable observers, there were no differences noted in their reliability during training. Unfortunately, no data were provided on their comparability when collecting data in the field.

If the presence of the observer functions, either as a conditioned or a discriminative stimulus, one would think that after four or five sessions in which the observer displays few, if any, reactions to their behavior, that the family might begin to habituate to the effects of their being present. Such a process could be detected by changes in mean levels over time for the various code categories. However, the two analyses discussed in the previous section showed no significant changes in mean level over sessions. These findings suggested that, if families habituated to observers' presence, the magnitude of the effect was too small to be detected by samples of that size.

While both parents and observers claim that observer presence is a significant variable, we have, as yet, no data which clearly demonstrate this effect.

DECISION RULES FOR THE CURRENT ANALYSIS

During coding each person was assigned a number, which was placed in front of the appropriate codes that characterized the behavior of each person interacting. The responses exhibited by the persons interacting were coded sequentially. Sometimes two behaviors occurred simultaneously. When this happened, both responses were coded. Similarly, more than one person could be coded. The details of these and other decision rules for coding are outlined in a procedures manual.

For the current analysis, noxious behaviors exhibited by boys between the ages of three and fourteen were identified. These included: Command Negative (CN), Disapproval (DI), Dependency (DP), Destructiveness (DS), High Rate (HR), Humiliate (HU), Ignore (IG), Noncomply (NC), Negativism (NE), Physical Negative (Hit) (PN), Tease (TE), Whine (WH), and Yell (YE). Each R_j that occurred was examined to determine if the family member whose presence preceded the behavior was the same family member who followed the interaction. For example, if the behavior was a hit (PN), the antecedent agent was young sister teasing, and the following behavior was also by young sister, then that PN was included in the analysis. If a different agent consequated the response, then it would seem less certain that that antecedent identified by the code system had, in fact, been the significant stimulus. All such potentially ambiguous episodes were dropped from the analysis.

It was our subjective impression that interactions in which

aversive stimuli were exchanged for extended periods of time may have been psychologically "different" from those interchanges made up of only one or two aversive stimuli. The stimuli controlling noxious behaviors during chained sequences may not only be different, but also have different conditional probability values attached. It seemed necessary, then, to carry out analyses of stimulus control separately for "chained" and "unchained" sequences. The analysis in the present report will focus only upon "unchained noxious responses."

If the noxious response occurring was at the beginning of a chain of behaviors, or isolated from a chain, it was included in the analysis. If any deviant behaviors involving the target subject occurred within the three prior time intervals (total of eighteen seconds), the noxious response was considered "chained." Three adjacent time sequences in which no deviant behavior occurred were required before a deviant response (R_j) could be included in the present analysis. Similarly, prosocial behaviors were said to be "chained" if they involved the same two agents. The analysis of stimulus control for prosocial responses required that the interaction involve two persons who had not interacted with each other during the preceding eighteen seconds.

If the original agent stopped interacting with the subject for three sequences, then a chain (of either deviant or prosocial behaviors) was considered terminated. Following such breaks, the first interaction of the target subject would be analyzed to determine the stimuli that controlled the occurrence of the response.

Dependent variable. The dependent variable used throughout the analysis was the probability of occurrence for a given R_j (noxious response). The base-rate value $p(R_j)$ was calculated for each of the thirteen responses for both samples of boys (See table 6.5, p. 181). This value described the proportion of occasions on which an R_j occurred, given that the target subject had not displayed any of the thirteen "aversive" behaviors during the previous three interaction episodes. In effect, $p(R_j)$ was concerned with the question of how likely it was that an aversive behavior would occur in "unchained" interaction. This meant that the behavior of both the target subject and the people with whom he had been interacting in the immediately preceding eighteen seconds had been "pleasant" or "neutral" to the target subject.

The value $p(R_j)$ was calculated by tabulating the total number of occasions that boys exhibited each of the twenty-nine code categories in "unchained" interactions. The sum of these was divided into the number of R_j's exhibited by boys.

Controlling stimuli. The significant antecedent stimuli for each R_j was determined by first identifying the event as an antecedent for all non-R_j events occurring in the code system. This was compared with the frequency with which the event occurred as an antecedent for R_j. The resulting fourfold table was subjected to a χ^2 analysis, with appropriate corrections for continuity, or Fisher's exact χ^2 when required. Those antecedents that produced χ^2 values significant at $p < .10$ were said to be significant controlling stimuli.

A significant χ^2 could mean that the antecedent stimulus significantly increased or decreased the rate of occurrence of the response, as compared with its corrected baseline value. The contribution of an event as an antecedent for R_j was subtracted from its contribution to all non-R_j events to calculate the corrected base rate as antecedent stimulus. Stimuli that increased the probability of occurrence of R_j were labeled facilitating stimuli (S^f), and those that decreased its probability were labeled as inhibitory stimuli (S^I).

While it would be useful to know that an antecedent stimulus was identified as significant, its contribution to prediction might be trivial. For example, the antecedent stimuli may have a very low base-rate probability. For boys from problem families, the base-rate value for a Hit was .010. The conditional probability of a Hit, given that the antecedent was that someone else in the family had hit him, was approximately .296. This increase in probability was significant; however, the fact that the antecedent occurred at the *very* low rate of approximately .007 suggested that only a limited explanation of the antecedents for Hit is being provided.

The information contained in the conditional probability of R_j, given the presence of the antecedent stimulus, could be combined with the information about the base rate for S^F or S^I to provide an estimate of the "importance" of the antecedent. Summing the compound probabilities resulting from multiplying $[p(R_j/\text{Antec}_i)]$ $[p(\text{Antec}_i)]$ for each of the code categories would account for all of the information available for $p(R_j)$, that is, sum to 1.00.

Controlling stimuli, then, may have two characteristics. They may be significant or nonsignificant, and they may also have differing importance. It is important to keep in mind that the two characteristics were not necessarily related. An antecedent stimulus that occurred only once, but that was followed by Hit, would generate a conditional probability $p(\text{Hit}/\text{Antec}_i)$ of 1.00. The χ^2 analysis would identify such a variable as nonsignificant. Similarly, the compound probability $[p(\text{Hit}/\text{Antec}_i)]$ $[p(\text{Antec}_i)]$ would be extremely low, and thus either process would identify such a variable as "not very important." On the other hand, all high-rate antecedents are likely to have relatively high-compound-probability values. However, the χ^2 analyses would determine whether they were significant. If a high-rate stimulus were shown to precede R_j significantly more often than it preceded all non-R_j's, then it would indeed be thought of as an important variable controlling R_j.

Simply collecting data on all the variables that preceded R_j and calculating their compound probabilities would sum to 1.00. The compound probabilities themselves do not identify a variable as significant; therefore, a two-step process was used to analyze stimulus control. Both steps were necessary conditions, but neither was a sufficient condition, for defining a variable as an important stimulus-controlling R_j. The first step determined whether the conditional probability value $p(R_j/\text{Antec}_i)$ was significant (the χ^2 analysis). The second involved the calculation of the compound probability $[p(\text{Antec}_i)]$ $[p(R_j/\text{Antec})]$.[7]

7. The programming used in the computer analysis was developed by Mark Layman, and the programs may be obtained by contacting him at the Oregon Research Institute, P. O. Box 3196, Eugene, Oregon 97403.

Results

STIMULUS CONTROL BY BEHAVIORAL EVENTS

A previous analysis of stimulus control for the responses Talk and Physical Negative (Patterson and Cobb 1971) had demonstrated that they were under the control of multiple stimuli. In this sense, the term *stimulus control* would refer to the matrix or network of stimuli that control a particular response. Each of the thirteen noxious responses was analyzed to determine the network of S^{F}'s and S^{I}'s which controlled its occurrence. To be included in such a network, the antecedent event must have been identified as exerting significant control (χ^2 significant at $p <$ .10 or better) over one of the noxious R_j's. Significant control would imply that the presence of the antecedent event would lead to appreciable increases or decreases in the probability of occurrence for that response. For any given R_j, the search for controlling stimuli was carried through each of the code categories, using the combined data from all family members.[8]

A total of 10,626 initiations of "new" responses for the boys from problem families produced 2,041 noxious responses. The comparable data for boys from the nonproblem families were 3,378 and 480, respectively. These figures provided the basis for estimating $p(R_j)$ for each of the noxious responses for both samples.[9]

8. Given that the stimuli controlling Hit and Talk would vary as a function of age, sex, and roles within families, then the data presented in the earlier report (Patterson and Cobb 1971) were confounded. At that time data were available from only twenty-four families; it was thought necessary to use the data from all family members in order to have a sample of events adequate for the analysis of stimulus control for Hit. While the earlier study analyzed the contribution of each code by each agent, the data for the dependent variables were summed across agents and thus may have been "confounded." In the present report, the data for the dependent variables were not confounded; but, to the extent that there was an agent by antecedent-event interaction, there may have also been a confounding in the present analysis. Data are now being collected in which neither possible confound will be present.

9. A summary of the details of the analyses of stimulus control for each of the R_js for both samples of boys may be obtained from the National Auxiliary Publications Service. Order document #02107 (13 pp.) from ASIS/NAPS c/o Microfiche Publications, 305 E. 46th St., NYC 10017. Re-

Assuming that a sample of fifteen to twenty events was sufficient, then adequate data were available to analyze the stimuli controlling all of the R_j's for the boys from problem families. Some of the R_j's occurred so infrequently for boys from nonproblem families that it was impossible to determine their controlling stimuli. The present analysis did not provide an adequate analysis of stimulus control for the variables Command Negative, Dependency, Destructiveness, High Rate, Humiliate, and Ignore for boys of nonproblem families.

The compound-probability values for each of the significant controlling stimuli were summed for each R_j. Dividing this value into the $p(R_j)$ gave a precise description of the extent to which the significant S^F's and S^I's accounted for the response. Given that our guesses were correct in constructing the original coding system, the relevant antecedent variables might have been built into the system, and thus a large proportion of some noxious responses could be accounted for. On other variables, for which either the guesses were more limited or the amount of data sampled inadequate, the proportion of $p(R_j)$ accounted for will be correspondingly lower.[10]

Table 6.5 summarizes for each R_j the frequency with which it occurred in the two samples, the $p(R_j)$ values, and the proportion of its base rate accounted for by the antecedent variables (S^F's and S^I's) identified as significant.

The existing code system and network of antecedent variables seemed to account for most of the occurrences of noxious responses such as Whine, Noncomply, Ignore, High Rate, Disapproval, Humiliate, and Negativism for the boys from problem families. Data from boys of nonproblem families showed somewhat lower levels and for a more restricted set of variables: Noncomply, Negativism, Disapproval, and Command Negative. With the exception of the latter, all of the noxious responses whose antecedents were well described for the nonproblem family boys

---

mit in advance for each NAPS accession number $1.50 for microfiche or $5.00 for photocopies up to 30 pages, 15¢ for each additional page. Make checks payable to Microfiche Publications.

10. There was, in fact, a correlation of .49 ($p < .10$) between the frequency with which a variable occurred and the amount of the base-rate value accounted for by the determinants sampled with this coding system.

TABLE 6.5. *The proportion of* $p(R_j)$*s accounted for by significant controlling stimuli*

Noxious Behaviors (R_j)	Problem Families: frequency R_j	Problem Families: $p(R_j)$	Problem Families: proportion of $p(R_j)$ accounted for	Nonproblem Families: frequency R_j	Nonproblem Families: $p(R_j)$	Nonproblem Families: proportion of $p(R_j)$ accounted for
Command Negative	21	.002	.472	7	.003	.715
Disapproval	646	.061	.780	159	.047	.798
Dependency	17	.002	.000	7	.002	0
Destructiveness	18	.002	.053	0	0	0
High Rate	88	.008	.850	6	.002	0
Humiliate	38	.004	.734	5	.001	.196
Ignore	72	.007	.956	7	.002	.280
Noncomply	404	.038	.997	128	.038	.999
Negativism	278	.026	.743	64	.019	.796
Physical Negative	106	.010	.673	11	.003	.631
Tease	117	.011	.584	25	.007	.596
Whine	120	.011	.939	39	.012	.256
Yell	116	.011	.326	22	.007	.091
Total	2,041	.192	----	480	.142	----

were also well described for the boys from problem families. Presumably, a greater incidence of such responses as High Rate, Humiliate, Ignore, and Whine would make it possible for the existing variables in the code system to contribute at the same level as they did for the other sample of boys.

Lacking any prior knowledge of what to expect, the authors were surprised at both the magnitude of the percentages describing these functional relations and at the number of responses for which they obtained. Presumably much of the information necessary to "understand" many of these noxious responses was to be found in the behavior of family members which occurred in the immediately prior six seconds. It had been expected that much larger time intervals would have to be involved in the sampling of antecedents before it was possible to account for that much information about a noxious response.

These data showed that for ten of the thirteen variables for boys from problem families, the existing network of antecedents accounted for greater than 40 percent of the base-rate information for the response. For that sample there were only three variables for which the present model seemed clearly inadequate in determining the stimuli that controlled their occurrence: Dependency, Destructiveness, and Yell.[11]

For each R_j the lists of significant determinants were compared in order to identify those events serving similar functions as S^F's or S^I's for the two samples. The compound probabilities were summed for these overlapping determinants for each sample; the sums were divided by their respective $p(R_j)$ values to determine the amount of the base-rate value accounted for by the overlapping variables. The data for overlap in determinants for the two samples are summarized in table 6.6 below.

11. It is conceivable that a larger sampling of DP and DS events would reveal clear patterns of stimulus control. However, in retrospect, DP and DS were not variables carefully studied in the preliminary field observations made in 1965 and 1966. However, we did believe we had done an adequate job of describing the antecedents for Yell. A proper study of these three behaviors would require beginning over with general field observations followed by designing a more appropriate coding system. It seems reasonable to expect that some new variables excluded from the present coding system would be identified by such an analysis.

There were no reasonable means for determining the overlap value to be exceeded before shared determinants might be said to be "psychologically significant." A figure of 40 percent was arbitrarily set as necessary in applying the label "common determinants." Using this criterion, four of the seven R_j's showed sufficiently high levels of overlap to constitute support for the hypothesis that problem and nonproblem families demonstrated similarities in stimuli that controlled noxious responses. Command Negative, Noncomply, Negativism, and Physical Negative all demonstrated common determinants for problem and nonproblem families.

These findings imply that for some noxious responses exhibited by boys, the process for producing and maintaining them may be comparable for problem and nonproblem families.

RESPONSE CLASSES

Presumably, responses under similar stimulus control may be, but are not necessarily under similar reinforcement control. For example, if the controlling stimulus were aversive, then its removal would constitute a negative reinforcement for all responses controlled by that stimulus. In this case, a single stimulus defines both the antecedent and the reinforcing events. In keeping with the earlier analysis of stimuli controlling Hit (Patterson and Cobb 1971), it was hypothesized that for the noxious responses most of the antecedents would be aversive stimuli.

TABLE 6.6. *Amount of overlap in determinants for* R_js *for boys from and nonproblem families*

Noxious Responses	*Number of Significant Variables in Common*	*Proportion of* p(R_j) *Accounted for by Compound Probabilities*	
		Problem families	*nonproblem families*
Command Negative	6	.472	.430
Disapproval	6	.270	.364
Noncomply	7	1.000	1.000
Negativism	4	.661	.718
Physical Negative	3	.422	.449
Tease	2	.332	.318
Whine	2	.232	.256

It was also assumed that some responses would prove to be under the control of equivalent sets of aversive stimuli and this constitute a class of behaviors. Those antecedent variables significant for each of two R_j's were summed. These values were then divided into their respective $p(R_j)$s to provide an overlap percentage for that pair. All pairs of R_j's were analyzed. Each comparison generated an overlap percentage for both members. Given that there was complete agreement for the stimuli controlling two R_j's, then the overlap percentages would be positive and 1.00 for both of them. If the S^F variables for one R_j were the S^I variables for the R_j's being compared, then the overlap percentage would be negative.

The magnitude of the overlap-percentage figure was determined both by the magnitude of $p(R_j)$ *and* the magnitude of the summed compound-probability values for each R_j. The magnitude of these summed compound-probability values would almost certainly be different from each member of a pair of R_j's; in addition, the base-rate probabilities for the two R_j's were likely to be different. For this reason, the magnitude of the overlap percentages could be radically different for two R_j's. The shared determinants might account for most of the information inherent in the base-rate data for one noxious response, while accounting for only a small proportion of the second. The overlap percentages for all pairs of R_j's are summarized in table 6.7.

Since very few of the determinants for Dependency, Destructiveness, and Yell had been identified by the present coding system, there was no appreciable overlap of these variables with any others. While possessing significant determinants, Noncomply, High Rate, and Command Negative showed limited overlap with any other variables.

Among the remaining variables, there were two general clusters. These clusters were defined by variables that showed overlap proportions equal to, or greater than 40 percent with all other members of the class.

The first cluster, labeled "Social Aggression," was defined by two variables, Tease and Physical Negative. Each was defined by a substantial network of significant S^F's and S^I's. The data in table 6.8 showed that 43 percent of p(PN) was accounted for by deter-

TABLE 6.7. *Overlap among determinants for R_j's for boys from problem families*

	Amount of $p(R_j)$ Accounted for by Compound Probabilities for Determinants Shared in Common with Y_j									
	CN	*DI*	*HR*	*HU*	*IG*	*NC*	*NE*	*PN*	*TE*	*WH*
CN	......	2.2	0.0	0.0	0.0	0.0	0.0	18.0	0.8	0.0
DI	18.8	......	40.8	68.4	88.8	100.0	66.8	16.8	−5.3	93.9
HR	−4.6	−49.7	......	−52.7	−56.9	−92.3	−56.1	20.7	24.7	−60.1
HU	0.0	46.1	−12.5	......	63.8	−0.2	59.6	−11.3	−19.7	61.6
IG	−4.6	87.6	−36.4	52.7	......	−92.8	66.8	−11.3	−12.0	93.9
NC	0.0	−49.8	−15.9	−52.7	−73.4	......	−53.2	22.6	23.0	−62.5
NE	0.0	75.5	−47.6	52.7	77.6	−0.2	......	−11.3	−19.7	84.9
PN	14.2	−50.7	12.4	−47.6	−72.2	−92.3	−32.5	......	46.7	−76.6
TE	4.6	−33.3	12.4	−47.6	−54.2	−92.3	−43.2	43.2	......	−60.8
WH	0.0	85.4	−40.8	52.7	84.6	−92.8	66.8	−15.1	−23.1	......

minants shared in common with Tease. Forty-six percent of p(TE) was accounted for by variables shared in common with PN.

Together, these events occurred at a rate of about two per 100 interactions; the p(PN) was .010 and p(TE), .011. Including data from chained interactions might produce a considerable increase in these values. Figure 6.3 summarizes the information for the significant S^F events controlling Social Aggressive responses for boys from problem families.

There was a set of five S^F's *shared* by the two responses. With the exception of Comply, they seem, a priori, to fit the label "aversive stimuli." In this context the antecedent event, Laugh, presumably has some aversive, teasing, implications. To a limited extent, then, Social Aggression and its shared network of aversive controlling stimuli fit the requirements for a definition of a

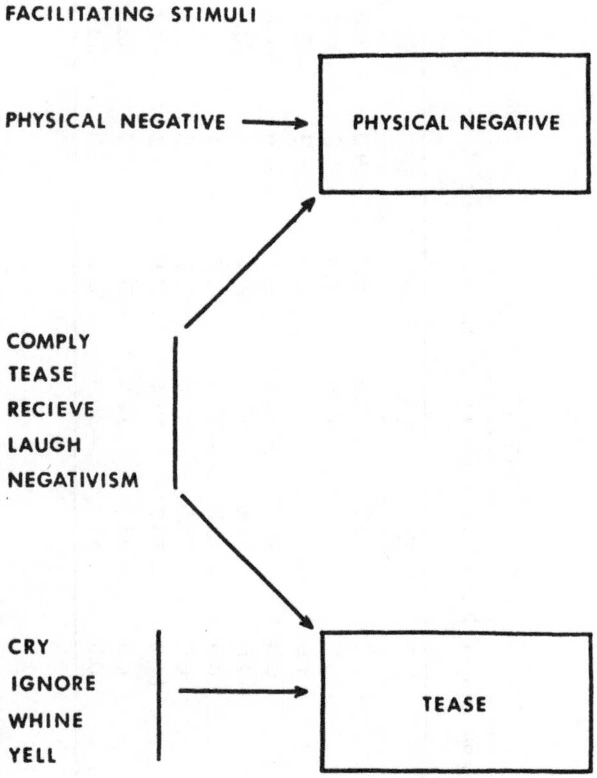

FIGURE 6.3. *Stimulus control for social aggression.*

class of coercive behaviors. Presumably, the primary contingencies maintaining its occurrence would be negative reinforcement, in that a Hit or a Tease response would likely terminate the presentation of the aversive stimuli that set the occasion for their initial occurrence. Needless to say, the eventual status of this class of responses hinges, in part, upon the outcome of attempts to establish the "aversiveness" of the stimuli controlling the behaviors. As these crucial tests have yet to be made, the status of this response class as coercive must remain in question.

Interestingly enough, the S^I's controlling the two responses were also highly similar. The antecedent events that significantly decreased the probability of occurrence of either a Hit or a Tease were Command, Dependency, Normative, and Talk.

A paper by Cobb and Patterson (in preparation) analyzed the status of various groups of family agents whose presence or absence significantly controlled the noxious response exhibited by three male family groups: the deviant child, the older brother, and the younger brother. Results indicated that the siblings provided the *only* significant S^F's for members of the Social Aggression class. For each group of boys, the parents either significantly inhibited the responses from occurring or had no effect upon their occurrence. In contrast, the siblings accounted for the major proportion of the occurrences of the responses by acting as significant facilitators within each of the three male groups. The finding that Social Aggression was a class of noxious responses under sibling control confirms the hypothesis presented in Patterson, Littman, and Bricker (1967).

The second cluster of noxious responses that exhibited shared determinants was labeled "Hostility." The responses that defined this class were Disapproval, Humiliate, Negativism, Ignore, and Whine. By and large, these were *verbal* behaviors. After examining these findings, the writers hypothesized that such responses are probably not as noxious as are those of the Social Aggression class; thus, their occurrence would be followed by reduced schedules of punishment from the victims. In this manner, the behaviors might be thought of as more subtle means of inflicting pain upon another person.

Presumably, people who displayed high rates of such behav-

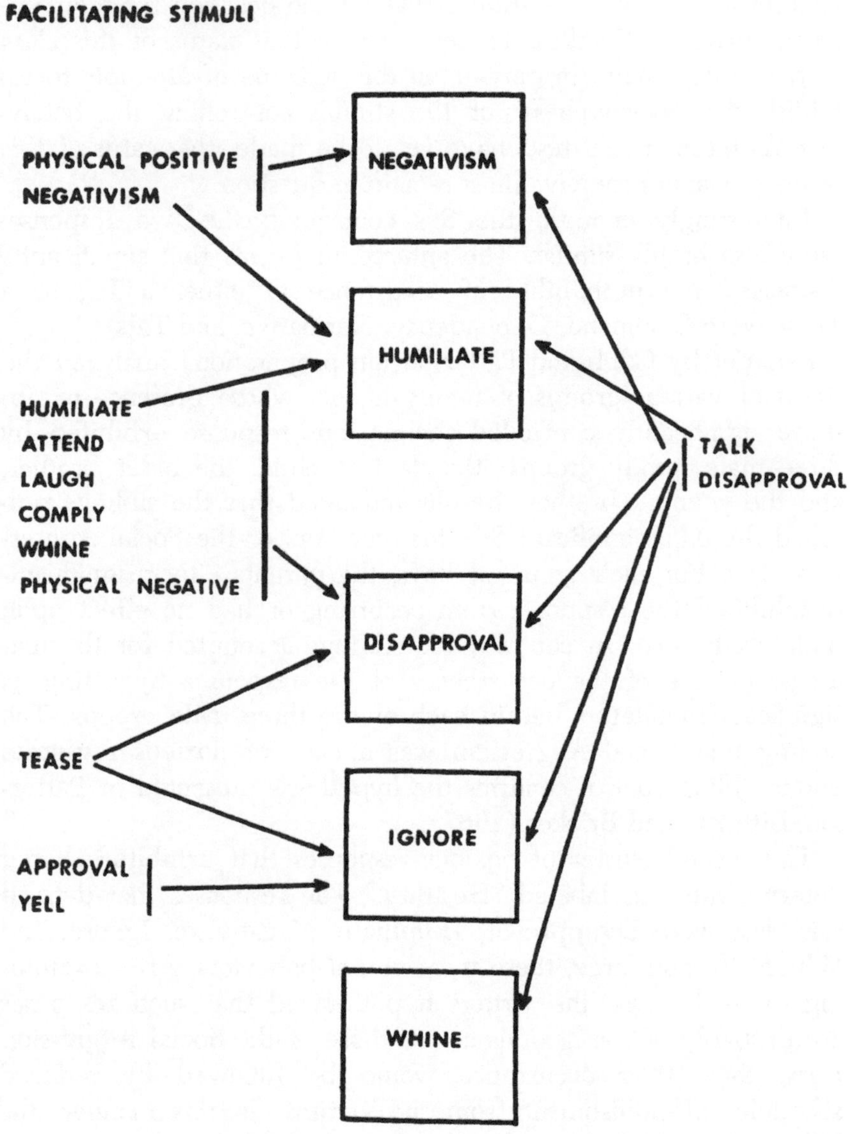

FIGURE 6.4. *Stimulus control for hostility.*

iors would be characterized as "unpleasant." A clinician observing such behavior might label such a person as "hostile." As used here, the term *Hostile* makes no necessary reference to underlying anger or frustration implied in the definition used by such writers as Berkowitz (1962). For the present, the term describes only a class of responses controlled by a specific network of stimuli.

The combined rate with which responses of this class occurred was very high; eleven per 100. The base rates (unchained) for the responses Disapproval, Humiliate, Negativism, Ignore, and Whine for boys from problem families were .061, .004, .026, .007, and .011, respectively. The S^F's controlling the occurrence of these responses are summarized in figure 6.4.

The ubiquitous antecedent for Hostile responses seemed to be Talk, which was identified as a significant S^F for *every* member of the class. With one exception, Disapproval also served as a general antecedent for all class members. Because both of these variables have relatively high base rates of occurrence, their compound-probability values for both R_j's were substantial. In fact, these two antecedents would account for most of the information available for each of the noxious responses. Taking this perspective, Hostile responses could be viewed as a class of verbal behaviors that themselves are under the control of verbal stimuli.

While some antecedents for some Hostile R_j's might be thought of as aversive (Negativism, Humiliate, Whine, Physical Negative, Tease, Yell, and Disapproval), the network of controlling stimuli was far too heterogeneous to merit any single label describing the S^F's. While comments from our observers suggested that some Talks are in fact quite aversive, they seemed "subtle," perhaps even idiosyncratic to each family. This would suggest some needed modifications in our current coding system, in order that these subtle aversive events could be coded. However, even if this were accomplished, it could still be the case that the class Hostile is not a case of coercive behaviors. The presence of Physical Positive, Attention, Comply, and Approval as S^F's for Hostile constitutes a disconfirmation for that hypothesis. In almost all instances, the R_j's were under the control of both aversive and nonaversive stimuli, which suggests the mixed control of Hostile responses.

The analysis of agents serving as S^F's for responses in this class was carried out separately for the deviant child and for younger and older brother (Cobb and Patterson, in preparation). One finding comes through very clearly: the females in the families served as significant agents for evoking each R_j in this class. For only one R_j were male family members identified as a facilitating stimulus. For the noxious responses Negativism and Whine, the mother was a significant S^F for *every* group of boys. She and the other females in the family constituted the stimuli controlling Hostile behaviors in boys.

Boys from nonproblem families. Comparable data on response class were also analyzed for the boys from nonproblem families. As noted earlier (table 5), only half the R_j's for this sample were defined by even modest frequencies of occurrence. The analyses were limited to those R_j's whose antecedents had previously been shown to be accounted for by variables in the present coding system. Unfortunately, there were only five R_j's that met this criterion. Some of these were based upon very low frequencies; thus the analyses should be thought of as *very* preliminary. The overlap percentages among Command Negative, Disapproval, Noncomply, Physical Negative, and Tease are summarized in table 6.8.

The data showed that there were no classes of noxious responses for the boys from nonproblem families. In that only a

TABLE 6.8. *Overlap among determinants for* R_js *for boys from nonproblem families*

	Proportion of $p(R_j)$ *Accounted for by Compound Probabilities Shared in Common with* Y_j				
	CN	*DI*	*NC*	*PN*	*TE*
CN	------	−.012	−.067	.363	−.198
DI	.285	------	−.947	.360	.278
NC	.000	.126	------	.089	−.041
PN	.140	.290	.000	------	−.080
TE	.000	.264	−.008	−.089	------

few of the responses were defined by a reasonable sampling of events, there is little that can be said about these findings. If it were true that classes of responses did not, in fact, exist for such samples, this would be of great interest.

In retrospect, it seems eminently unreasonable to test hypotheses about low-base-rate events by using samples of children who were selected because they presumably were "normal" and thus likely to display few noxious R_j's. For the present, it must be assumed that the hypotheses about coercive processes among normal boys have not been adequately explored by these analyses.

Discussion

This exploratory analysis of stimulus control was highly productive, in that it showed that the procedures could identify social stimuli that controlled some noxious social responses exhibited by boys. For boys from problem families, the sheer quantity of significant controlling stimuli attests to the power of the approach. The findings underscore the fact that some (not all) important determinants of behavior are to be found in the immediately impinging social stimuli observed in on-going social interaction. Concurrent measures of internal states and/or cognitions might account for additional components of variance in the R_j's. Given adequate means for measuring these internal events, they might also be shown to interact with the observable inputs from the immediate social environment. Certainly, a satisfactory "theory" of aggression must eventually be able to integrate such a composite set of variables. The present findings, however, constitute a promising initial stage in analyzing the external stimuli that control some noxious children's behaviors. It is not clear, of course, that such a simplistic approach would be equally efficacious in accounting for stimuli that control the noxious behaviors of adults.

The mode of data collection and analysis demonstrated its utility for the general problem of identifying stimuli that control children's behavior. The fact that classes of responses controlled by comparable stimuli were also identified suggests that this general approach would not necessarily lead to a description that is completely idiosyncratic to each response and to each child. This preliminary analysis encourages us to believe that other, and even more clearly defined, classes of noxious behaviors could be identified.

Data from the present coding system for boys from problem families suggest the presence of two interesting classes of responses, Social Aggression and Hostility. The S^F's controlling the occurrence of responses included in the class Social Aggression seemed, a priori, to be primarily aversive in character. It is assumed that a means can be found for determining the "aversiveness" of the stimuli controlling response events of this class. For the present, however, face validity for these stimuli would suggest that the class constitutes an operational definition for the behaviors described in the coercion process. Tentatively, it would also be assumed that these responses are primarily under the control of negative reinforcement. The occasion for these behaviors was set by siblings, not by parents. This finding was in keeping with the outcome of the previous analysis of preschool aggressive interactions in emphasizing the contribution of children as agents responsible for teaching children deviant behaviors (Patterson, Littman, and Bricker 1967).

Hostility category was comprised primarily of verbal behaviors that were, in turn, controlled by verbal stimuli. The data suggested that the antecedents for responses of this class were only partially aversive in nature. Therefore, this class cannot be considered as support for a ubiquitous coercive process.

In that the stimuli that controlled the two classes were quite different, it can be said that these are two different classes of noxious behaviors. In addition, the agents whose presence sets the occasion for the behaviors tended to be somewhat different. While siblings' presence set the occasion for Social Aggressive behaviors, it was the mothers and older females in the family who were primarily responsible for the hostile behaviors. It was curious in this regard to note that the father did not serve as an S^F agent for responses in either of these classes.

These preliminary explorations in applying the procedures were productive in that they brought into focus the enormous amounts of event sampling requisite for analyses of sequential dependencies. In retrospect, this characteristic should have been clear at the outset; the fact that it was not means that the current attempt to analyze stimulus-control processes for "normal" boys was simply premature.

To obtain a clear idea of stimulus control, with all possible confounds removed, requires enormous amounts of data. In the earlier analysis of stimulus control for Hit and Talk (Patterson and Cobb 1971), the analysis was carried out using Hits contributed by any, and all family members. To the extent that these R_j's for children of different sexes, or for parents, are under different stimulus control, then the attempt to build up a sufficient sample of events by combining data for R_j's across agents produced some possible confounds in the analysis of stimulus control.

Two comparable problems exist in the present analysis. While the data for R_j's were provided by only a single class of agents (boys) and thus avoided the previous "error," there remains yet another potential source of confounding. This lay in the fact that individual subjects may have contributed differentially to the R_j's. For a sample of ten or twenty events, it is conceivable that *all* of them were contributed by one or two subjects. Because small samples of events provide less stable estimates and are more likely to be confounded, they must therefore be interpreted with extreme caution.

The second problem concerns the fact that the data for the antecedents for R_j's were obtained by pooling information from all agents as they contributed to an R_j. To the extent that there exists an interaction between agents' presence and antecedent event in controlling R_j, then some confounding still exists in the present data. Obviously the "cure" for this problem is to obtain larger samples of R_j events, so that appropriate breakdown is feasible. As a preliminary test for this mode, a minimum of fifty hours of baseline data is currently being collected for high-rate "aggressive" boys.

While these analyses may have implications for personality theory, the implications for practical treatment strategies are very clear. Up to this point, the behavior-modification literature was focused upon reinforcement control in altering deviate behavior. As an alternative, a type of "precursor intervention" more oriented toward stimlus-control problems would begin by first analysizing the S^F's, S^F agents, and agent behaviors within families to determine the antecedents that trigger the problem behaviors.

Our own current family intervention has been profoundly affected by these findings. Given prior information about stimulus control, the planning strategies now include provisions for altering the behavior of the controlling agents (typically siblings), as well as that of the deviant boy. Analyses are now being planned to determine what increments in efficiency, if any, accrue from such practices. It is conceivable, for example, that an understanding of stimulus-control and response-class compositions for a given child would make it possible to identify the target responses that would produce the greatest spread of behavior change.

In passing, it might also be noted that the existence of classes constitutes something of a problem for investigators using multiple-response-baseline designs. The current strategy outlined here assumes that alterations in the stimulus and reinforcement contingencies controlling an R_j should generalize to all other R_j's that are members of that class. This would somewhat vitiate the power of multiple-response-baseline designs unless one chooses R_j's that were not class members.

Glossary

Coercion process: A process characterizing dyadic interchanges in which one or more persons applies aversive stimuli to control the behavior of the other. The painful stimulus is presented until the desired changes are produced in the behavior of the other person. At this point, the aversive stimulus is withdrawn.

Controlling stimulus: Observable, external stimuli which occur in time intervals immediately adjacent to the target response. Their occurrence is accompanied by alterations in the probability of the occurrence for the target response in the immediately following time interval.

Facilitating stimulus: The occurrence of this antecedent event is accompanied by increases in the probability of occurrence of the target response. Its status is determined by comparing the conditional probability of the target response given the antecedent to the corrected base rate probability of the targeted response.

Inhibitory stimulus: This is an antecedent event whose occurrence is associated with a reduced probability of occurrence of the target response. As the case for the identification of a facilitating stimulus, it is necessary to have four kinds of information in identifying such an event: (1) the frequency with which the antecedent precedes the target response; (2) the frequency with which the antecedent precedes all non-target responses; (3) the frequency with which the target response occurs; and (4) the frequency with which the antecedent precedes the target response.

Accelerator: An accelerator is a consequence for a target response whose presence signifies an increased probability that the target response will occur in the immediately following time interval. To be identified as an accelerator, the conditional probability of the target response's recurrence given that the previous response had been consequated by this particular event is compared to the base rate probability of the target response's recurrence given that it had occurred in the immediately preceeding time interval.

Decelerator: A decelerator is defined as a consequence event whose presence is associated with a decrease in the conditional probability of the target response. This status is determined by comparing the conditional probability value with the base rate probability value for the target response.

Response class: The class of responses is defined as a set of responses which is under comparable stimulus control. Conceivably, one could define classes on the basis of similarities among responses in terms of facilitating, accelerating, or reinforcing stimuli.

References

Atkinson, J. "Brief Deprivation of Mother-Attention as an Antecedent Event for Coercive Demands in the Preschool Child." Master's thesis, University of Oregon, 1971.

Azrin, N. H.; Hutchinson, R. R.; and Hake, D. F. "Pain-induced Fighting in the Squirrel Monkey." *Journal of Experimental Analysis of Behavior* 6 (1963): 620.

Azrin, N.; Ulrich, R.; Hutchinson, R.; and Norman, D. "Effect of Shock Duration on Shock-Induced Fighting." *Journal of the Experimental Analysis of Behavior* 7 (1964): 9–11.

Berkowitz, L. *Aggression: A Social Psychological Analysis.* New York: McGraw-Hill Book Co. 1962.

——. "Control of Aggression." In *Review of Child Development Research,* edited by B. Caldwell and H. Riccuti. Vol. 3. New York: Russell Sage Foundation, 1971.

Buss, A. H. *The Psychology of Aggression.* New York: John Wiley & Sons, 1961.

——. "The Effect of Harm on Subsequent Aggression." *Journal of Experimental Research in Personality* 1 (1966): 249–55. *(a)*

——. "Instrumentality of Aggression, Feedback, and Frustration as Determinants of Physical Aggression." *Journal of Personality and Social Psychology* 3 (1966): 153–62. *(b)*

Church, R. M. "The Varied Effects of Punishment on Behavior." *Psychological Review* 70 (1963): 369–402.

Devine, V. D. "The Coercion Process: A Laboratory Analog." Ph.D. dissertation, State University of New York at Stony Brook, 1971.

Ebner, M. "An Investigation of the Role of the Social Environment in the Generalization and Persistence of the Effect of a Behavior Modification Program." Ph.D. dissertation, University of Oregon, 1967.

Flory, R. K.; Ulrich, R. E.; and Wolff, P. C. "The Effects of Visual Impairment on Aggressive Behavior." *Psychological Record* 15 (1965); 185–90.

Graham, F. K.; Charivat, W. A.; Honig, A. S.; and Weltz, P. C. "Aggression as Function of the Attack and the Attacker." *Journal of Abnormal and Social Psychology* 46 (1951): 512–20.

Harris, A. "Observer Effect on Family Interaction." Ph.D. dissertation, University of Oregon, 1969.

Hartmann, D. P. "The Influence of Symbolically Modelled Instrumental Aggression and Pain Cues on the Disinhibition of Aggressive Behavior." Ph.D. dissertation, Stanford University, 1965.

Hokanson, J. E., and Eddman, R. "Effect of Three Social Responses on Vascular Processes." *Journal of Personality and Social Psychology* 3 (1966): 442–47.

Hokanson, J. E.; Willus, K. R.; and Korolsak, E. "The Modification of Autonomic Responses during Aggressive Interchanges." *Journal of Personality* 36 (1968): 386–404.

Hollingshead, A. B., and Redlich, F. C. *Social class and mental illness: A community study.* New York: John Wiley, 1958.

Hops, H. "Covariation of Social Stimuli and Interaction Rates in the Natural Preschool Environment." Ph.D. dissertation, University of Oregon, 1971.

Hutchinson, R. R.; Ulrich, R. E.; and Azrin, N. H. "Effects of Age and Related Factors on Reflexive Aggression." *Journal of Comparative and Physiological Psychology* 59 (1965): 365–69.

Kass, R. E., and O'Leary, K. D. "The Effects of Observer Bias in Field-experimental Settings. Paper presented at the Behavior Analysis in Education Symposium, University of Kansas, Lawrence, April 1970.

Kopfstein, D. "Effects of Accelerating and Decelerating Consequences on the Social Behaviors of Trainable Retarded Children." Manuscript. Atlanta: Department of Psychology, Emory University, 1971.

Lewis, O. *Five Families*. New York: Basic Books, 1965.

Littman, R.; Pierce-Jones, J.; and Stern, T. "Child-Parent Activities in the Natural Setting of the Home: Results of a Methodological Pilot Study." Mimeographed Manuscript. Eugene: Department of Psychology, University of Oregon, 1957.

LoLordo, V. M. "Positive Conditioned Reinforcement from Aversive Situations." *Psychological Bulletin* 72 (1969): 193–203.

Patterson, G. R. "Intervention in the Homes of Predelinquent Boys: Steps toward Stage Two." paper presented at the meeting of the American Psychological Association, Washington, D.C., September 1971.

Patterson, G. R., and Cobb, J. A. "A Dyadic Analysis of "Aggressive" Behaviors: An Additional Step Toward a Theory of Aggression." In *Minnesota Symposia on Child Psychology*, edited by J. P. Hill, pp. 72–129. Vol. 5. Minneapolis: University of Minnesota Press 1971.

Patterson, G. R.; Cobb, J. A.; and Ray, R. S. "Direct Intervention in the Classroom: A Set of Procedures for the Aggressive Child." In *Critical Issues in Research and Practice: Proceedings of the Fourth International Conference on Behavior Modification*, edited by F. Clark and L. Hamerlynck. Champaign, Ill.: Research Press, 1972.

——. "A Social Engineering Technology for Retraining the Families of Aggressive Boys." In *Georgia Symposium in Experimental Clinical Psychology*, edited by H. Adams and L. Unikel. Vol. 2. Springfield, Ill.: Charles C. Thomas, in press.

Patterson, G. R., and Harris, A. "Some Methodological Considerations for Observation Procedures." Paper presented at the meeting of the American Psychological Association, San Francisco, September 1968. Mimeographed.

Patterson, G. R.; Littman, R. A.; and Bricker, W. "Assertive Behavior in Children: A Step toward a Theory of Aggression." *Monographs of the Society for Research in Child Development,* vol. 32 (5, serial no. 113) (1967).

Patterson, G. R., and Reid, J. B. "Reciprocity and Coercion: Two Facets of Social Systems." In *Behavior Modification in Clinical Psychology,* edited by C. Neuringer and J. Michael, pp. 133–77. New York: Appleton-Century-Crofts, 1970.

Paul, J. S. "Observer Influence on the Interaction of a Mother and a Single Child in the Home." Master's thesis, Oregon State University, 1964.

Rapp, D. W. "Detection of Observer Bias in the Written Record." Cited in R. Rosenthal, *Experimenter Effects in Behavioral Research.* New York: Appleton-Century-Crofts, 1966.

Raush, H. L. "Interaction Sequences." *Journal of Personality and Social Psychology* 2 (1965): 487–99.

Reid, J. B. "Reciprocity and Family Interaction." Ph.D. dissertation, University of Oregon, 1967.

———. "Reliability Assessment of Observation Data: A Possible Methodological Problem." *Child Development* 41 (1970): 1143–50.

Rosenthal, R. *Experimenter Effects in Behavioral Research.* New York: Appleton-Century-Crofts, 1966.

Schalock, H. D. "Observer Influence on Mother-Child Interaction in the Home: A Preliminary Report." Paper presented at the meeting of the Western Psychological Association, Carmel, California, 1958. Mimeographed.

Scott, J. P. *Aggression.* Chicago: University of Chicago Press, 1958.

Scott, J. P., and Fredericson, E. "The Causes of Fighting in Mice and Rats." *Physiological Zöology* 24 (1951): 273–309.

Scott, P.; Burton, R.; and Radke-Yarrow, M. "Social Reinforcement under Natural Conditions." *Child Development* 38 (1967): 54–63.

Shah, S., and Weber, G. H. "The Problem of Individual Violence: A Review of Some Major Issues." Report to National Commission on Causes and Prevention of Violence. Washington, D. C.: Center for Studies of Crime and Delinquency, NIMH, 1968. Mimeographed.

Shaw, D. A. "Family Maintenance Schedules for Deviant Behavior." Ph.D. dissertation, University of Oregon, 1971.

Skindrud, K. "A Preliminary Evaluation of Observer Bias in Multivariate Studies of Social Interaction." Mimeographed Manuscript. Eugene: Oregon Research Institute, 1970.

Thomas, D. S.; Loomis, A. M.; and Arrington, R. *Observational Studies of Social Behavior.* Vol. 1, *Social Behavior Patterns.* New Haven, Conn.: Institute of Human Relations, Yale University, 1933.

Toch, H. *Violent Men*. Chicago: Aldine Publishing Co., 1969.
Ulrich, R., and Azrin, N. "Reflexive Fighting in Response to Aversive Stimulation." *Journal of the Experimental Analysis of Behavior* 5 (1962): 511–21.
Ulrich, R.; Wolff, P. C.; and Azrin, N. H. "Shock as an Elicitor of Intra- and Inter-Species Fighting Behavior." *Animal Behavior* 12, no. 1 (1964): 14–15.
Wahl, G. L. "Operant Analysis of Family Interaction." Ph.D. dissertation, University of Oregon, 1971.
Wilson, J. A. B. *A Clockwork Orange*. London: Heinemann, 1962.

Albert Bandura received his bachelor's degree from the University of British Columbia and his Ph.D. degree from the University of Iowa. After receiving his Ph.D. and completing a postdoctoral internship, Dr. Bandura joined the faculty at Stanford University where he is currently professor of psychology. He has been a fellow at the Center for Advanced Studies in the Behavioral Sciences, and a recipient of a special research fellowship of the National Institute of Mental Health and of a Guggenheim fellowship. He has served on the editorial board of nine professional journals including Journal of Personality and Social Psychology, Journal of Experimental Social Psychology, Journal of Experimental Child Psychology, Journal of Applied Behavioral Analysis, *and* Behavior Therapy. *In 1972 he received the Distinguished Scientist Award of Division 12, American Psychological Association, and in 1973 received the Distinguished Scientist Award of the California Psychological Association. He is now the president of the American Psychological Association. Interests in social learning theory, psychotherapy, and personality development are reflected in his extensive research history as well as in the publication of five books.*

7

Social Learning Theory of Aggression

ALBERT BANDURA

Until recent years psychological theories depicted behavior as impelled by inner forces in the form of drives and impulses. Different theories proposed diverse sets of motivators, some containing a few all-purpose motives, others embracing a varied assortment of specific drives. Since the principal causes of behavior resided in the individual, that is where one looked for the explanations of man's actions. It is therefore not surprising that aggression has traditionally been explained by recourse to drive forces.

According to the instinct theory, man is by nature aggressive. Presumably he comes equipped with an autonomous aggression-generating system that requires periodic discharge through some form of aggressive behavior. Freud (1933) hypothesized a death instinct that keeps regenerating itself. More recently, Lorenz (1966) postulated an aggressive urge that builds up in the absence of releaser stimuli, which presumably function as innate instigators of aggressive actions.

Freud won few adherents to his position. Apparently the notion that people harbored an inborn impulse constantly striving to kill them exceeded the bounds of credibility. On the other hand, Lorenz's view, and aspects of the instinct doctrine promul-

Preparation of this chapter was facilitated by research grant M-5162 from the National Institutes of Health, U.S. Public Health Service. Some of the material contained here is drawn from Bandura (1973).

gated by Ardrey (1966), gained widespread popular acceptance. Among researchers working in the field, however, Lorenz's publication was admired for its literary quality, but severely criticized for its weak scholarship. In an edited volume, Montagu (1968) marshaled considerable evidence to dispute most of Lorenz's nativistic interpretations.

Complex behavior does not emerge as a unitary pattern, but is formed through integration of many component activities of differing origins. For this reason, the innate-learned dichotomy has long been discarded as misleading. Lorenz's hydraulic motivational model is open to even more serious criticism than his speculations about the origins of behaviors. As Hinde (1956) and Lehrman (1953) show, there exists no neurophysiological evidence to indicate that functional activities generate their own motivating energy, which builds up in the absence of releasers.

It is interesting that people vigorously disclaim that instincts cause them to behave the way they do, but are quick to believe that man is instinctively aggressive. One possible explanation is that most people find it difficult to understand how socialized human beings could repeatedly commit atrocities, often at the risk of self-extermination, unless driven by an inherent viciousness. Also, by attributing aggression to inherited tendencies, people are absolved from the responsibility of changing social conditions that benefit their self-interests while fostering aggression in others.

Since, in the instinct view, aggression is internally generated, no amount of improvement of the conditions of life can alter the level of aggression. Aggression is inevitable. In an exchange of letters with Einstein on how mankind may be spared future wars, Freud (1950) reiterated his belief that destruction satisfies an instinctual inclination and that it is, therefore, fruitless to attempt to eliminate aggressiveness. The most that society can do is to provide safe outlets for it. Occupying privileged positions in society, theorists usually prescribe gladiatorial combat for mass viewing and other recretional activities supposedly conducive to the release of pent-up aggressive impulses. To the less advantaged who rely on aggression to improve their life circumstances, the recreational prescriptions would constitute ineffectual remedies for misdiagnosed causes.

For years, the standard explanation of aggression was in terms of frustration. According to this theory (Dollard et al. 1939; Feshbach 1964, 1970), frustration produces an aggressive drive, which, in turn, motivates aggressive behavior. Aggression is considered a naturally dominant response to frustration, but nonaggressive reactions can occur if aggression has been inhibited through punishment. Reactive drives replaced autonomous instincts as the source of aggression, but the two theories are much alike in their implications for the regulation of aggressive behavior. Since frustration, in one form or another, is ever present, in both approaches man is burdened with a continuous source of aggressive energy that requires periodic release. Both theories assume that aggression is reduced by behaving aggressively.

The widespread acceptance of the frustration-aggression notion is perhaps attributable more to its simplicity than to its demonstrated predictive power. In point of fact, the formula that frustration breeds aggression does not hold up well under empirical scrutiny (Bandura 1973). Frustration subsumes such a diverse set of conditions that it no longer has a specific meaning. In experimental studies, for example, people are frustrated by being personally insulted, subjected to physically painful treatment, deprived of valued rewards, blocked from reaching desired goals, or by failure experiences. There exists a large body of evidence that punishment, extinction, delay of reward, and response obstruction do not have uniform behavioral effects (Bandura 1969). Even the same treatment at different intensities and under different learning histories can elicit markedly different responses.

Not only is there great heterogeneity on the antecedent side of the relationship, but the consequent part of the formula—the aggressive behavior—also subsumes a vast array of activities colored by value judgments. Whether a given activity is considered aggressive depends on a variety of factors, many of which reside in the definer rather than in the performer. Aggression is typically defined as behavior that has injurious consequences, accompanied by ten to twenty qualifiers. The same destructive behavior can be labeled aggressive or otherwise depending on subjective judgments of whether it was intentional or accidental. If the dispenser of aggression is a sanctioned authority, his injurious behavior is minimized as vigorous pursuit of duty; but if a free-lancing individual does it, he is judged to be acting violently. The same act is regarded differently, depending upon, among other factors, the sex, age, and socioeconomic level of the performer. Value orientations of the judges affect the way in which particular patterns are interpreted. The rhetoric of recent years demonstrates how one man's violence is another man's social righteousness. People ordinarily do not aggress in blatant, direct ways that carry high risk of punishment. The injurious consequences of their behavior are often remote, circuitous, and impersonal. An individual who votes for social practices that have injurious physical and psychological effects on others is, in his view, engaging in democratic action, but, to the victims who must endure the harmful consequences, he is behaving aggressively.

Considering the mixed items that get included under frustration and aggression, it is questionable whether any general statements about the relationship between these nebulous events have much meaning or validity.

AGGRESSIVE DRIVE OR GENERAL EMOTIONAL AROUSAL

The diverse events subsumed under the omnibus term *frustration* do have one feature in common: they are all aversive in varying degrees. In social learning theory (Bandura 1973) it is not that frustration creates aggression, but that aversive experiences produce emotional arousal that can elicit a variety of behaviors, depending on the types of reactions people have learned for coping with stressful conditions. When distressed, some people seek help and support; others display achievement behavior; others show withdrawal and resignation; some aggress; others exhibit heightened somatic activity; others anesthetize themselves with drugs or alcohol; and most intensify constructive efforts to overcome their problems.

As will be shown later, aversive stimulation is only one of many instigators of aggressive behavior. When other persons aggressed and social scientists theorized about it, aggression tended to be viewed as an impulsive, emotional, pathological manifestation. More recently, as social scientists and their associates themselves have begun to participate in coercive protest and to take action against deleterious social policies, a more balanced view of aggression and its determinants has emerged. What appears irrational and pathological to onlookers, and to the targets of aggression, often serves the aggressor as a method for getting what he wants when other options have failed or remain unavailable. Human aggression is activated by anticipated positive consequences as well as by aversive experiences. The major differences among the instinctual, reactive drive, and social learning theories in the ways they conceptualize the motivational component of aggression are depicted schematically in figure 7.1.

There are several lines of evidence that lend support to the social learning formulation. Psychophysiological studies have been conducted in which people undergo fear- and anger-provoking experiences while changes in their physiological reactions are simultaneously recorded. Results show that fear and anger have similar physiological correlates (Ax 1953; Schachter 1957). By looking at the physiological records alone, one could not distinguish whether the individuals had been frightened or angered. The varied array of emotions experienced phenomenologically

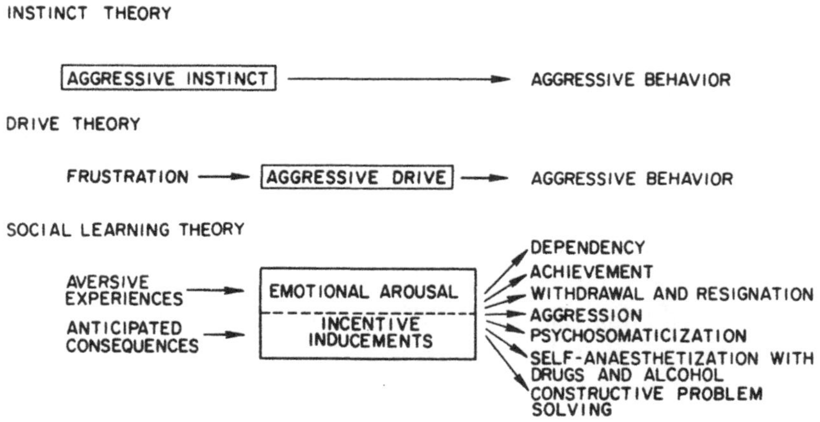

FIGURE 7.1. *Schematization of alternative motivational analysis of aggression.*

apparently stem from a common diffuse state of emotional arousal, rather than from distinct drive states. Whether people experience their emotional arousal as fear, anger, euphoria, or some other state depends not on internal somatic cues, but on a number of external defining influences.

People judge their emotions partly from the nature of the instigating conditions. Visceral arousal generated by threat is experienced as fear; arousal produced by thwarting is experienced as anger; and that resulting from irretrievable loss of valued objects, as sorrow (Hunt, Cole, and Reis 1958). Even the same source of physiological arousal may be experienced as different emotions, depending on the emotional reactions of models. Affective modeling cues can give definition to emotional states of uncertain origin or provide direction in ambiguous situations where people know the source of their arousal but are unsure about how they are supposed to react to it. Schachter and Singer (1962) provide suggestive evidence that people under drug-induced arousal who do not know to what to attribute the excitation experience the arousal as aggression when others respond hostilely, but they experience the same state as euphoria when they see others behaving in a jocular way. To some extent, emotional states produced by environmental stimuli are likewise susceptible to relabeling (Nisbett and Schachter 1966; Ross, Rodin, and Zimbardo 1969).

DIFFERENTIAL PREDICTIONS OF DRIVE AND SOCIAL LEARNING THEORIES

A number of predictions follow from the social learning formulation which differ from the traditional frustration-aggression hypothesis. Under conditions where individuals are prone to behave aggressively, any source of emotional arousal can enhance aggressive behavior. Results of several experiments have bearing on this prediction. Zillman (1969) produced anger arousal, sex arousal, or no arousal in adults, and then provided them with an opportunity to behave punitively by shocking another person. Compared with the behavior of nonaroused subjects, both anger and sex arousal enhanced punitiveness. Indeed, aggressiveness was determined more by level of arousal than by its source.

Geen and O'Neal (1969) similarly found that aversive, though nonirritating, noise increased subjects' punitiveness, especially if they had had prior exposure to aggressive models.

It might be argued that high sex arousal and noise have some frustrating properties. An experiment performed by Christy, Gelfand, and Hartmann (1971) provides a more definitive test of predictions from the frustration-aggression and the arousal-prepotent-response formulations. After observing aggressive or nonaggressive models, groups of children engaged in competitive activities in which one member consistently won and the other was a consistent loser. Other pairs played noncompetitively. Following these experiences, the children's imitative aggressiveness was measured. Competitors showed more imitative aggression than noncompetitors; however, victors increased their aggression just as much as those who experienced failure-induced frustration. These findings are especially interesting since Lorenz (1966) prescribes competitive activities as a means of reducing aggressive behavior.

The social learning formulation further predicts that arousal decreased through nonaggressive means will reduce aggression as much as, or even more than, will acting aggressively. In drive theories, the aroused aggressive drive presumably endures until discharged by some form of aggressive activity. From the social learning perspective, anger arousal dissipates, but it can be repeatedly regenerated on later occasions through ruminating on the anger-provoking incidents. Thus, by thinking about past insulting treatments, a person can work himself into a rage long after the original emotional reactions have subsided. The persistence of elevated anger arousal is attributed to self-generated arousal rather than to the existence of an undischarged reservoir of aggressive energy. To illustrate the different views, let us consider the example of a person who becomes angered by an apparent social slight, but discovers that the invitation to the social function has arrived in the next mailing. He is likely to show an immediate drop in anger arousal and aggressiveness without having to assault or denounce someone in order to reduce a lingering aggressive drive.

A number of investigators have compared the relative effectiveness of different treatment experiences in reducing aggressive behavior. Mallick and McCandless (1966) found that explanation of why a provocateur behaved obnoxiously reduced children's aggression toward him, whereas the children's free expression of physical aggression did not decrease their punitive behavior. This finding is in agreement with Kaufmann and Feshbach (1963), who reduced students' inclination to behave aggressively by cognitively restructuring the provocative situation.

The literature contains more evidence on the effects that expressions of aggression, either in fantasy or in action, have on subsequent aggressive behavior. Controlled studies with children (Feshbach 1956; Freeman 1962; Kenny 1952; Nelson 1969) indicate that, far from producing cathartic reductions, participation in aggressive activities within a permissive setting maintains the behavior at its original level and may actually increase it. In a study of adults, Kahn (1966) found that angered students who ventilated their resentment to a sympathetic listener increased their dislike for the antagonist significantly more than controls who merely sat for an equivalent time, and that during the recovery period the catharted subjects were generally more aroused physiologically.

The research cited above suggests that ventilative therapies, aimed at draining aggressive drives, may be inadvertently reinforcing aggressive tendencies. By contrast, social learning treatments, which have proved highly successful (Bandura 1969), help people from the outset to acquire better ways of dealing with social problems so that they have less to get angry about. Aggressive behavior of long standing is reliably reduced by a variety of procedures, including modeling alternative modes of response (Chittenden 1942); selective reinforcement in which aggressive actions are nonrewarded while constructive coping methods are actively supported (Hawkins et al. 1966; Patterson, Cobb, and Ray 1971; Sloane, Johnston, and Bijou 1967; Zeilberger, Sampen and Sloane 1968), elimination of fantasied instigators of violent outbursts (Agras 1967), and development of competencies that provide new sources of reward (Staats and Butterfield 1965).

Under certain conditions expression of aggression can decrease its incidence, although the reductive effects do not occur through drainage of aggressive-drive forces. Angry displays, especially if accompanied by threats, may so intimidate antagonists that they cease behaving in provocative ways. Interpersonal interactions are somewhat ambiguous as to exactly who does what to whom and why, with the result that events can be easily misjudged or distorted. When malign intent is misattributed to the actions of others, anger arousal can be ruminatively generated to the point where the aggrieved person acts with inappropriate hostility, as if he were designedly maltreated. To the extent that verbalized resentment clarifies matters, it can diminish autistically produced aggression. Moreover, behaving aggressively can arouse fear and self-censure over the injurious consequences of one's actions, and thus have reductive effects through inhibitory processes. Finally, aggressive protest often achieves desired changes in social prartices, thereby removing chronic instigators of the behavior. The belief that human behavior is impelled by inner aggressive forces is nonetheless so strongly ingrained in psychological thinking that aggression decrements, when they do occur, are automatically attributed to cathartic drive discharges without the consideration of more plausible processes.

Frustration-aggression theory predicts that vicarious participation in aggression, as in watching televised violence, similarly drains the aggressive drive, thereby reducing the likelihood of aggressive behavior. This issue was debated by the illustrious Greek savants long before the advent of commercial television. Aristotle contended that emotional displays purged emotions, whereas Plato maintained that they aroused them. As in most of their disputes over the nature of man, Plato turned out to be the better psychologist. Numerous studies show, almost without exception, that exposure to aggressive modeling tends to increase, rather than to reduce, aggressive tendencies in observers (Bandura 1973; Goranson 1970; Siegel 1970).

Although there is little evidence to support cathartic reduction of aggression, it is not uncommon for people subjectively to experience relief as a result of viewing violence. From the self-arousal view, people feel better after watching televised programs not because their aggressive drives have been drained, but because engrossment in absorbing activities provides relief from self-generated distress. They could experience equally salutary effects by getting involved in an absorbing book, an interesting talk, or other activities lacking violent content which effectively turn off upsetting trains of thought.

There is a third implication of social learning theory that differs from traditional views. Frustration or anger arousal is a facilitative but not a necessary condition for aggression. Frustration is most likely to provoke aggression in people who have learned to respond to aversive experiences with aggressive attitudes and actions. In an early study bearing on this issue, Davitz (1952) demonstrated that, following arbitrarily insulting treatment, aggressively trained children behaved more aggressively, whereas cooperatively trained children behaved more cooperatively.

The influential role of social learning experiences in determining aggressive responses is strikingly revealed in research by Delgado (1967). It has been repeatedly shown that electrical stimulation of the hypothalamus evokes attack-like behavior in animals. Delgado added a social dimension to the research which threw new light on thalamic control of aggression. He recorded the social behavior of a small colony of monkeys at normal times and at periodic intervals when a member of the colony was electrically stimulated through radio-transmission procedures.

Thalamic stimulation of a monkey was assumed a dominant role in the colony instigated him to attack subordinate male members, but the stimulated boss monkey did not assault the females. By contrast, thalamic stimulation elicited cowering and submissive behavior in a monkey of low social rank. Even more impressive is evidence that electrical stimulation of the same cerebral mechanism can evoke markedly different behavior in the same animal as his social rank is modified by changing the membership of the colony. Thus, thalamic stimulation elicited submissiveness in the animal when he occupied a low hierarchical position, but elicited marked aggressiveness when he was the dominant member in the group.

People do not have to be angered or emotionally aroused to behave aggressively. As will be shown later, a culture can pro-

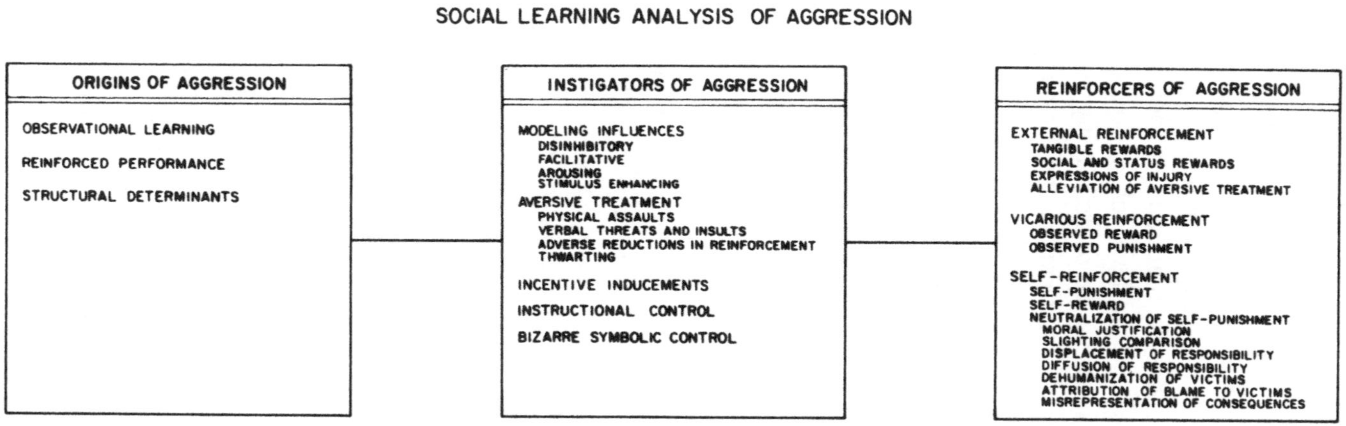

FIGURE 7.2. *Schematic outline of the origins, instigatiors, and reinforcers of aggression in social learning theory.*

duce highly aggressive people, while keeping frustration at a low level, by valuing aggressive accomplishments, furnishing successful aggresive models, and ensuring that aggressive actions secure adequate rewarding consequences. Since it does not hold aggression to be an inevitable or unchangeable aspect of man, but a product of aggression-promoting conditions operating within a society, social learning theory maintains a more optimistic view of man's power to reduce his level of aggressiveness. Whether this capability is used wisely or destructively is another matter.

A complete theory of aggression, whatever its orientation, must explain how aggressive patterns of behavior are developed, what provokes people to behave aggressively, and what maintains their aggressive actions. The determinants of these three separable aspects of aggression are summarized in figure 7.2. The remainder of this article is addressed to these three major issues.

Acquisition of Aggressive Modes of Behavior

People are not born with preformed repertoires of aggressive behavior. They must learn them in one way or another. Some of the elementary forms of aggression can be perfected with minimal guidance, but most aggressive activities—whether they be dueling with switch-blade knives, sparring with opponents, military combat, or vengeful ridicule—entail intricate skills that require extensive learning. In the social learning system, aggressive modes of response are acquired either through observation of aggressive models or on the basis of direct experience.

New modes of behavior are not fashioned solely through experience, either of a direct or observational sort. Biological structure obviously sets limits on the types of aggressive responses that can be perfected, and genetic endowment influences the rate at which learning progresses. Biological determination of aggression varies across species, however. Animals must rely for combat successes on their biological equipment, which is partly determined by genetic and hormonal factors. In contrast, man's capacity to use destructive weapons and the organized power of numbers has greatly reduced his dependence upon physical characteristics for aggressive attainments.

OBSERVATIONAL LEARNING

Most of the behaviors that people display are learned observationally, either deliberately or inadvertently, through the influence of example. By observing the actions of others, one acquires an idea of how the behavior can be performed, and on later occasions the representation serves as a guide for action. Numerous laboratory studies have demonstrated that children readily acquire novel modes of aggression on the basis of examples set by aggressive models (Bandura 1965a; Bandura, Ross, and Ross 1963*a;* Hicks 1965; Nelson, Gelfand and Hartmann 1969).

Exposure to aggressive models does not automatically ensure observational learning for a variety of reasons. First, some people do not profit much from example, because they fail to observe the essential features of the model's behavior. Second, persons cannot be much influenced by observation of a model's behavior if they have no memory of it. After aggressive responses are acquired through modeling, whether they are retained or lost with the passage of time depends on the extent to which memory aids are employed. Past modeling influences can achieve some degree of permanence if they are represented in memory in symbolic form (Bandura and Jeffery in press; Gerst 1971). In a study including observational learning of aggression (Bandura, Grusec, and Menlove 1966), children reproduced a high proportion (62 percent) of modeled aggressive responses that they had translated into words, whereas responses never coded verbally were much less likely to be retrieved (26 percent). Covert rehearsal is another means of retaining what has been learned observationally. Evidence for the stabilizing effects of symbolic rehearsal appears frequently in naturalistic reports. Some assassins in mass slayings originally get the idea from descriptive accounts of a mass killing. The incident remains salient in their thinking long after it has been forgotten by others, and it is repeatedly revivified and elaborated in thought until, under appropriate instigating conditions, it serves as the basis for an analogous murderous action (*New York Times* 1966).

Even if symbolic representations of modeled activities are developed and retained, behavioral enactment may be impeded because the individual lacks the physical capabilities necessary for its accomplishment. Social learning theory distinguishes between acquisition of behaviors that have destructive and injurious potential and factors that determine whether a person will perform what he has learned. This distinction is important because not all the things learned are expressed in action. A person can acquire, retain, and possess the capability to skillfully execute modeled aggressive behavior, but the learning may rarely be expressed if the behavior has no functional value for him, or if it is negatively sanctioned. In such circumstances, the introduction of positive incentives promptly translates observational learning into action (Bandura 1965*b;* Madsen 1968).

People can learn through observation not only the specific responses exhibited by aggressive models, but also the general strategy guiding the models' behavior in different situations. Responses embodying the observationally derived principle are likely to resemble the model's style of behavior even if the observer has never seen the model responding in the new situations. In a modern society there are three major sources of aggressive behavior, which are drawn upon to varying degrees. These different modeling influences are discussed in the following sections.

Familial influences. One prominent source is the aggression modeled and reinforced by family members. Investigators who have studied the familial determinants of antisocial aggression report a much higher incidence of familial aggressive modeling for delinquent than for nondelinquent boys (Glueck and Glueck 1950; McCord, McCord, and Zola 1959). Most assaultive youngsters, however, do not have criminally violent parents.

In middle-class families that produce violence-prone offspring, parental aggressive modeling usually takes less blatant forms. Parents of such children favor aggressive solutions to problems, although their actions rarely extend to unlawful performances (Bandura 1960; Bandura and Walters 1959). There is evidence also that otherwise-conforming parents often foster aggressive modes of response by modeling aggressive orientations in word and attitude, rather than in deed (Johnson and Szurek 1952).

Subcultural influences. Although familial influences play a major role in setting the direction of social development, the family is embedded in a network of other social systems. The subsculture in which a person resides and with which he has repeated contact may provide a second important source of aggression. Not surprisingly, the highest rates of aggressive behavior are found in environments where aggressive models abound and where aggressiveness is regarded as a highly valued attribute (Short 1968; Wolfgang and Ferracuti 1967). In these aggressive subcultures one gains status primarily through fighting prowess. Consequently, good aggressors are the prestigious models upon whom members pattern their behavior.

Symbolic modeling. Much social learning occurs through casual or directed observation of real-life models. However, styles of behavior can be conveyed through pictures and words as well as through action. Comparative studies, in fact, show that response patterns portrayed either pictorially or verbally can be learned observationally about as well as those presented through social demonstration (Bandura and Mischel 1965; Bandura, Ross, and Ross 1963*a*).

The third source of aggressive behavior is the symbolic modeling provided by the mass media—especially television, because of its ubiquity and its vivid portrayal of events. The advent of television has greatly expanded the range of models available to the growing child. Whereas his predecessors, especially those in middle-class homes, had limited opportunity to observe brutal aggression, the modern child has witnessed innumerable stabbings, beatings, stompings, stranglings, muggings, and less blatant but equally destructive forms of cruelty before he has reached kindergarten age. Thus, both children and adults, regardless of their backgrounds, have unlimited opportunities to learn from televised modeling aggressive coping styles and the whole gamut of felonious behavior within the comfort of their homes.

The powerful influence of symbolic modeling is most noticeable in the shaping and spread of collective aggression. Social contagion of new styles and tactics of aggression conforms to a pattern that characterizes the transitory changes of most other types of collective activities: New behavior is initiated by a salient example; it spreads rapidly in a contagious fashion; after it has been widely adopted, it is discarded, often in favor of a new form that follows a similar course.

Modeled solutions to problems which achieve some measure of success are not only widely adopted by people facing similar difficulties, but they tend to spread to other troublesome areas as well. The civil rights movement, which itself was modeled after Gandhi's crusades of nonviolent resistance, in turn provided the sample for other protest campaigns aimed at eliminating injustices and undesired social practices. The model of collective protest as a means of forcing social reforms spread to the antiwar movement and to disadvantaged groups, including Chicanos, homosexuals, and women.

The recent years provide numerous additional illustrations of the rapid contagion of the style of collective aggression. The campus protest movement at Berkeley served as the model for the sit-in method of protest in universities throughout the country. The peaceful sit-in was supplanted by progressively more violent forms, graduating to combative disruptions of university functions, and eventually to destruction of buildings. Following a New York rally, where hard-hatted construction workers beat up antiwar demonstrators, assaults on students by hard-hatters spread nationwide.

Airline hijacking provides another striking example of the rapid rise and decline of modeled aggression. Air piracy was unheard of in the United States until a commercial airliner was hijacked to Havana in 1961. Prior to this incident there was a rash of hijacking of Cuban airliners to Miami. These incidents were followed by a wave of hijackings, both in the United States and abroad, reaching its height in 1969, when a total of eighty-seven airplanes was pirated. Thereafter, hijackings declined in the United States, but continued to spread to other countries, so that international air piracy became relatively common (fig. 7.3). News of an inventive hijacker who successfully parachuted from an airliner with a bundle of extorted money temporarily revived a declining phenomenon in the United States, as others became inspired by his successful example.

In Brazil a new form of political collective bargaining was devised when a U.S. ambassador was abducted and later freed in exchange for political prisoners. This practice quickly spread across Latin America as other consular and ambassadorial envoys were kidnapped in Argentina, Brazil, Guatemala, Uruguay,

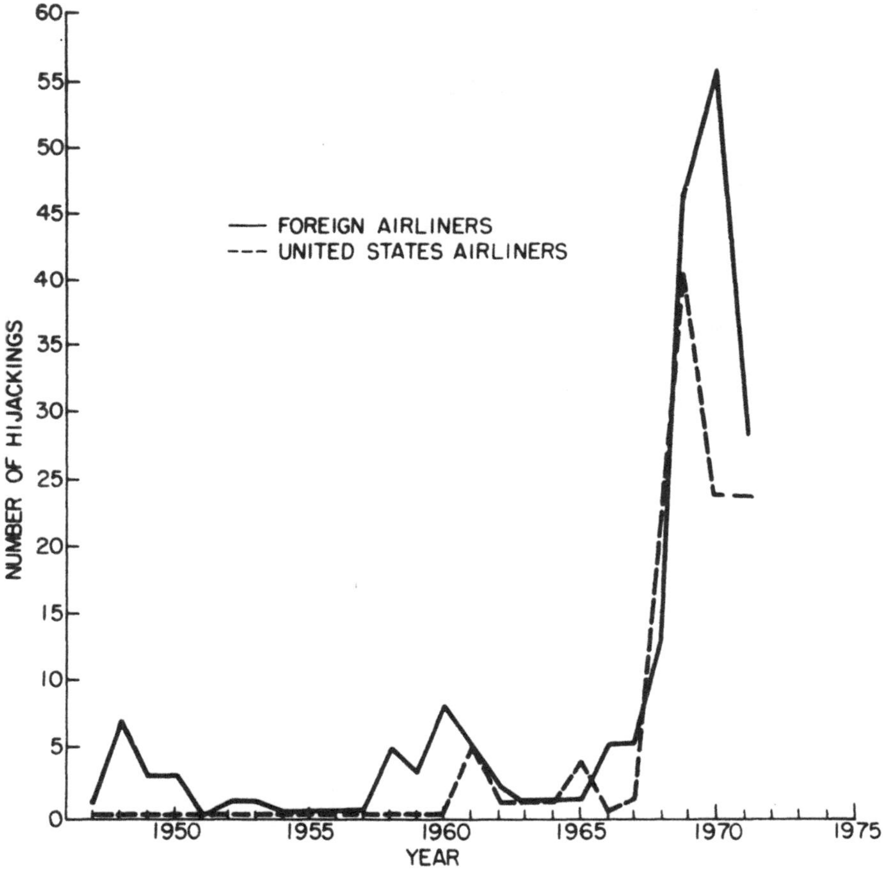

FIGURE 7.3. *Incidence of hijackings over a span of twenty-five years. The rise in foreign hijackings during the 1949–50 period occurred in Slavic countries at the time of the Hungarian uprising, and the second flare-up in 1958–61 comprised almost entirely Cuban hijackings to Miami. A sudden widespread diffusion of hijackings occurred in 1969–70, involving airliners from a total of forty-two different countries.*

and the Dominican Republic and held hostage for the release of political prisoners. Canada, Spain, and Turkey, containing dissident political factions, soon joined the ranks of South American countries in consular abductions.

There are several possible explanations for the abrupt decline of contagious aggression. First, the targets of aggression develop effective countermeasures. As hijacking escalated, airlines added screening procedures and concealed armed guards as deterrents. College administrators similarly improved their methods of countercontrol through court injunctions and new judicial procedures on the basis of repeated experience in dealing with coercive group action. Just as aggressive tactics are widely modeled, so are the methods of countercontrol. Second, the discrepancy between anticipated and experienced consequences plays an important role in determining the future courses of aggression. Direct observation and media reports of mass aggression are largely confined to the dramatic episodes, not to the intervening long hours of boredom and fatigue. What is seen of the group's functioning generally conveys the sense of camaraderie and principled dedication rather than the stress of pressures for conformity, the feeling of isolation that accompanies estrangement from the larger community, and the discouragement arising from failure to achieve fundamental changes. Participants who are drawn into protest activities mainly by their apparent excitement may drop out after experiencing first-hand the full consequences of the endeavor. Third, a new style of behavior rapidly loses its positive value through overuse. When the same rhetoric and tactics are used repeatedly, protest activities take on the quality of staged productions rather than genuine expressions of principle. Stereotyped exhortations are generally viewed as manipulative and increasingly resisted.

LEARNING BY DIRECT EXPERIENCE

Patterns of behavior can also be shaped through a more rudimentary form of learning which relies on the rewarding and punishing consequences of trial-and-error performance. There have been few experimental attempts to fashion novel forms of aggression by differential reinforcement alone. It would be foolhardy to instruct novices in how to handle firearms or hand grenades by selectively reinforcing their trial-and-error efforts. Where the consequences of errors can be dangerous or fatal, demonstration rather than unguided experience is the best teacher.

Learning through combat experience has been explored to a limited extent in experiments with lower species designed to train docile animals into ferocious fighters (Ginsburg and Allee 1942; Scott and Marston 1953). This outcome is achieved by arranging a series of bouts with progressively more experienced fighters under conditions where the trainee can win fights without being hurt. As fighting skills are developed and reinforced through repeated victories, formerly noncombative animals become more and more vicious in their aggressive behavior. While successful fighting produces brutal aggressors, severe defeats create enduring submissiveness (Kahn 1951).

Patterson, Littman, and Bricker (1967) report a field study illustrating how passive children can be shaped into aggressors through a process of victimization and successful counteraggression. Passive children who were repeatedly victimized and whose counteraggression often proved effective in halting attacks, not only increased defensive fighting, but eventually began to initiate attacks of their own. On the other hand, passive children who were seldom maltreated because they avoided others, and those whose counteraggressive responses were unsuccessful, remained submissive in their behavior.

Modeling and reinforcement influences operate jointly in the social learning of aggression in everyday life. Styles of aggression are largely learned through observation and refined through reinforced practice. The powerful effects that these two determinants have on the form and incidence of aggression are most strikingly revealed in ethnographic reports of societies that pursue a warlike way of life and those that display a pacific style of behavior. In cultures where interpersonal aggression is discouraged and devalued, people live peaceably (Alland, 1972; Levy 1969). In other societies that provide extensive training in aggression and make it an index of manliness or personal worth, people spend a great deal of time threatening, fighting, maiming, and killing each other (Gardner and Heider, 1969).

Instigators of Aggression

People rarely aggress in blind indiscriminate ways. Rather, aggressive actions tend to occur at certain times, in certain settings, toward certain objects or individuals, and in response to certain forms of provocation. Most of the events that evoke aggressive behavior in humans gain this capacity through learning experiences rather than from genetic endowment. Some formerly neutral stimuli acquire aggression-arousing potential through contiguous association with combative encounters. After a number of such paired experiences, the stimulus alone tends to elicit aggressive responsiveness (Creer, Hitzing, and Schaeffer 1966; Farris, Gideon, and Ulrich 1970).

The learning histories of different individuals often vary substantially; hence, the incidents that set off aggressive actions in one person may have relatively little effect on another. One of a number of chronic assaulters studied by Toch (1969) illustrate this conditioning process. As a youngster, he suffered a humiliating beating at the hands of an imposing opponent, a painful incident that determined this selection of future victims. Thereafter, he would become violent at any slight provocation by a large-sized person. People learn to dislike and to attack certain types of individuals on the basis of symbolic and vicarious experiences as well as through direct encounters with them. In the symbolic form, words and pictures that conjure up hatreds are used to endow persons and places with aggression-arousing value. In vicarious conditioning, events take on evocative properties through association with emotions aroused in observers by affective experiences of others (Bandura 1965*a*).

A second way in which aggressive actions are brought under stimulus control is through association with differential response consequences. When the same behavior is treated differently depending on the times, places, or persons toward whom it is directed, these informative cues signify the probable consequences accompanying certain actions, and people regulate their behavior accordingly. They tend to aggress toward persons and in contexts where it is relatively safe and rewarding to do so, but they are disinclined to display such behavior when it carries a high risk of punishing consequences. The following sections review the different forms that aggression elicitors ordinarily take.

MODELING INFLUENCES

Most human behavior is under modeling-stimulus control. People applaud when others clap, they laugh when others laugh, they exit from social functions and meetings when they see others leaving, and on countless other occasions their behavior is prompted and channeled by modeling stimuli. One effective way to get people to aggress is to have others do it.

The aggression-eliciting function of modeling influences is typically studied by providing individuals with socially sanctioned opportunities to engage in physically injurious actions, but in which, unknown to the aggressor, the victim experiences no pain (Buss 1961). Results of numerous studies generally show that both children (Hoelle 1969; Walters and Llewellyn Thomas 1963) and adults (de Charms and Wilkins 1963; Epstein 1966; Hartmann 1969) behave more punitively if they have seen others act aggressively than if they have not been exposed to aggressive models. The elicting power of modeling stimuli is enhanced under conditions where observers are angered (Berkowitz 1965; Hartmann 1969; Wheeler 1966), they have strong authoritarian tendencies (Epstein 1966), the modeled aggression is socially justified (Berkowitz 1965), and where the victim invites attack through his prior association with aggression (Berkowitz 1965).

Social learning theory distinguishes four processes through which aggressive modeling influences may serve as external inducements for aggressive behavior. In most instances, behaving like others is rewarding, whereas divergent actions are less effective or may even bring disapproval. As a result of such differential reinforcement, models' actions come to serve as informative cues that similar performances have functional value (Bandura and Barab 1971). Conversely, when contingencies are reversed, so that matching responses are never reinforced but dissimilar behavior is consistently rewarded, imitativeness is rarely exhibited (Miller and Dollard, 1941). Through correlation with positive reinforcement, the actions of others operate as discriminative stimuli signifying probable consequences for observers, thus prompting them to behave in similar ways.

Aggressive behavior, especially when cruel and lacking adequate justification, is socially disapproved if not self-condemned. Anticipated censure can exert restraining influence on aggressive actions. When people respond approvingly or even indifferently to the actions of assailants, it conveys the impression that aggression is not only acceptable but expected in the situation. Moreover, exposure to models engaging in threatening activities without experiencing any untoward effects produces vicarious extinction fears and behavioral inhibitions (Bandura 1971*c;* Cline 1970). Seeing modeled aggression punished strengthens inhibitions in observers, whereas seeing it rewarded or go without any adverse consequences reduces observers' restraints toward behaving in a like manner (Bandura 1971*b).* In social groups where aggressive conduct is regarded as emulative behavior, aggressive modeling is primarily instigational. In groups that censure aggressive actions, modeling may also serve a disinhibitory function. Usually, both *instigational* and *disinhibitory* processes are involved.

Aggressive modeling can enhance aggressive responding in other ways as well. The behavior of models directs observers' attention to the particular objects used by the performer. This *stimulus-enhancing effect* may prompt observers to use the same instruments to a greater extent, though not necessarily in an imitative way (Bandura 1962). It has been further shown that the observation of others aggressing produces *emotional arousal* as measured physiologically, in children (Cline 1970), in adults (Zillman 1969), and in animals (Welch and Welch 1968). The resultant emotional arousal, as previously shown, can augment aggressive responding. The empirical evidence, considered together, reveals that modeling influences can function as teachers, instigators, inhibitors, disinhibitors, stimulus enhancers, and as emotion arousers.

AVERSIVE TREATMENT

Aggressive behavior is often aversively controlled by unpleasant, thwarting, offensive, and physically painful treatment. Since these different forms of aversive stimulation can, and often do, have dissimilar behavioral effects, social learning theory relates injurious behavior to specific aversive antecedents rather than to the omnibus term frustration.

Physical assaults. If one wished to provoke aggression, a dependable way to do so would be simply to hit another person, who would then be likely to oblige with a counterattack. To the extent that counteraggression discourages further assaults, it is reinforced by pain reduction and thereby assumes high functional value. Although naturally occurring contingencies favor the development of a strong pain-aggression relationship, there is some dispute over whether it is innate or acquired.

Azrin and Ulrich, the major proponents of the nativistic view, have extensively investigated the relationship between shock-produced pain and aggression (Azrin 1967; Ulrich 1966). Pairs of animals placed in a small chamber will attack each other when subjected to aversive stimulation in the form of electric shock, intense heat, or physical blows. Azrin and Ulrich conclude that since combative behavior is elicited by aversive stimuli with some regularity, emerges without any prior training, and persists without any evident reinforcement, pain-induced aggression must be an unlearned reflexive behavior.

Although the pain-aggression relationship appears to have some generality, there exists substantial evidence that disputes the view that animals are genetically programmed to respond aggressively to painful stimulation. Shocks fail to produce fighting in both certain docile and certain vicious species (Azrin 1967; Ulrich and Azrin 1962). Young animals rarely, if ever, fight when shocked unless they have had some fighting experience (Hutchinson, Ulrich, and Azrin 1965; Powell and Creer 1969); in some studies shocks produce little or no fighting in 20 to 30 percent of mature animals. If aggression is an unlearned dominant response to pain, then initial shocks should produce attack, which is not generally the case (Azrin, Hutchinson, and Hake 1963). Noncontingent painful stimulation may provoke aggression, but—contrary to the reflexive-elicitation hypotheses—when attack responses are shocked, the painful consequences reduce and eliminate rather than increase aggressive responding (Azrin 1970; Baenninger and Grossman 1969). Moreover, given a choice, animals would rather escape than fight (Logan and Boice 1969). The final, and most striking, evidence that pain-aggression reactions are determined more by fortuitous situational factors than by innate organization is the finding that in a small enclosure approximately 90 percent of the shocks provoke fighting, whereas in a slightly larger chamber animals ignore each other and only 2 percent of the shocks elicit attack (Ulrich and Azrin 1962). The overall results support the conclusion that physically painful experiences are facilitative but not sufficient to provoke aggression in animals (Bandura 1973).

Painful stimulation is an even less consistent elicitor of aggression in humans. Whether or not people counteraggress in the face of physical assaults depends upon their combat success and the power of their assailant. Those who have been successful in controlling people through force escalate their counterattacks to compell acquiescence (Edwards 1967; Peterson 1971). Given other options, low aggressors are easily dissuaded from making counterattacks under retaliative threats. In studying the aversive activation of aggression, it is of greater import to identify the events that initiate an injurious response before any actual physical pain has been delivered, than to demonstrate that physical assaults have a high likelihood of eliciting defensive reactions. Rausch (1965), for example, has shown that a hostile response has a 75 percent chance of evoking reciprocal aggression. Of greater interest, however, is the finding that friendly gestures iniated aggressive responses 45 percent of the time in hyperaggressive boys but rarely did so in nonaggressive children. A complete casual analysis must be concerned with what provokes people to hit in the first place as well as the probability that a hit will produce a counterhit. Aggression is often initiated by threats that forebode painful experiences. It is not uncommon for people who have come to expect rejection to respond to friendly expressions with anticipatory distrust and aggression (Bandura and Walters 1959).

Verbal threats and insults. Social interchanges are typically escalated into physical aggression by verbal threats and insults. Toch (1969) retrospectively analyzed sequences of actions and reactions of chronic assaulters to determine what set them off on a course productive of violence. In his sample, which included assault-prone police officers, parolees, and prison inmates, humiliating affronts and threats to reputation and manly status emerged as major precipitants of violence. High sensitivity to embarrassing treatment is usually combined with deficient skills for resolving disputes and restoring self-esteem by verbal means without having to dispose of antagonists physically. In fighting gangs, status threats, from challengers either within the group itself or from rival gangs, are quick to provoke aggressive actions.

Insult alone is less effective in provoking counterattack in individuals who ordinarily eschew aggression, but it does heighten aggressive responding when supported by hostile modeling and other disinhibitory influences (Hartmann 1969; Wheeler and Caggiula 1966).

No one has traced, either developmentally or experimentally, the process whereby insults acquire aggression-eliciting potential. The most plausible explanation is in terms of foreseen consequences. Affronts that are not successfully counteracted can have far-reaching effects for victims. Not only do they become easy targets for further victimization, but they are apt to forfeit their social standing, along with the rewards and privileges that go with it. To the extent that punishment of insults by counteraggression reduces the likelihood of further maltreatment, the insult-aggression reaction becomes well established.

Adverse conditions of reinforcement. Aversive conditions of life can also provoke people to take aggressive action. Explanations of collective aggression characteristically invoke impoverishment and discontent arising from privations as principal causal factors. Since most discontented people do not aggress, the view that discontent breeds disorders requires certain qualifications. This issue is well illustrated in interpretations of urban riots in ghetto areas. Despite condemnation of their degrading and exploitive conditions of life, comparatively few of the sufferers take active measures to force warranted changes. A vast majority of the disadvantaged blacks did not engage in disruptive public protest, and even in cities experiencing civil disturbances only about 15 to 20 percent of ghetto residents actively participated in the aggressive activities (Lieberson and Silverman 1965; McCord and Howard 1968; Sears and McConahay 1969).

The critical question for social scientists to answer is not why some people subjected to adverse conditions aggress, but rather why a sizable majority of them acquiesce to dismal living conditions in the midst of affluent styles of life. To facilely invoke the frustration-aggression hypothesis, as is commonly done, is to disregard the more striking evidence that severe privation generally results in feelings of hopelessness and massive servility. Pervasive discontent may be a necessary but not a sufficient cause of collective aggression.

The evidence indicates that discontent produces aggression not in those who have lost hope, but in the more successful members whose assertive efforts at social and economic betterment have been periodically reinforced; consequently, they have some reason to expect that coercive action will force additional social change.

Current explanations of violent protest emphasize relative deprivation rather than the actual level of aversive conditions as the instigator of collective aggression. In an analysis of conditions preceding major revolutions, Davies (1969) reports that revolutions are most likely to occur when a period of social and economic advances that instills rising expectations is followed by a sharp reversal. People not only judge their present gains in relation to those they secured in the past; they also compare their lot in life with the benefits accruing to others (Bandura, 1971*b*). Unfavorable discrepancies between observed and experienced outcomes tend to create discontent, whereas individuals may be satisfied with limited rewards as long as they are as good as, or better than, what others are receiving.

Since most people who feel relatively deprived do not resort to violent action, aversive privations contribute to aggression in interaction with other inducements rather than as an independent determinant. Gurr (1970) examined three determinants of the magnitude of civil disorders. These included the level of social discontent, traditional acceptance of tactical force to achieve desired reforms, and the balance of coercive power between the regime and the challengers. In less extreme forms of collective aggression, acceptance of forcible tactics and coercive power were equally strong determinants, whereas variations in discontent had less effect. Widespread discontent combined with dissident coercive power emerged as the important determinants of revolutionary violence.

Response to inequitable deprivation is further influenced by, among other factors, the social justification and promise of social reforms. Considering the complex interplay of influences, it is hardly surprising that level of deprivation alone, whether defined in absolute or relative terms, is a weak predictor of collective aggression (McPhail, 1971).

Thwarting of goal-directed behavior. Proponents of the frustration-aggression theory define frustration in terms of interference or blocking of goal-seeking activities. In this view, people are provoked to aggression when obstructed, delayed, or otherwise thwarted in getting what they want. Research bearing on this issue shows that thwarting can lead people to intensify their efforts, which, if sufficiently vigorous, may be construed as aggression. However, thwarting fails to provoke forceful actions in people who have not experienced sufficient positive reinforcement to develop reward expectations, and in those who are blocked so far from the goal that it appears unattainable (Haner and Brown 1955; Holton 1961; Longstreth 1966).

In instances where thwarting provokes aggression, it is probably attributable more to the implied personal insult than to blocking of ongoing behavior. Consistent with this interpretation, people report more aggression to hypothetical thwartings that appear unwarranted than to those for which excusable reasons exist, even though both involve identical blocking of goal-directed behavior (Cohen 1955; Pastore 1952).

INCENTIVE INDUCEMENTS

The preceding discussion was concerned solely with aversively motivated aggression, which occupies a more prominent role in psychological theorizing than is warranted empirically. The cognitive capacity of humans to represent future consequences enables them to guide their behavior by outcomes extended forward in time. A great deal of human aggression in fact is prompted by anticipated positive consequences. Here, the instigator is the pull of expected reward, rather than the push of painful treatment. This positive source of motivation for aggression represents the second component in the motivational analysis depicted schematically in figure 7.1.

The consequences that people anticipate for their actions are derived from, and therefore usually correspond to, prevailing conditions of reinforcement. The powerful anticipatory activation and reinforcement control of aggression receives detailed consideration later. It should be noted, however, that expectation and actuality do not always coincide because anticipated outcomes are also partly inferred from observed consequences of others, from what one reads or is told, and from many other cues that in past experience were reliable forecasters of likely outcomes. Since judgments are fallible, aggressive actions are sometimes prompted and temporarily sustained by erroneous anticipated consequences. Habitual offenders, for example, often err by overestimating the chances of success for transgressive behavior (Claster, 1967). In collective protest, coerceive actions are partly sustained, even in the face of punishing consequences, by expectations that continued pressure may eventually produce social reforms.

INSTRUCTIONAL CONTROL

During the process of socialization, people are extensively trained to obey orders. By the rewarding of obedience to directives and the punishing of noncompliance, orders eventually acquire eliciting power. After this form of social control is established, legitimate authorities can successfully command aggression from others, especially if actions are presented as justified and necessary and the agents possess strong coercive power. As Snow (1961, p. 24) has perceptively observed, "When you think of the long and gloomy history of man, you will find more hideous crimes have been committed in the name of obedience than have been committed in the name of rebellion."

Milgram (1963) has shown in a series of experiments that well-meaning adults will administer increasingly severe shocks on command from an experimenter, despite their victims' desperate pleas. Adults find it difficult to behave counter to peer pressures calling for increasingly hurtful actions, just as they are averse to defying legitimized authority (Milgram 1964). It is relatively easy to hurt a person on command when his suffering is not visible and when causal actions seem physically or temporally remote from their deleterious effects. Mechanized forms of warfare, by which masses of people can be put to death by destructive forces released remotely, illustrate such depersonalized aggression. When the injurious consequences of one's actions are fully evident, vicariously aroused distress and loss of self-respect serve as restraining influences over aggressive conduct that is otherwise authoritatively sanctioned. Milgram (1965) obtained diminishing obedience as the harmful consequences of punitive actions became increasingly more salient and personalized. Results of these studies, and others to be cited later, show that it requires particular social conditions rather than monstrous people to produce heinous deeds.

DELUSIONAL CONTROL

In addition to the various external instigators, aggressive behavior can come under bizarre symbolic control. Every so often, tragic episodes occur in which individuals are led by delusional beliefs to commit acts of violence. Some follow divine inner voices commanding them to murder. Others are instigated to self-protective attacks by paranoid suspicions that the victim is conspiring to harm them. And still others are prompted by grandiose convictions that it is their heroic responsibility to eliminate maleficent individuals in positions of power.

A study of presidential assassins (Weisz and Taylor 1970) shows that, with one exception, the murderous assaults were partly under delusional control. The assassins acted either under divine mandate, through alarm that the president was in a conspiracy with treacherous foreign agents to overthrow the government, or on the conviction that their own adversities resulted from presidential persecution. Being unusually seclusive in their behavior, the assassins effectively shielded their erroneous beliefs from corrective influences.

Maintaining Conditions

The third major feature of the social learning formulation is concerned with the conditions that sustain aggressive responding. It has been amply documented in psychological research that behavior is largely controlled by its consequences. This principle applies equally to aggression. Aggressive modes of response, like other forms of social behavior, can be induced, eliminated, and reinstated by altering the effects they produce (Bandura 1973).

People aggress for a variety of reasons. Essentially the same aggressive actions may thus have markedly different functional value for different individuals, and for the same individual on different occasions. In traditional theories of learning, reinforcement influences are largely confined to the effects of external outcomes impinging directly upon the performer. Social learning theory, on the other hand, distinguishes three forms of reinforcement control: the influence of direct external reinforcement, vicarious or observed reinforcement, and self-reinforcement.

DIRECT EXTERNAL REINFORCEMENT

Aggression is strongly influenced by its direct consequences, which take many forms. Extrinsic rewards assume special importance in interpersonal aggression, because such behavior, by its very nature, generally creates certain painful outcomes. A person who gets into fights will suffer some injury even though he eventually triumphs over his opponents. Under noncoercive conditions, positive incentives are needed to overcome the inhibitions aroused by the aversive side effects of aggression.

Tangible rewards. People often resort to aggressive action because it is an effective means of securing desired tangible rewards. Ordinarily docile animals will fight when aggressive attacks produce food or drinks (Azrin and Hutchinson 1967; Ulrich et al. 1963). Children will persist in punching behavior that gets them playthings, but discontinue such responses when the payoff is withdrawn (Cowan and Walters 1963; Walters and Brown 1963). Indeed, observation of children's interactions disclosed that approximately 80 percent of the aggressors' assaultive actions produced rewarding consequences for them (Patterson, Littman, and Bricker 1967). Given this surprisingly high level of positive reinforcement of aggressive behavior, there is no need to invoke an aggressive drive to explain the prevalence of such actions.

There are other forms of aggression which are sustained by their material consequences, although, for obvious reasons, they are not easily subject to systematic analysis. Delinquent and adult transgressors, for example, can support themselves on income derived from aggressive pursuits; protestors can secure through forceful collective response social reforms that affect their lives materially; and nations are sometimes able to gain control over prized territories through warfare.

Social and status rewards. Some aggressive behaviors are maintained because they win approval and status rewards. Children who are praised for hitting become more aggressive than those who receive no approval for such behavior (Patterson, Ludwig, and Sonoda 1961). The effects of social reinforcement on aggression are by no means confined to children. Adult males and females commended for punitive actions toward another person become progressively more aggressive, whereas nonreinforced subjects display a relatively low level of aggression (Geen and Stonner 1971; Staples and Walters 1964). Aggressive responses, if socially reinforced, not only increase in frequency, but the reinforcement can enhance other forms of aggression as well (Geen and Pigg 1970; Loew 1967).

Analyses of social renforcement of aggressive behavior in natural settings are in general agreement with results of laboratory studies. Parents of assaultive children are generally nonpermissive with respect to aggressive behavior in the home, but condone, actively encourage, and reinforce provocative and aggressive actions toward others in the community (Bandura 1960; Bandura and Walters 1959). In aggressive gangs, members achieve status and recognition through their skill in fighting (Short 1968). Police apprehended a gang in the San Francisco area which used attacks upon strangers, without provocation, as its main admission requirement. Each physical assault, which had to be witnessed by a club member to be valid, was valued at ten points, and a total of 100 points was required for full-fledged membership. During wartime, otherwise compassionate societies offer medals, promotions, and social commendations on the basis of skill in killing. In the Nazi structure of reinforcement, where enslavement and execution of racial minorities were viewed as meritorious acts of patriotism, promotions in concentration camps were made partly on skill in performing mass murders. Camp commandants proudly compared execution rates like industrial production figures (Andrus 1969).

Lest the Nazi atrocities be dismissed as an anomalous product of a deranged social system, it should be noted that otherwise socialized people can be led to behave brutally and to take pride in such actions under circumstances where reinforcement practices that favor sadistic forms of behavior are instituted. A U.S. infantry battalion in South Vietnam adopted its own reward system for eliminating Viet Cong (*San Francisco Chronicle* 1970). Infantrymen who could prove they had killed an enemy were not only rewarded with rest and recreation, but were also decorated with specially designed "Kill Cong" emblems, formally presented at company formations. The barbarity of this reinforcement system is revealed in what had to be submitted as evidence of a kill. To lay claim to a badge, one had to bring back an enemy ear. A string of ears was proudly displayed at the headquarters like huntsmen's trophies.

Alleviation of aversive treatment. People are frequently subjected to distressing treatment from which they seek relief. Coercive action that is not unduly hazardous is the most direct and quickest means of alleviating adverse conditions, if only temporarily. Defensive forms of aggression are often reinforced by their capacity to terminate humiliating and painful treatment. Reinforcement through pain reduction is well documented in studies cited earlier showing that children who are often victimized but who terminate the maltreatment by successful counter-aggression eventually become highly aggressive in their behavior (Patterson, Littman, and Bricker 1967).

In the social learning analysis, defensive aggression is sustained to a greater extent by anticipated consequences than by its instantaneous effects. People will endure painful treatment on the expectation that their aggressive efforts will eventually succeed. Aggressive actions may also be partly maintained in the face of hurtful counterattack by anticipated costs of timidity. In aggression-oriented circles, failure to fight back can arouse fear of future victimization and humiliation. A physical pummeling may, therefore, be far less distressing than repeated social derision or self-contempt. In other words, humans do not behave like unthinking servomechanisms directed solely by immediate response feedback. Rather, they partly regulate their actions on the basis of probable future consequences. Under aversive conditions of life, people will persist, at least for a time, in aggressive behavior that produces immediate pain but the prospect of relief from misery.

Expressions of injury. Proponents of drive theories contend that injury is the goal of aggression. It is, therefore, widely assumed that aggressive behavior is reinforced by signs of suffering in the victim. According to Sears, Maccoby, and Levin (1957), pain cues become rewarding through their repeated association with tension relief and removal of frustrations. Feshbach (1970), on the other hand, interprets the rewarding value of pain expressions in terms of self-esteem processes: perception of pain in one's tormentors is experienced as satisfying because successful retaliation restores the aggressor's self-esteem.

A contrasting view is that signs of suffering ordinarily function as inhibitors rather than as positive reinforcers of aggressive behavior. Because of the potential dangers of violence, all societies severely punish cruel and destructive acts of aggression, except under special circumstances. In the course of socialization, most people adopt for self-evaluation societal standards that designate ruthless aggression as morally reprehensible. Consequently, aggression that produces suffering in others elicits both fear of retaliation and self-condemnation, which tend to inhibit injurious attacks.

Laboratory studies of the influence of pain expressions on further physical assaults on suffering victims support the inhibitory view. Aggressors behave less punitively toward their victims when the latter express anguished cries than when they suffer in silence (Baron 1971*a*, 1971*b*; Geen 1970). Pain cues exert their suppressive effects under angered and nonangered conditions alike. Moreover, people are less inclined to behave cruelly when they see their suffering victims than when they merely hear the distress they have caused them (Milgram 1965).

The scope of the experimental treatments and the populations studied are too limited to warrant the strong conclusion that pain expressions never serve as positive reinforcers of aggressive behavior. A gratuitous insult from a stranger in a laboratory may not create sufficient animosity for the victim to derive satisfaction from injurious retaliation. It is a quite different matter in situations in which an antagonist repeatedly tyrannizes others or wields, his power in ways that make life miserable for them. In such instances, news of the misfortune, serious illness, or death of an oppressor is joyfully received by people who ordinarily respond more compassionately to the adversities befalling others. However, the alleviation of aversive treatment from an injured oppressor rather than his suffering may be the primary source of satisfaction. In experimental investigations pain expressions occur without the other extraneous rewards accompanying victory over antagonists.

From the standpoint of social learning theory, the suffering of one's enemy is most apt to be rewarding when hurting him relieves discomfort or benefits aggressors in other ways. On the other hand, when aggressors suffer reprisals or self-contempt for harming others, signs of suffering function as negative reinforcers that deter injurious attacks.

There are certain conditions under which pain expressions may assume positive reinforcing properties. Examples can be cited of societal practices in which cruel, monstrous acts are considered praiseworthy by persons in positions of power. Such bizarre reinforcement contingencies can breed people who take pleasure in inflicting pain and humiliation. Some of the most horrid illustrations of this phenomenon are documented in the proceedings of the Nuremberg trials. Rudolph Hoess, a former commandant of Auschwitz, for example, had a window installed in a gas chamber so he could watch the gruesome massacres (Andrus 1969). In addition, clinical studies of sexual perversion have disclosed numerous cases in which pain cues acquire powerful rewarding value through repeated association with sexual gratification. As a result, erotic pleasure is derived from inflicting pain on others or on oneself.

There are no conceptual or empirical grounds for regarding aggression maintained by certain reinforcers to be more genuine or important than that supported by other reinforcers. A comprehensive theory must account for all aggressive actions, whatever the purposes they serve. To restrict analysis of aggression to behavior that is reinforced by expressions of injury is to exclude from consideration some of the most violent forms of interpersonal assault where injury is an inevitable by-product rather than the major function of the behavior. Questions also arise about the distinction traditionally drawn (Berkowitz 1962; Feshbach 1970) between "instrumental" aggression, which is supposedly aimed at securing extraneous rewards, and "hostile" aggression, the sole purpose of which is presumably to inflict suffering. Since, in all instances, the behavior is instrumental in producing certain desired outcomes, be they pain, status rewards, or material gain, it would be more accurate to designate aggressive behaviors in terms of their functional value rather than on the basis of whether they are instrumental.

VICARIOUS REINFORCEMENT

People repeatedly observe the actions of others and the occasions on which they are rewarded, ignored, or punished. Observed outcomes influence behavior in much the same way as do directly experienced consequences (Bandura 1971*b*; Kanfer 1965). People, therefore, not only regulate their behavior on the basis of direct experience, but they also profit greatly from the successes and mistakes of others. In general, seeing aggression rewarded in others increases, and seeing it punished decreases, the tendency to behave in similar aggressive ways (Bandura 1963*b*; Bandura, Ross, and Ross 1963*b*). The more consistent the observed response consequences, the greater the faciliatory and inhibitory effects on the viewer (Rosekrans and Hartup 1967).

Vicarious reinforcement produces its behavioral effects through several mechanisms (Bandura 1971*a*). Response consequences accruing to others convey information to observers about the types of actions likely to be approved or disapproved and the specific conditions under which it is appropriate to perform them. Observed reinforcement is not only informative. Seeing others securing desired outcomes can function as a motivator by arousing in observers expectations that they can gain similar rewards for analogous performances. Some of the changes in responsiveness may result from the vicarious conditioning and extinction of emotional arousal which occurs when one observes the affective consequences accruing to models. In addition to the aforementioned effects, valuation of the performer and the reinforcing agent can be significantly altered by observing their rewarding and punishing interactions.

There are a number of social factors that may substantially alter the customary effects of observed consequences. Models and observers often differ in distinguishable ways, so that behavior considered approvable for one may be punishable for the other, depending on discrepancies in sex, age, and social status. When the same behavior produces unlike consequences for different members, observed reward may not enhance the level of imitative aggressiveness.

Under some circumstances, observed punitive treatment raises rather than lowers aggression. When societal agents misuse their power to reward and punish, they undermine the legitimacy of their authority and generate strong resentment. Seeing inequitable punishment, rather than prompting compliance, may free incensed observers from self-censure of their own actions and thus increase aggressive behavior. Indeed, leaders of protest movements sometimes attempt to rally supporters to their cause by selecting aggressive tactics calculated to provoke authorities to punitive actions.

Ordinarily, observed punishment tends to devalue the model

and his behavior, whereas the same model assumes emulative qualities when his actions are rewarded. However, an aggressor may gain rather than lose status in the eyes of his peers when he is punished for a style of behavior valued by the group or when he aggresses against social practices that violate the professed values of society. It is for this reason that authoritative agencies are usually careful not to discipline deviators in ways that might martyr them.

The manner in which an aggressor responds to the effects of his behavior can also influence the way observers later react when they themselves are rewarded for displaying similar responses. Ditrichs, Simon, and Greene (1967) report that children who had observed models express progressively more hostility for social approval later increased their own output of hostile responses under positive reinforcement. However, when models appeared oppositional by reducing hostile responses that brought them praise, or reacted in random fashion as though they were uninfluenced, observers did not increase their expression of hostility even though they were praised whenever they did so. Thus, susceptibility to direct reinforcement was increased by observed willing responsiveness, but reduced by observed resistance.

SELF-REINFORCEMENT

A great deal of human behavior is regulated by the self-evaluative consequences it produces. People set themselves certain standards of behavior and respond to their actions in self-approving or self-critical ways, in accordance with their self-prescribed demands (Bandura 1971*a*, 1971*b*). Having adopted a self-monitoring reinforcement system, they do things that give them self-satisfaction and a feeling of self-worth; conversely, they refrain from behaving in ways that result in self-criticism and other self-devaluative consequences. Because of self-reactive tendencies, aggressors must contend with themselves as well as with others when they behave in an injurious fashion.

SELF-REWARD FOR AGGRESSION

One can distinguish several ways in which self-generated consequences enter into the self-regulation of aggressive behavior. At one extreme are individuals who have adopted a self-reinforcement system in which aggressive behavior is a source of personal pride. Such individuals readily engage in aggressive activities and experience self-satisfaction and other positive feelings for aggressing successfully. Members of fighting gangs compile scrapbooks of newspaper articles about their aggressive exploits, which they regard with pride. In the Nazi regime, where horrific massacres were politically sanctioned, commandants of extermination camps felt tremendous pride when they surpassed the kill rates of other crematoriums (Andrus 1969). Indeed, Eichmann confessed that death lists were his favorite reading before he went to sleep.

SELF-PUNISHMENT FOR AGGRESSION

In the course of socialization, most individuals acquire, through example and precept, negative sanctions against cruel actions. As a result, they are restrained from injurious aggression by anticipated self-criticism. There is no more devastating punishment than self-contempt.

Results of the study by Bandura and Walters (1959) reveal how anticipatory self-reproach for repudiated aggression serves as a motivating influence to keep behavior in line with adopted standards. Adolescents who were normally compassionate in their dealings with others responded with self-disapproval, remorse, and attempts at reparation even when their aggressive activities were minor in nature. Assaultive boys, on the other hand, experienced relatively few negative self-reactions over rather serious aggressive activities.

NEUTRALIZATION OF SELF-CONDEMNATION FOR AGGRESSION

Aggression is rarely uniformly self-rewarded or self-punished, irrespective of the victim or the circumstances under which it is performed. By engaging in a variety of self-deceptive cognitive maneuvers, humane, moral people can behave cruelly without self-condemnation. The self-absolving practices assume numerous forms.

Slighting aggression by advantageous comparison. A practice that is widely employed is to slight one's aggressive actions by comparison with more hideous deeds. American executors of Asian warfare and their ardent supporters, for example, minimized the slaying of countless Indochinese on the ground that it checked massive Communist enslavement. Given such a benevolent definition of destructive practices, aggressors remained unperturbed by the fact that the intended beneficiaries were exterminated at an alarming rate. Radical protestors, on the other hand, defined their domestic violence as trifling, or even laudable, by comparing it with the widespread carnage perpetrated by Americans in Southeast Asia.

Justification of aggression in terms of higher principles. A closely related form of self-vindication is to construe one's aggression in terms of higher values. Given sufficiently noble aims, almost any form of aggression can be justified as righteous. To take an historical example, many massacres were devotedly perpetrated by crusading Christians in the service of high religious principles. Similarly, in contemporary times violence is frequently espoused in the name of freedom, social justice, equality, and civil order.

Displacement of responsibility. People can be led to behave in an injurious way provided that a legitimate authority is willing to assume responsibility for their actions. Participants in Milgram's (1963) experiments, who were deterred from further punitive assaults by distress over the suffering they had inflicted, continued to escalate shocks to hazardous levels despite their victims' agonizing cries after the experimenter assured them he would be fully accountable for the consequences of their behavior. Guiltless obedience to horrific orders is most evident in military atrocities.

Diffusion of responsibility. Exemption from self-criticism can be achieved to some extent by obscuring and diffusing responsibility for aggressive practices. Collective aggression depends on many task functions that must be supported by an organizational apparatus. Departmentalization of destructive activities works in several ways to reduce participants' sense of personal responsibility for their behavior. Through division of labor, division of decision making, and collective action, people can be contributors to cruel practices and bloodshed without feeling personally responsible or self-contemptuous for their part in it.

Dehumanization of victims. A further means of protection against self-devaluation is to dehumanize the victim. People selected as targets are often divested of human qualities by being viewed not as individuals with sensitivities, but as stereotyped objects bearing demeaning labels such as "gooks" or "niggers." If dispossessing victims of humanness does not fully eliminate self-reproof, it can be further reduced by attributing subhuman or degrading characteristics to them. Foes become "degenerates," "pigs," and other bestial creatures. After victims have been so devalued, they can be cruelly attacked without much risk of self-punishment.

Attribution of blame to victims. Attribution of blame to victims is still another expedient that can be used for self-assuaging purposes. In this process, aggressors see themselves essentially as persons of good will who are forced into punitive actions by villainous adversaries. Victims are condemned for bringing the suffering on themselves either by their character defects or by their witless and provocative behavior. Observers of victimization can be affected in much the same way as the aggressors. Seeing victims suffer punitive treatment for which they are held partially responsible leads observers to devalue them (Lerner, 1971; Piliavin, Hardyck, & Vadum, 1967). The indignation aroused by ascribed culpability, in turn, provides moral support for even more brutal acts by aggressors.

Misrepresentation of consequences. After people have aggressed, additional self-placating measures are available that operate principally through misrepresentation of the consequences of one's actions. When people are prompted to self-disapproved conduct under conditions in which they have some choice on whether or not to behave that way, they tend to minimize injurious consequences and to recall the potential benefits but not the harms of punishing courses of action (Brock and Buss, 1962, 1964). As long as the damages that aggressors cause are disregarded or belittled, they have little reason to engage in self-censuring reactions.

Graduated desensitization. The aforementioned practices will not instantaneously transform a gentle person into a brutal aggressor. Rather, the change is usually achieved through a gradual desensitization process, in which the participants may not fully recognize the marked changes they have undergone. Initially, individuals are prompted to perform aggressive acts they can tolerate without excessive self-censure. After their discomfort and self-reproof are extinguished through repeated performance, the level of aggression is progressively increased in this manner until eventually gruesome deeds, originally regarded as abhorrent, can be performed without much distress.

Examples taken either from military atrocities or political violence convey the impression that sanctioning of human cruelty occurs only under extraordinary circumstances. Quite the contrary. Many societal practices causing widespread harm are routinely performed for financial profit by decent people under self-exonerating justifications.

The presence of friendly bonds between people serves to inhibit aggression toward each other in the face of provocation from external sources (Davitz 1952; Wright 1942). However, just as high moral principles can be used to support ruthless behavior, positive bonds can heighten aggressiveness under certain conditions. The mutual support of close friendship reduces restraints against aggressing toward a common foe. As Wright (1942) has demonstrated, close friends are more abusive toward their antagonists than groups with weaker bonds of friendship.

Given the variety of self-absolving devices, a society cannot rely solely on individuals, however noble their convictions, to safeguard against brutal deeds. Just as aggression is not rooted in the individual, neither does its control reside solely there. Humaneness requires, in addtion to benevolent codes of self-reinforcement, social reinforcement systems that uphold compassionate behavior and discourage cruelty.

References

Agras, W. S. "Behavior Therapy in the Management of Chronic Schizophrenia." *American Journal of Psychiatry* 124 (1967): 240–43.

Alland, A., Jr. *The Human Imperative*. New York: Columbia University Press, 1972.

Andrus, B. C. *The Infamous of Nuremberg*. London: Fravin, 1969.

Ardrey, R. *The Territorial Imperative*. New York: Atheneum Publishers, 1966.

Ax, A. F. "The Physiological Differentiation between Fear and Anger in Humans." *Psychosomatic Medicine* 15 (1953): 433–42.

Azrin, N. H. "Pain and Aggression." *Psychology Today* 1 (1967): 27–33.

——. "Punishment of Elicited Aggression." *Journal of Experimental Analysis of Behavior* 14 (1970): 7–10.

Azrin, N. H., and Hutchinson, R. R. "Conditioning of the Aggressive Behavior of Pigeons by a Fixed-Interval Schedule of Reinforcement." *Journal of the Experimental Analysis of Behavior* 10 (1967): 395–402.

Azrin, N. H.; Hutchinson, R. R.; and Hake, D. F. "Pain-induced Fighting in the Squirrel Monkey." *Journal of the Experimental Analysis of Behavior* 6 (1963): 620.

Baenninger, R. and Grossman, J. C. "Some Effects of Punishment on Pain-elicited Aggression." *Journal of the Experimental Analysis of Behavior* 12 (1969): 1017–22.

Bandura, A. "Relationship of Family Patterns to Child Behavior Disorders." Progress report, Stanford University Project no. M-1734. U.S. Public Health Service, 1960.

——. "Social Learning through Imitation." In *Nebraska Symposium on Motivation, 1962*, edited by M. R. Jones, pp. 211–69. Lincoln: University of Nebraska Press, 1962.

——. "Vicarious Processes: A Case of No-Trial Learning." In *Advances in Experimental Social Psychology*, edited by L. Berkowitz, 2:1–55. New York: Academic Press, 1965. *(a)*

——. "Influence of Models' Reinforcement Contingencies on the Acquisition of Imitative Responses." *Journal of Personality and Social Psychology* 1 (1965): 589–95. *(b)*

——. *Principles of Behavior Modification*. New York: Holt, Rhinehart & Winston, 1969.

——. "Vicarious and Self-Reinforcement Processes." In *The Nature of Reinforcement*, edited by R. Glaser, pp. 228–78. New York: Academic Press, 1971. *(a)*

——. *Social Learning Theory.* New York: General Learning Press, 1971. *(b)*

——. "Psychotherapy Based upon Modeling Principles." In *Handbook of Psychotherapy and Behavior Change,* edited by A. E. Bergin and S. L. Garfield, pp. 653–708. New York: John Wiley & Sons, 1971. *(c)*

——. *Aggression: A Social Learning Analysis.* Englewood Cliffs, N.J.: Prentice-Hall, 1973.

Bandura, A., and Barab, P. G. "Conditions Governing Nonreinforced Imitation." *Developmental Psychology* 5 (1971): 244–55.

Bandura, A.; Grusec, J. E.; and Menlove, F. L. "Observational Learning as a Function of Symbolization and Incentive Set." *Child Development* 37 (1966): 499–506.

Bandura, A., and Jeffery, R. "Role of Symbolic Coding and Rehearsal Processes in Observational Learning." *Journal of Personality and Social Psychology,* in press.

Bandura, A., and Mischel, W. "Modification of Self-imposed Delay of Reward through Exposure to Live and Symbolic Models." *Journal of Personality and Social Psychology* 2 (1965): 698–705.

Bandura, A.; Ross, D.; and Ross, S. A. "Imitation of Film-mediated Aggressive Models." *Journal of Abnormal and Social Psychology* 66 (1963): 3–11. *(a)*

——. "Vicarious Reinforcement and Imitative Learning." *Journal of Abnormal and Social Psychology* 67 (1963): 601–7. *(b)*

Bandura, A., and Walters, R. H. *Adolescent Aggression.* New York: Ronald Press, 1959.

Baron, R. A. "Magnitude of Victim's Pain Cues and Level of Prior Anger Arousal as Determinants of Adult Aggressive Behavior." *Journal of Personality and Social Pscyhology* 17 (1971): 236–43. *(a)*

——. "Aggression as a Functon of Magnitude of Victim's Pain Cues, Level of Prior Anger Arousal, and Aggressor-Victim Similarity." *Journal of Personality and Social Psychology* 18 (1971): 48–54. *(b)*

Berkowitz, L. *Aggression: A Social Psychological Analysis.* New York: McGraw-Hill, 1962.

——. 'The Concept of Aggressive Drive: Some Additional Considerations." In *Advances in Experimental Social Psychology,* 2:301–29. New York: Academic Press, 1965.

Brock, T. C., and Buss, A. H. "Dissonance, Aggression, and Evaluation of Pain." *Journal of Abnormal and Social Psychology* 65 (1962): 197–202.

——. "Effects of Justification for Aggression and Communication with the Victim on Postaggression Dissonance." *Journal of Abnormal and Social Psychology* 68 (1964): 403–12.

Buss, A. H. *The Psychology of Aggression.* New York: John Wiley & Sons, 1961.

Chittenden, G. E. "An Experimental Study in Measuring and Modifying Assertive Behavior in Young Children." *Monographs of the Society for Research in Child Development,* vol. 7 (1, serial no. 31) (1942).

Christy, P. R.; Gelfand, D. M.; and Hartmann, D. P. "Effects of Competition-induced Frustration on Two Classes of Modeled Behavior." *Developmental Psychology* 5 (1971): 104–11.

Claster, D. S. "Comparison of Risk Perception between Delinquents and Non-delinquents." *Journal of Criminal Law, Criminology, and Police Science* 58 (1967): 80–86.

Cline, V. B. "Plethysmographic Heart Response of High and Low Television Exposure Children While Watching a Violent Movie." Manuscript. Salt Lake City: University of Utah, 1970.

Cohen, A. R. "Social Norms, Arbitrariness of Frustration, and Status of the Agent of Frustration in the Frustration-Aggression Hypothesis." *Journal of Abnormal and Social Psychology* 51 (1955): 222–26.

Cowan, P. A., and Walters, R. H. "Studies of Reinforcement of Aggression, I.: Effects of Scheduling." *Child Development* 34 (1963): 543–51.

Creer, T. L.; Hitzing, E. W.; and Schaeffer, R. W. "Classical Conditioning of Reflexive Fighting." *Psychonomic Science* 4 (1966): 89–90.

Davies, J. C. "The J-Curve of Rising and Declining Satisfactions as a Cause of Some Great Revolutions and a Contained Rebellion." In *Violence in America: Historical and Comparative Perspectives,* edited by H. D. Graham and T. R. Gurr, 2:547–76. Washington, D.C.: Government Printing Office, 1969.

Davitz, J. R. "The Effects of Previous Training on Postfrustration Behavior." *Journal of Abnormal and Social Psychology* 47 (1952): 309–15.

de Charms, R., and Wilkins, E. J. "Some Effects of Verbal Expression of Hostility." *Journal of Abnormal and Social Psychology* 66 (1963): 462–70.

Delgado, J. M. "Social Rank and Radio-stimulated Aggressiveness in Monkeys." *Journal of Nervous and Mental Disease* 144 (1967): 383–90.

Ditrichs, R.; Simon, S.; and Greene, B. "Effect of Vicarious Scheduling on the Verbal Conditioning of Hostility in Children." *Journal of Personality and Social Psychology* 6 (1967): 71–78.

Dollard, J.; Doob, L. W.; Miller, N. E.; Mowrer, O. H.; and Sears, R. R. *Frustration and Aggression.* New Haven, Conn.: Yale University Press, 1939.

Edwards, N. L. "Aggressive Expression under Threat of Retaliation." Ph.D. dissertation, University of Iowa, 1967.

Epstein, R. "Aggression toward Outgroups as a Function of Authoritarianism and Imitation of Aggressive Models." *Journal of Personality and Social Psychology* 3 (1966): 574–79.

Farris, H. E.; Gideon, B. E.; and Ulrich, R. E. "Classical Conditioning of Aggression: A Developmental Study." *Psychological Record* 20 (1970): 63–68.

Feshbach, S. "The Catharsis Hypothesis and Some Consequences of Interaction with Aggressive and Neutral Play Objects." *Journal of Personality* 24 (1956): 449–62.

Feshbach, S. "The Function of Aggression and the Regulation of Aggressive Drive." *Psychological Review* 71 (1964): 257–272.

——. "Aggression." in *Carmichael's Manual of Child Psychology,* edited by P. H. Mussen, 2:159–259. New York: John Wiley & Sons, 1970.

Freeman, E. "Effects of Aggressive Expression after Frustration on Performance: A Test of the Catharsis Hypothesis." Ph.D dissertation, Stanford University, 1962.

Freud, S. *New Introductory Lectures on Psycho-Analysis.* New York: W. W. Norton & Co., 1933.

——. "Why War?" in *Collected Papers,* edited by J. Strachey, 5:273–87. London: Hogarth Press, 1950.

Gardner, R., and Heider, K. G. *Gardens of War.* New York: Random House, 1968.

Geen, R. G. "Perceived Suffering of the Victim as an Inhibitor of Attack-induced Aggression. *Journal of Social Psychology* 81 (1970): 209–16.

Geen, R. G., and O'Neal, E. C. "Activation of Cue-elicited Aggression by General Arousal." *Journal of Personality and Social Psychology* 11 (1969): 289–92.

Geen, R. G., and Pigg, R. "Acquisition of an Aggressive Response and Its Generalization to Verbal Behavior." *Journal of Personality and Social Psychology* 15 (1970): 165–70.

Geen, R. G., and Stonner, D. "Effects of Aggressiveness Habit Strength on Behavior in the Presence of Aggression-related Stimuli." *Journal of Personality and Social Psychology* 17 (1971): 149–53.

Gerst, M. S. "Symbolic Coding Processes in Observational Learning." *Journal of Personality and Social Psychology* 19 (1971): 7–17.

Ginsburg, B., and Allee, W. C. "Some Effects of Conditioning on Social Dominance and Subordination in Inbred Strains of Mice." *Physiological Zoology* 15 (1942): 485–506.

Glueck, S., and Glueck, E. *Unraveling Juvenile Delinquency.* Cambridge, Mass.: Harvard University Press, 1950.

Goranson, R. E. "Media Violence and Aggressive Behavior: A Review of Experimental Research." In *Advances in Experimental Social Psychology,* edited by L. Berkowitz, pp. 1–31. New York: Academic Press, 1970.

Gurr, T. R. "Sources of Rebellion in Western Societies: Some Quantitative Evidence." *Annals of the American Academy of Political and Social Science* 391 (1970): 128–44.

Haner, C. F., and Brown, P. A. "Clarification of the Instigation to Action Concept in the Frustration-Aggression Hypothesis." *Journal of Abnormal and Social Psychology* 51 (1955): 204–6.

Hartmann, D. P. "Influence of Symbolically Modeled Instrumental Aggression and Pain Cues on Aggressive Behavior." *Journal of Personality and Social Psychology* 11 (1969): 280–88.

Hawkins, R. P.; Peterson, R. F.; Schweid, E.; and Bijou, S. W. "Behavior Therapy in the Home: Amelioration of Problem Parent-Child Relations with the Parent in a Therapeutic Role." *Journal of Experimental Child Psychology* 4 (1966): 99–107.

Hicks, D. J. "Imitation and Retention of Film-mediated Aggressive Peer and Adult Models." *Journal of Personality and Social Psychology* 2 (1965): 97–100.

Hinde, R. A. "Ethological Models and the Concept of "Drive." *British Journal of Philosophical Science* 6 (1956): 321–31.

Hoelle, C. "The Effects of Modeling and Reinforcement on Aggressive Behavior in Elementary School Boys." *Dissertation Abstracts* 29B (1969): 3483–84.

Holton, R. B. "Amplitude of an Instrumental Response Following the Cessation of Reward." *Child Development* 32 (1961): 107–16.

Hunt, J. McV.; Cole, M. W.; and Reis, E. E. S. "Situational Cues Distinguishing Anger, Fear, and Sorrow." *American Journal of Psychology* 71 (1958): 136–51.

Hutchinson, R. R.; Ulrich, R. E.; and Azrin, N. H. "Effects of Age and Related Factors on the Pain-Aggression Reaction." *Journal of Comparative and Physiological Psychology* 59 (1965): 365–69.

Johnson, A. M., and Szurek, S. A. "The Genesis of Antisocial Acting Out in Children and Adults." *Psychoanalytic Quarterly* 21 (1952): 323–43.

Kahn, M. "The Physiology of Catharsis." *Journal of Personality and Social Psychology* 3 (1966): 278–86.

Kahn, M. W. "The Effect of Severe Defeat at Various Age Levels on the Aggressive Behavior of Mice." *Journal of Genetic Psychology* 79 (1951): 117–30.

Kanfer, F. H. "Vicarious Human Reinforcement: A Glimpse into the Black Box." In *Research in Behavior Modification,* edited by L. Krasner and L. P. Ullmann, pp. 244–67. New York: Holt, Rinehart & Winston, 1965.

Kaufmann, H., and Feshbach, S. "The Influence of Antiaggressive Communications upon the Response to Provocation." *Journal of Personality* 31 (1963): 428–44.

Kenny, D. T. "An Experimental Test of the Catharsis Theory of Aggression." Ph.D. dissertation, University of Washington, 1952.

Lehrman, D. S. "A Critique of Konrad Lorenz's Theory of Instinctive Behavior." *Quarterly Review of Biology* 28 (1953): 337–63.

Lerner, M. J. "Observer Evaluation of a Victim: Justice, Guilt, and Veridical Perception." *Journal of Personality and Social Psychology* 20 (1971): 127–35.

Levy, R. I. "On Getting Angry in the Society Islands." In *Mental Health Research in Asia and the Pacific*, edited by W. Caudill and T.-Y. Lin, pp. 358–80. Honolulu: East-West Center Press, 1969.

Lieberson, S., and Silverman, A. R. "The Precipitants and Underlying Conditions of Race Riots." *American Sociological Review* 30 (1965): 887–98.

Loew, C. A. "Aquisition of a Hostile Attitude and Its Relationship to Aggressive Behavior." *Journal of Personality and Social Psychology* 5 (1967): 335–41.

Logan, F. A., and Boice, R. "Aggressive Behaviors of Paired Rodents in an Avoidance Context." *Behaviour* 34 (1969): 161–83.

Longstreth, L. E. "Distance to Goal and Reinforcement Schedule as Determinants of Human Instrumental Behavior." In *Proceedings of the 74th Annual Convention of the American Psychological Association, 1966*, pp. 39–40. 1966.

Lorenz, K. *On Aggression*. New York: Harcourt, Brace & World, 1966.

McCord, W., and Howard, J. "Negro Opinions in Three Riot Cities." *American Behavioral Scientist* 11 (1968): 24–27.

McCord, W.; McCord, J.; and Zola, I. K. *Origins of Crime: A New Evaluation of the Cambridge-Somerville Youth Study*. New York: Columbia University Press, 1959.

McPhail, C. "Civil Disorder Participation: A Critical Examination of Recent Research." *American Sociological Review* 36 (1971): 1058–72.

Madsen, C., Jr. "Nurturance and Modeling in Preschoolers." *Child Development* 39 (1968): 221–36.

Mallick, S. K., and McCandless, B. R. "A Study of Catharsis of Aggression." *Journal of Personality and Social Psychology* 4 (1966): 591–96.

Milgram, S. "Behavioral Study of Obedience." *Journal of Abnormal and Social Psychology* 67 (1963): 371–78.

——. "Group Pressure and Action against a Person." *Journal of Abnormal and Social Psychology* 69 (1964): 137–43.

———. "Some Conditions of Obedience and Disobedience to Authority." *Human Relations* 18 (1965): 57–76.

Miller, N. E., and Dollard, J. *Social Learning and Imitation*. New Haven, Conn.: Yale University Press, 1941.

Montagu, M. F. A. *Man and Aggression*. New York: Oxford University Press, 1968.

Nelsen, E. A. "Social Reinforcement for Expression versus Suppression of Aggression." *Merrill-Palmer Quarterly* 15 (1969): 259–78.

Nelson, J. D.; Gelfand, D. M.; and Hartmann, D. P. "Children's Aggression Following Competition and Exposure to an Aggressive Model." *Child Development* 40 (1969): 1085–97. *New York Times*. November 13, 1966, p. 1.

Nisbett, R. E., and Schachter, S. "Cognitive Manipulation of Pain." *Journal of Experimental Social Psychology* 2 (1966): 227–36.

Pastore, N. "The Role of Arbitrariness in the Frustration-Aggression Hypothesis." *Journal of Abnormal and Social Psychology* 47 (1952): 728–31.

Patterson, G. R.; Cobb, J. A.; and Ray, R. S. "A Social Engineering Technology for Retraining Aggressive Boys." In *Georgia Symposium in Experimental Clinical Psychology*, edited by H. Adams and L. Unikel, vol. 2. New York: Pergamon Press, 1971.

Patterson, G. R.; Littman, R. A.; and Bricker, W. "Assertive Behavior in Children: A step toward a Theory of Aggression." *Monographs of the Society for Research in Child Development*, vol. 32 (5, serial no. 113) (1967).

Patterson, G. R.; Ludwig, M.; and Sonoda, B. "Reinforcement of Aggression in Children." Manuscript. Eugene: University of Oregon, 1961.

Peterson, R. A. "Aggression Level as a Function of Expected Retaliation and Aggression Level of Target and Aggressor." *Developmental Psychology* 5 (1971): 161–66.

Piliavin, I., Hardyck, J., and Vadum, A. Reactions to the Victim in Just or Non-just World." Paper presented at the meeting of the Society of Experimental Social Psychology, Bethesda, Maryland, August, 1967.

Powell, D. A., and Creer, T. L. "Interaction of Developmental and Environmental Variables in Shock-elicited Aggression." *Journal of Comparative and Physiological Psychology* 69 (1969): 219–25.

Rausch, H. L. "Interaction sequences". *Journal of Personality and Social Psychology* 2 (1965): 487–499.

Rosekrans, M. A., and Hartup, W. W. "Imitative Influences of Consistent and Inconsistent Response Consequences to a Model of Aggressive Behavior in Children." *Journal of Personality and Social Psychology* 7 (1967): 429–34.

Ross, L.; Rodin, J.; and Zimbardo, P. G. "Toward an Attribution Therapy: The Reduction of Fear through Cognitive-Emotional

Misattribution." *Journal of Personality and Social Psychology* 12 (1969): 279–88.

San Francisco Chronicle. June 11, 1970, p. 23.

Schachter, J. "Pain, Fear, and Anger in Hypertensives and Normotensives: A Psychophysiological Study." *Psychosomatic Medicine* 19 (1957): 17–29.

Schachter, S., and Singer, J. E. "Cognitive, Social and Physiological Determinants of Emotional State." *Psychological Review* 69 (1962): 379–99.

Scott, J. P., and Marston, M. V. "Nonadaptive Behavior Resulting from a Series of Defeats in Fighting Mice." *Journal of Abnormal and Social Psychology* 48 (1953): 417–28.

Sears, D. O., and McConahay, J. B. "Participation in the Los Angeles Riot." *Social Problems* 17 (1969): 3–20.

Sears, R. R.; Maccoby, E. E.; and Levin, H. *Patterns of Child Rearing*. Evanston, Ill.: Row, Peterson, 1957.

Short, J. F., ed. *Gang Delinquency and Delinquent Subcultures*. New York: Harper & Row, 1968.

Siegel, A. E. "Violence in the Mass Media." In *Violence and the Struggle for Existence*, edited by D. N. Daniels, M. F. Ochberg, and F. M. Ochberg, pp. 193–239. Boston: Little, Brown & Co., 1970.

Sloane, H. N.; Johnston, M. K.; and Bijou, S. W. "Successive Modification of Aggressive Behaviour and Aggressive Fantasy Play by Management of Contingencies." *Journal of Child Psychology and Psychiatry and Allied Disciplines* 8 (1967): 217–26.

Snow, C. P. "Either-Or." *Progressive* 25, no. 2 (1961): 24–25.

Staats, A. W., and Butterfield, W. H. "Treatment of Nonreading in a Culturally Deprived Juvenile Delinquent: An Application of Reinforcement Principles." *Child Development* 36 (1965): 925–42.

Staples, F. R., and Walters, R. H. "Influence of Positive Reinforcement of Aggression on Subjects Differing in Initial Aggression Level." *Journal of Consulting Psychology* 28 (1964): 547–52.

Toch, H. *Violent Men*. Chicago: Aldine Publishing Co., 1969.

Ulrich, R. E. "Pain as a Cause of Aggression." *American Zoologist* 6 (1966): 643–62.

Ulrich, R. E., and Azrin, N. H. "Reflexive Fighting in Response to Aversive Stimulation." *Journal of the Experimental Analysis of Behavior* 5 (1962): 511–20.

Ulrich, R.; Johnston, M.; Richardson, J.; and Wolff, P. "The Operant Conditioning of Fighting Behavior in Rats." *Psychological Record* 13 (1963): 465–70.

Walters, R. H., and Brown, M. "Studies of Reinforcement of Aggression, III: Transfer of Responses to an Interpersonal Situation." *Child Development* 34 (1963): 563–71.

Walters, R. H., and Llewellyn Thomas, E. "Enhancement of Punitiveness by Visual and Audiovisual Displays." *Canadian Journal of Psychology* 17 (1963): 244–55.

Weisz, A. E., and Taylor, R. L. "American Presidential Assassinations." In *Violence and the Struggle for Existence,* edited by D. N. Daniels, M. F. Gilula, and F. M. Ochberg, pp. 291–307. Boston: Little, Brown & Co. 1970.

Welch, A. S., and Welch, B. L. "Reduction of Norepinephrine in the Lower Brainstem by Psychological Stimulus." *Proceedings of the National Academy of Sciences* 60 (1968): 478–81.

Wheeler, L. "Toward a Theory of Behavioral Contagion." *Psychological Review* 73 (1966): 179–92.

Wheeler, L., and Caggiula, A. R. "The Contagion of Aggression." *Journal of Experimental Social Psychology* 2 (1966): 1–10.

Wolfgang, M. E., and Ferracuti, F. *The Subculture of Violence.* London: Tavistock Publications, 1967.

Wright, M. E. "Constructiveness of Play as Affected by Group Organization and Frustration. *Character and Personality* 11 (1942): 40–49.

Zeilberger, J.; Sampen, S. E.; and Sloane, H. N., Jr. "Modification of a Child's Problem Behaviors in the Home with the Mother as Therapist." *Journal of Applied Behavior Analysis* 1 (1968): 47–53.

Zillman, D. "Excitation Transfer in Communication-mediated Aggressive Behavior." *Journal of Experimental Social Psychology* 7 (1971): 419–34.

John F. Knutson received his bachelor's degree from Augustana College (Illinois) and his Ph.D. from Washington State University. After completing a post-doctoral fellowship in Medical Psychology at the University of Oregon Medical School, he joined the faculty of the Department of Psychology at the University of Iowa. In addition to aggressive behavior, his research interests include experimental psychopathology and behavior modification.

8

Aggression as Manipulatable Behavior

JOHN F. KNUTSON

Seven chapters have provided explications of research paradigms and data directed toward an understanding of aggression. There are many obvious similarities as well as differences among the findings, which may eventually provide a data base upon which to build programs to control human aggression. Both similarities and differences should be examined before considering programs.

On Defining Aggression

Research in any area of psychology always presents problems that are unique to the subject matter under consideration, and aggression research is no exception. Here, one ubiquitous problem has been that of arriving at a suitable definition of the phenomenon being investigated. There seems to be no other specific area of research which has developed more idiosyncratic defini-

The experiments of this chapter were made possible by funds provided through the Graduate College and the Old Gold Foundation of the University of Iowa.

tions of the area itself. Issues in the definition of *reinforcement* are classic in psychology; but when those disagreements are compared with the diverse definitions of *aggression*, the positions on the former appear to be almost in accord. How have the authors here defined aggression and how do their definitions relate to definitions of aggression in general?

Part of the problem in defining aggression relates to the fact that the defining individual frequently affixes a definition to the particular theoretical predilections operating in his laboratory. It is not surprising to find that definitions of aggression formulated by neobehaviorists are different from those of psychodynamically oriented clinical researchers. Obviously, definitions applicable to a particular theory might lack a useful generality. An additional problem is the fact that the term is not a technical one, and the word seems to have more connotative than dennotative meanings. It appears that many authors have been unable to develop operational definitions of aggression which are independent from their own theories and from the nontechnical, connotative meanings of the word. Both the theoretically based definitions and the nontechnical connotations of the word have resulted in a major disagreement revolving about the concept of intent.

The intention of an organism can only be inferred from its behavior, either motor or verbal. Because of the influences of behaviorism and the predominant philosophy of science upon scientific psychology, inferences about a subject's intent are usually eschewed. This is not true in aggression research. The issue of intent has been paramount—and not just in aggression research using human subjects. Consideration of an unobserved intentional inner state is reflected in many definitions of aggression. Reviewing the issues raised in defining the term, Kaufmann (1965, 1970) concluded that any time *aggression* is used an inference regarding intent is implicitly made. While Kaufmann sees intent as implicit in any use of the word *aggression,* some writers have explicitly included intent in their definitions of aggression. Feshbach (1971), for example, distinguished between *instrumental* and *hostile* aggression on the basis of whether the aggressing organism engages in the behavior for an ultimate positive consequence or for the purpose of injuring the target. Other recent definitions of aggression (e.g., Daniels, Gilula, and Ochberg 1970) have also included a consideration of the intent of the attacking organism. When viewing shock-elicited aggression in rats or schedule-induced aggression in pigeons in my laboratory, visitors almost always ask why the attacking subject should *want* to attack the target. These questions are almost as frequently asked by behavioral scientists as by visitors from the general public.

If inferences regarding intent seem to lie outside the predominantly accepted research strategy, why are so many authors in this area of research so insistent on the inclusion of intent? Perhaps it is due to the basic issue of the validity of their research, or more correctly the *face validity* of their research. That is, if the laboratory behavior defined as aggression does not necessarily appear to be aggression, the reader is assured that the behavior is aggression because the author has specified the aggressive intent of the subject. Conversely, behavior that appears to be aggression can be excluded from the definition because of the nonaggressive intent of the subject. Concern for the face validity of an operational definition is scientifically unreasonable, yet it seems that many of the definitions found in the aggression literature could have resulted from such a concern. The essential problems in defining aggression relate not to face validity of operational definitions, but rather to *criterion validity*.

Research on aggression is directed to an experimental analysis of a particular behavior that occurs with some frequency in the natural world. Ostensibly, that research should say something about the variables that influence aggression in a natural environment. If the operational definition of a behavior does not coincide with that behavior in the natural environment, then the research incorporating that definition will be suspect with respect to its implications. Criterion validity of the definition is required before the research can be assessed relative to its implications for the understanding and controlling of aggressive behavior. Critics of laboratory aggression research have often criticized the artificiality of the variables used in the laboratory (e.g., Singer 1971); however, an assessment of the criterion validity of the definitions used seems to be just as important but far less common.

If the major concern is with the criterion validity of definitions as they relate to the natural world, then an examination of natural-environment analyses of aggression would seem to be a useful first step in defining aggression. Ethologists and behavioral biologists (e.g., Carthy and Ebling 1964; Lorenz 1966; Tinbergen 1953) have observed and recorded naturally occurring behavior patterns in many species of animals. From these observations, classes of interorganism behaviors and their salient features have been catalogued. Intraspecific behaviors, grouped according to such functions as defending broods, securing territory and mates, or establishing social hierarchies within a group, are usually subsumed under labels of aggression, agonistic behaviors, or often merely "fighting." Interspecific predatory responses are usually excluded from these labels (e.g., Carthy and Ebling 1964). The ethologists usually have not become immersed in major considerations associated with defining aggression (e.g., Carthy and Ebling 1964), because global, all-inclusive definitions are often inappropriate to their tasks.

The naturalistic observation of behavior by ethologists involves a functional analysis of particular classes of behavior, such as dispersive or defensive responses, and the conditions under which they emerge. In analyzing such naturally occurring behaviors according to function, ethologists have identified species-specific stereotyped response patterns which characterize the naturally occurring behaviors of particular species. Often, the stereotyped dispersive or defensive classes of responding are characterized by identifiable topographies. Many laboratory researchers have adopted these characteristic intraspecific response topographies as their operational definitions of aggression (e.g., Scott and Fredericson 1951; Ulrich and Azrin 1962). By dealing with laboratory behavior that is isomorphic with ethologically defined aggressive or agonistic behaviors, these experimenters aligned their research with the naturally occurring phenomenon. The validity of the definition of laboratory aggression is then assumed on the basis of parallel topography. This strategy seems reasonable only if the response topography is unique to an ethologically defined fighting response and not characteristic of other organism responses, and if it is not an epiphenomenon of some laboratory manipulation or stimulus condition. The first qualification is obvious; the second requires an example. Data from a recent experiment by Knutson and Hynan (1972) demonstrated that a very close approximation to the upright response of rats, which has often been scored as aggression (threat posture) in the shock-elicited aggression research, may occur with a high frequency among some rats when shocked alone. That is, the threat posture occurred in the absence of a suitable target. Therefore, one may question the merit of recording upright posture as aggression in shock-elicited aggression research with rats, even if it is topographically similar to the defensive boxing included in the fighting repertoire of rats (Barnett 1963). If a response topography is characteristic of a particular naturally occurring interorganism class of behaviors, and if that topography is not an artifact of a laboratory manipulation, then the use of a particular response topography may be one step in the direction of establishing the criterion validity of a laboratory definition of aggression.

In this book, topography plays a major role in the aggression definitions in the chapters dealing with nonhuman aggression. McClearn and DeFries' adoption (chap. 3) of the Lagerspetz (1964) scale of mouse fighting makes considerable use of response topography. Similarly, Denenberg (chap. 2) and Moyer (chap. 1) incorporate response topographies in definitions of aggression. It is interesting Ulrich, Dulaney, Arnett and Mueller (chap. 4) comment upon the advantage of an experimental analysis of behavior without an emphasis upon topography, thus permitting a general understanding of behavior. Yet, this chapter incorporates an obviously topographically delineated response as the definition of aggression in the primate-research paradigm they describe. With the exception of considerations of "Hit" in the Patterson and Cobb chapter and of several studies to which Bandura refers, topographical definitions of *aggression* are not used in the studies of human subjects. As a rule, human-aggression research has not used response topography as an operational definition of aggression, although there are exceptions (e.g., Kelly and Hake 1970; Peterson 1970).

Difficulties in obtaining close approximations of the stereotyped naturally occurring response topographies in the laboratory, difficulties in observational recording of those behaviors, or problems associated with consequential tissue damage resulting from an attack topography combine to present many problems for the aggression researcher. Consequently, many laboratory analyses of aggression have adopted paradigms that include only some salient feature of naturally occurring, ethologically defined aggressive or agonistic behavior. For example, a salient feature of aggressive behavior in some primates is biting. This can result in severe tissue damage to subjects and requires observational recording, with the consequent potential for unreliability. Thus, as Ulrich, Dulaney, Arnett and Mueller have reported in chapter 4, an automated bite-recording device has been used to record a response that seems to be characteristic of naturally occurring primate aggression. They cited a series of studies that supported the use of bite recording as a definition of aggression. This research demonstrated that the automatically recorded biting phenomenon is influenced by independent variables in the same manner as the interorganism laboratory aggressive response, which has many of the essential species-specific topographical characteristics. The obvious advantages of the bite-recording methodology resulted in widespread adoption of biting as the definition of aggression in laboratory primate research. Its success in the primate situation prompted Azrin, Rubin, and Hutchinson (1968) to attempt automated bite recording in the rat, and those authors recommended it for further aggression research in rats. Unfortunately, just as naturally occurring, ethologically defined aggression topographies cannot necessarily be generalized among species (cf. Kimbrell 1968), Hutzell and Knutson (1972) demonstrated that the automatically recorded biting behavior is an inadequate definition of aggression in rats. The bite-recording definition of aggression obscured the influence of postweaning rearing conditions and sex. These variables had previously been demonstrated to be important determiners of intraspecific fighting behavior (Conner and Levine 1969; Hutchinson, Ulrich, and Azrin 1965), and in this experiment were variables that exerted a strong influence upon aggression defined in terms of interorganism topographies. These data suggest that without an unequivocal demonstration that the salient feature is equivalent to the ethologically defined phenomenon, the salient feature should not be assumed to be equivalent to the total behavior pattern. Currently, there seems to be more data to recommend using ethologically described response topographies as aggression definitions than to adopt the salient-feature strategy.

Interestingly, the Patterson and Cobb study (chap. 6), with the heavy emphasis upon the recording of behavior in the natural environment, does not incorporate a definition of aggression based on ethological techniques. Instead, these authors have adopted the more common strategy in human-aggression research of using a priori definitions assumed to be obvious characteristics of aggression. They consider the use of noxious social stimulation in an interorganism interaction to be "aggressive." They are careful, however, to avoid the use of the word *aggressive* and prefer to consider only specific classes of noxious interactions. To consider aggression to be noxious or painful stimulation does not involve a specific response topography, but instead is to adopt as the definition a salient characteristic considered to be ubiquitous in all aggression. By doing so, the Patterson and Cobb study parallels much of the laboratory aggression research using human subjects. Buss (1961) and many other investigators (e.g., Baron 1971*a;* Williams et al. 1967) have defined aggression as merely one subject presenting painful stimulation to another subject. This simple, unambiguous, operational definition of aggression has much to recommend it. This is especially true in human research, where species-specific, stereotyped aggressive responses are not characteristic. Indeed, in all the chapters in this volume which deal with human data, there is some consideration of aggression as the presentation of noxious stimulation. Similarly, the mouse-killing response of the rat, flank and tail biting of the mouse, and other tissue-damaging responses of animal subjects could also be considered as presentations of aversive stimulation. Then, in the broadest sense, all the authors here to some degree consider aggression to be the presentation of noxious stimulation.

Defining aggression as the presentation of aversive stimuli has had considerable support. Aversiveness appears to be a characteristic of many of the stereotyped behaviors recorded by ethologists. It is not inconsistent with many topographical definitions, and it does not have implications of intent. The aversiveness of stimuli can be independently assessed transituationally, and this definition should be reasonably easy to specify in a laboratory. The presentation of aversive stimulation is a broad and widely used definition of aggression, but in most research situations embellishments have been added. For example, Buss (1961) chose to exclude from his definition both the accidental delivery of noxious stimulation and the administration of painful stimuli for socially acceptable reasons. While Buss (1961) explicitly argued against the use of intent in aggression definitions, his two exclusions certainly raise the question of intent. An additional problem with this definition has arisen from a standard procedure in which it is used. In the aggression-machine procedure, a subject performs a task in which his response supposedly presents noxious noise or electric shock to another subject (a confederate of the experimenter). Rarely is aversive stimulation actually given, and rarely is the subject given feedback on the consequences of his responding. Since the subject neither actually presents noxious stimulation nor is given feedback on his behavior, it could be argued that this paradigm does not really meet the boundary conditions of aggression as the presentation of noxious stimulation. Buss has argued that his data indicate that the subjects are not aware that aversive stimulation is not actually presented and, therefore, this operational definition of aggression is met. Kaufmann (1970) has met the same criticism by defining aggression to be the response of individuals having a subjective probability greater than zero that their behavior will not fail to provide aversive stimulation to a target subject. By emphasizing subjective probabilities greater than zero of not failing to provide aversive stimulation, excluding accidental delivery of noxious stimulation, and excluding socially acceptable behavior in these definitions of aggression, the idea of intent has been coupled with presentation of aversive stimulation.

It is interesting that "accidental" occurrences of behavior in aggression research are considered differently than in other areas of research. If accidental delivery means random or chance occurrences, perhaps accidental deliveries of aversive stimulation can be treated as other random sources of variation which do not systematically influence results. That is, specific definitional exclusion seems unnecessary, and such random occurrences ought to be treated probabilistically as error variance or random fluctuation upon a behavioral baseline. If the "presentation of aversive stimulation" is the definition of *aggression*, then when an organism delivers noxious stimulation it is behaving aggressively. Whether that definition is meaningful and useful is a function of whether criterion validity for that operational definition can be established, not whether some of the behavior is excluded on the grounds of the possible nonaggressive intent of the subject.

Some consideration should also be given to suggestions that behavior presented for socially acceptable reasons which results in painful stimulation should be excluded from definition of aggression. Recently, the Surgeon General's Scientific Advisory Committee on Television and Social Behavior (1972) noted the sociopolitical aspects of definitions of aggression. A scientific analysis of behavior has to be apolitical and amoral. Operational definitions of aggressive behavior must transcend political and moral criteria. That a political or social group chooses to value particular behaviors or condemn particular behaviors should not determine the operational adequacy of defining those behaviors as aggression, nor should that determine the essential criterion validity of the definition. In commenting on the violent and aggressive behaviors committed in support of noble causes, Bandura (chap. 7) seems to provide considerable support for this position. Other recent publications (e.g., Daniels, Gilula, and Ochberg 1970) have also eliminated the distinction between socially acceptable and socially unacceptable aggressive behaviors.

The frequency with which qualifiers have been added to the presentation-of-pain definition of aggression accurately reflects the degree to which researchers often find this definition to be too broad and nonspecific to be scientifically useful. Qualifiers other than accidental delivery and social desirability have been incorporated. The qualification of amplitude has often been invoked, such that only a high-amplitude, painful stimulus or response is termed aggressive. This tactic is frequently adopted in the aggression-machine literature (e.g., Baron 1971*a;* Buss 1961; Williams et al. 1967). Several of the present authors include aspects of the amplitude or the magnitude of response in their definitions; however, for none of them is amplitude the primary defining characteristic.

While the "presentation of a painful stimulus" is probably one of the more widely used definitions of aggression, another common strategy has been to level any behavior aggressive if it has a consequence falling into a particular category. For example, Dollard et al. (1939 considered aggression to be behavior that results in injury. More recently, the Surgeon General's Scientific Advisory Committee on Television and Social Behavior (1972, p. 9) defined aggression as "the inflicting of harm, injury, or discomfort on persons, or damage to property." Although closely related to the concept of presentation of aversive stimulation, definitions of this type are based only on the consequences of the behavior. While concern might be expressed that *consequence* is just another word for *intent,* no intent is necessarily implied. The consequence of a behavior may be as objectively specified as the behavior itself. Aggression definitions based on specific consequences, rather than on broad, general effects, are closely related to functional analyses of behavior and functional definitions of aggression consistent with the naturalistic observations of ethologists. In much the same manner that ethologists note classes of behavior in terms of their functional relationships to particular interorganism consequences, Denenberg (chap. 2) and McClearn and DeFries (chap. 3) functionally define aggression in terms of consequences, such as dispersion or tissue damage. Obviously, flank wounds during mouse-mouse interactions, dead mice during rat-mouse interactions, or tissue damage in any interorganism situation are easily recorded and perhaps constitute reasonable definitions of aggression. Indeed, Denenberg suggests that operational definitions based on natural consequences of behavior have a very high probability of criterion validity. The tissue-damage definition has much to recommend it, but it also poses serious problems for laboratory research. While it seems obvious that tissue damage may not be the definition of choice in laboratories investigating human interactions, it is also problematic in nonhuman research. Most of the intraspecific behaviors described as agonistic or aggressive rarely result in tissue damage (cf. Carthy and Ebling 1964; Lorenz 1966). Consequently, tissue damage as a consequence is too narrow and restrictive for use as the only definition of aggression.

Closely related to the functional-analysis strategy is the definitional program suggested by Moyer (chap. 1). In his chapter, he considers the possibility of eight different kinds of aggression, delineated in terms of consequences and the stimulus conditions under which the behavior occurs. The concern with the specificity of the consequences of behavior reflected in the Moyer chapter is considerably different from the Dollard et al. (1939) strategy, which incorporated a broad-consequence definition. General operational definitions of aggression are being supplanted by definitions of particular behaviors having particular consequences. Moyer not only indicates the consequence of the behavior but also suggests the precise conditions under which the behavior occurs. According to Moyer, aggressive behaviors are stimulus bound: a specified behavior has a particular consequence and only occurs under particular conditions. This approach to defining aggression is consistent with ethological definitions. In addition, the definition can have topographical specificity, it can be sufficiently specific to be useful in the laboratory, and it is suggestive of a high probability of criterion validity. In a recent symposium, Barnett (1969) indicated that the general term *aggression* is meaningless and that functional behavioral descriptions and operational definitions should be used. Barnett suggested that the analysis of particular behavior patterns, such as intermale, territorial, or dispersive, might be accomplished in terms of consequences. Such behavior patterns and specific consequences would then be substituted for the global, imprecise label of aggression. This position is strongly supportive of Moyer.

Moyer has suggested that eight different and independent kinds of aggression exist. The obvious implication of his position is that data based upon the operational definition of a particular kind of aggression may have no relationship to another kind. We might consider how the behaviors studied by the other authors fit into Moyer's categories. Since the other authors have not specifically attempted to develop operational definitions in terms of different kinds of aggression, there are sufficient ambiguities to prevent simple classification. For example, predatory aggression would seem to be primarily an interspecies response, yet it could involve intraspecies behavior. Although the rat is not permitted to consume the prey, the mouse-killing behavior of rats is probably predatory, but the rat-pup killing by male rats described by Denenberg (chap. 3) might also be predatory behavior. A college student presenting electric foot shock to a rat constitutes an interspecific behavior, but it is obviously not predatory. Consequently, the data of Ulrich, Dulaney, Arnett and Mueller (chap. 4) seem to involve primarily irritable and instrumental aggression, rather than predatory aggressive behavior. Intermale aggression obviously characterizes the mouse-mouse interactions described by McClearn and DeFries (chap. 3). This intermale pattern could also be involved in the behavior described by Patterson and Cobb (chap. 6), Berkowitz (chap. 5), or Bandura (chap. 7). With the exception of that of Moyer (chap. 1), none of the chapters seem to be addressed to fear-induced aggression. Territorial aggression is probably operating in the McClearn and DeFries triad chambers, and perhaps sex-related aggression is also involved. Territorial behavior and sex-related aggression seem far less obvious in the other studies. Both irritable and instrumental aggression were considered by Ulrich, Dulaney, Arnett and Mueller; Patterson and Cobb; Berkowitz; and Bandura. In reviewing them from the standpoint of Moyer's approach to definitions of aggression, one notes the differences among chapters and foresees the problems that might arise if one assumed that all of them dealt with a single kind of aggression.

Problems in developing adequate definitions of aggression have been reviewed several times (e.g., Feshbach 1964; Kahn and Kirk 1968; Kaufman 1965, 1970), but the definitional problems in the laboratory are continuously reflected in the literature. Barnett (1969) has made several good points in favor of discarding the term *aggression* to describe a general broad class of behavior. Similarly, Moyer (1968) has marshaled considerable support for operationalizing the concept of aggression in terms of restricted stimulus-bound behaviors having specific consequences. I concur with a position that emphasizes concepts of very specific and very restricted classes of behaviors as operational definitions of aggression. While the use of unambiguous and functionally derived operational definitions with a high degree of specificity should enhance the probability of establishing criterion validity of definitions, this in itself does not assure validity.

Ideally, the validity of a particular operational definition of an aggressive behavior would be established by an analysis of the behavior pattern under naturally occurring stimulus conditions. If a laboratory definition includes aspects of response topography, that topography should be demonstrated to be transituationally isomorphic with the topography of the organism under natural situations appropriate for the emergence of that behavior pattern. An assessment of topographical isomorphy obviously emphasizes species-specific definitions and mitigates against interspecies definitions. In addition to transituational demonstrations of topographical isomorphy, transituational demonstrations of the interorganism consequences of the response pattern are necessary for validation of the definition. It is the consequence of a behavior, together with the stimulus conditions under which it emerges, that distinguishes it among the kinds of aggression. Broad definitions, such as the "presentation of aversive stimulation," without additional delineation of stimulus conditions would not be appropriate to this strategy of formulating definitions. Similarly, concern for intent, social desirability, or accidental attack is unnecessary. Traditionally problematic aspects of the validity of aggression definitions, such as inanimate targets or property damage, can be easily considered as consequences of specific behaviors. Human verbal behavior can be treated as aggressive, providing the characteristics, stimulus conditions, and consequences are specified.

Emphasizing narrow and highly specific definitions of aggression would seem to argue against the development of general laws of aggression. While such general laws will not easily emerge, definitions reflecting a high degree of specificity and established validity should enhance the development of laws of behavior directed at specific kinds of aggression, which is a reasonable goal. Whether established laws are applicable to more than a single kind of aggression could be subsequently determined.

The Same Variables and Different Kinds of Aggression

When seven different studies related to a similar topic are examined concurrently, it is impossible not to look for examples of convergence as well as points of disagreement. With the marked array of operational definitions and research paradigms, it would seem that searches for common variables and generalizable laws would be unproductive. And yet, in spite of the wide range of operational definitions and research procedures, there are dimensions shared commonly by several of the studies. When the same independent variables similarly influence two different behaviors, there is perhaps the urge to go beyond a statement to the effect that different behaviors are being influenced similarly. Attempts at an extrapolation indicating the two behaviors reflect the same underlying behavioral trait are often made. While it is exciting to discover variables that similarly influence different kinds of aggression and that suggest the possibility of a few potent variables influencing many kinds of aggression, such findings can pose serious interpretative problems.

Common experimental procedures for the investigation of aggressive behavior in rats include shock-elicited aggression, considered by Ulrich, Dulaney, Arnett and Mueller (chap. 4), and mouse killing, described by Denenberg (chap. 2). Denenberg attempted to build a case for the use of mouse killing in lieu of shock-elicited aggression in rat research. The mouse-killing response of rats seems to be an interspecific, predatory behavior, while the shock-elicited aggression is probably an intraspecific, irritable aggressive behavior. Moyer (chap. 1) would suggest that these two behaviors are unrelated. Similarly, Denenberg seems to have taken the position that the mouse-killing response is independent of the laboratory phenomenon of shock-elicited aggression. Since these two behaviors have been investigated independently, with few parallels in variables, attempts to relate the two areas are infrequent.

Two attempts using electric shock to induce mouse-killing behavior in nonkiller rats were unsuccessful (Karli 1956; Myer and Baenninger 1966). These data provided support for the position that mouse killing and shock-elicited aggression are unrelated. Individual differences in fighting behavior under shock-elicited-aggression conditions are apparent in the literature (e.g., Powell et al. 1969). Perhaps the individual differences in aggressivity which emerge in a shock-elicited-aggression paradigm are related to the individual differences in aggressivity which emerge under mouse-killing situations. Support for such a hypothesis can be generated by reviewing data similarities among studies using the two different paradigms and the same independent variables. For example, Whalen and Fehr (1964) and Paul, Miley, and Baenninger (1971) presented data indicating that the rate of mouse-killing behavior in a population of rats was significantly increased by submitting the subjects to cycled food-deprivation schedules. These results were paralleled in the shock-elicited-aggression literature when food deprivation resulted in greater frequencies of fighting than those obtained in nondeprived control subjects (Cahoon et al. 1971; Lester and Cheses 1968). Interestingly, the Paul, Miley, and Baenninger (1971) study was unable to increase mouse killing with a water-deprivation schedule; and Hamby and Cahoon (1971) did not appreciably influence shock-elicited biting in rats with a water-deprivation schedule. Male rats kill mice at a higher frequency than do female rats (Myer 1971). These data are paralleled by demonstrations that male rats display more shock-elicited aggression than female rats (Conner and Levine 1969; Hutzell and Knutson 1972; Knutson and Hynan, 1972). Recently, Myer (1969) assessed the influence of postweaning isolation on the mouse-killing behavior of rats. Although the differences did not reach statistical significance, the percentage of killers among the postweaning-isolation animals was less than among those that had been maintained in community cages. Similarly, Hutchinson, Ulrich, and Azrin (1965) and Hutzell and Knutson (1972) demonstrated that rats housed in isolation after weaning displayed less shock-elicited aggression as adults than did rats maintained in community cages between weaning and the initiation of shock-elicited-aggression testing. Considered as a group, these studies suggest there are variables that influence both mouse-killing behavior and aggression resulting from foot-shock presentation. Also, they offer support for the hypothesis that individual differences in shock-elicited aggression and mouse killing can be related. Additional support for such a hypothesis could be inferred from recent hypothalamic lesion work of Panksepp (1971). In order to directly assess whether individual differences in mouse-killing behavior and shock-elicited aggression are related, an experiment was undertaken by Knutson and Hynan (In Press).

If shock-elicited aggression and mouse-killing behavior reflect individual differences in aggressivity, it would be expected that rats displaying high frequencies of shock-elicited aggression would be drawn from a population of mouse-killing rats and, conversely, that rats displaying a low frequency of fighting would be drawn from a population of nonkillers. Such a hypothesis is numerically consistent with the mouse-killing literature, indicating that a smaller proportion of domestic rats are killers, and shock-elicited-aggression data from this laboratory, indicating that a smaller proportion of rat pairs meet a rigorous criterion of high-frequency-rate fighting during foot-shock stimulation (Hynan 1971).

In a series of replications, 314 100–12-day-old experimentally naïve male hooded rats from the colony of the Department of Psychology, University of Iowa, were submitted to an assessment for mouse-killing behavior. A genetically heterogeneous colony of laboratory mice was used to provide targets. The pool of targets included mice having pigmented, dilute, or nonpigmented coat coloration. At the start of the experiment, each rat was transferred from a community-rearing cage to an 8 × 10 × 11-inch isolation cage, with food and water continuously available.

Following three days of adaptation to the isolation-cage conditions, the rats were tested daily for mouse killing. Experimenters placed a mouse in the home cage of the rat and observed the rat-mouse interactions. If the mouse was killed, it was immediately removed from the cage, and the length of time required to complete the kill was recorded. Mice that were unharmed by the rats were removed after two hours and returned to the mouse colony. Rats were submitted to two-hour test sessions daily for mouse killing until they either failed to kill on ten consecutive days or killed on ten consecutive days. All mouse-killing rats were retained for subsequent shock-elicited-aggression testing, as were an equal number of randomly selected rats that never killed. Extra nonkilling rats and unreliable killers—those that failed to achieve the killing criterion within twenty-five days—were discarded. An assessment of these mouse-killing data indicated that the occurrence of mouse killing was influenced neither by the sex of the mouse nor by the coat pigmentation. These data provide a systematic replication of data reported by Denenberg (chap. 2).

Following testing for mouse-killing behavior, killer and nonkiller rats were tested for shock-elicited aggression. Fifteen pairs of killer rats and fifteen pairs of nonkiller rats were constructed by pairing subjects that were closest in weight within a group. These pairs of rats were then submitted to shock-elicited-aggression test sessions in a 9 × 11½ × 7½ inch fighting chamber, constructed with Plexiglas walls and lid and a grid floor consisting of 3/32-inch stainless steel rods spaced ½ inch apart center to center. This fighting chamber was housed in a sound-attenuated chamber fitted with observation windows. Shock was delivered to the grid floor by means of a tube-type constant-current-DC supply and scrambled through a Gerbrands Model G5820 scrambler. Shock duration and frequency were programmed by means of conventional electronic timers and relay circuitry. Killer-rat pairs and nonkiller-rat pairs were submitted to ten daily shock-elicited-aggression test sessions consisting of 100 2-milliampere shocks of 0.5-second duration, programmed at a rate of twenty per minute. Trained observers, uninformed as to the group membership of the pair, recorded the occurrence of aggressive behavior. Because of previous research in this laboratory, upright postural responses, frequently labeled as "threat posture," were not recorded as aggression, and only stereotyped aggressive responses involving physical contact made by boxing or biting were recorded. Occasionally, rats under shock-elicited-aggression test conditions develop postures that serve to effectively avoid shock presentations. Observers concurrently recorded the occurrence of avoidance behavior. The data obtained are based upon the proportion of shocks actually administered to both members of the pair which elicited aggression.

The proportion of shocks eliciting aggressive behavior were analyzed, using a repeated-measures analysis of variance. There were no statistically significant differences between the killer- and nonkiller-rat groups ($F = 1.26$; $df = 1/28$; n.s.). Figure 8.1 *(left)* shows the shock-elicited fighting behavior of these groups of rats. The obviously increasing frequency of shock-elicited aggression in both groups was statistically significant ($F = 7.1$; $df = 9/252$; $p < .001$). Thus, killer and nonkiller rats did not differ with respect to shock-elicited-aggression frequencies when tested at a 2-milliampere shock intensity. However, it is possible that the 2-milliampere shock level produces such a high frequency of fighting that it is not sensitive to subtle differences in aggressivity reflected in the mouse-killing behavior. Consequently, it would seem reasonable to use a shock level that ordinarily results in a lower overall fighting frequency. Previous experience in this laboratory has indicated that high frequency of aggression is obtained with a 2-milliampere shock intensity, and that markedly lower fighting frequencies are obtained with 1-milliampere current levels.

The second experiment was a systematic replication of the preceding one. One hundred one 110–20-day-old experimentally naïve male rats were assessed for mouse-killing behavior, using the same procedure as in the preceding experiment. From this pool of subjects, ten pairs of killer and ten pairs of nonkiller rats were obtained. Subsequently, these pairs were submitted to ten shock-elicited-aggression test sessions, which were identical to the conditions in the preceding experiment except that the shock intensity was adjusted to 1 milliampere. Then these rats were

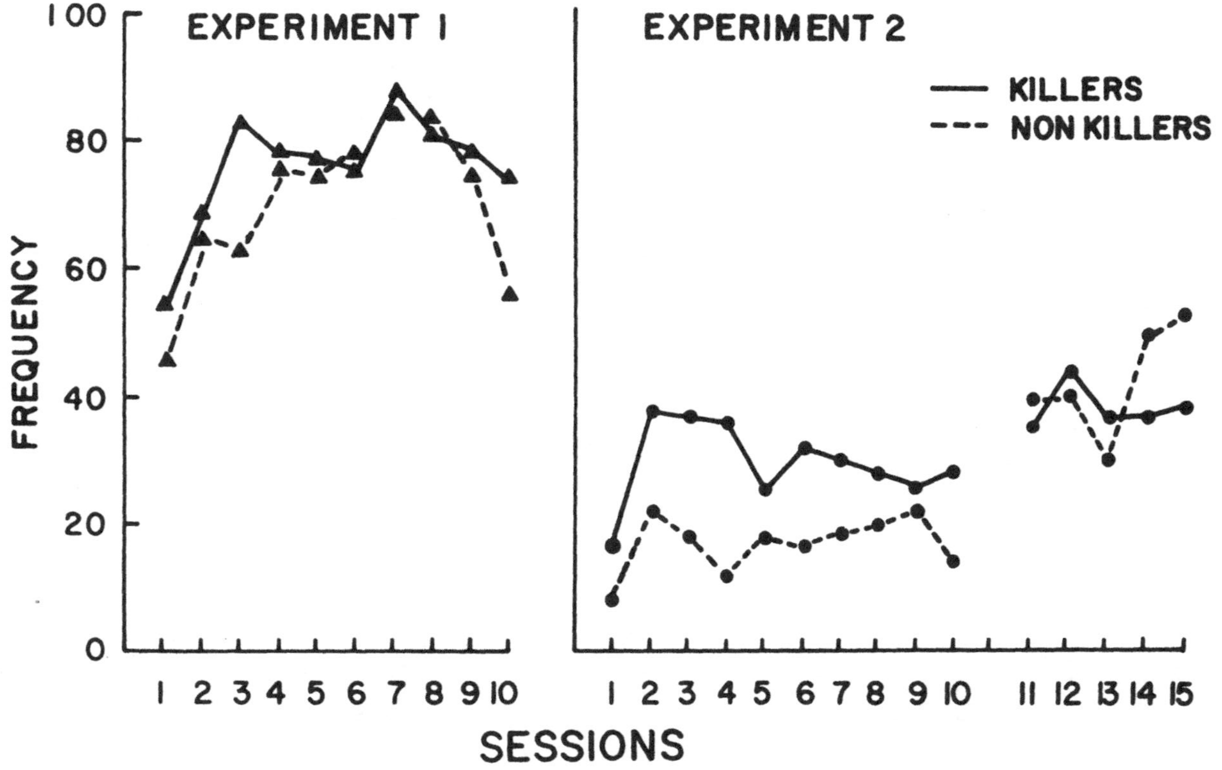

FIGURE 8.1. *Shock-elicted fighting displayed by pairs of mouse-killing and non-mouse-killing rats. Experiment 1 used 2-milliampere shocks. Experiment 2 used 1-milliampere shocks during sessions 1–10 and 2-*milliampere shocks during sessions *11–15*. (After Knutson and Hyman, in press)

tested for five sessions, using the 2-milliampere current level. Data recording and analysis was accomplished, using the same procedures as in the preceding experiment.

Figure 8.1 *(right)* shows the frequency of shock-elicited aggression displayed by the groups of killer and nonkiller rats in this experiment. The slight increase in fighting frequency across the ten 1-milliampere trials was statistically significant ($F = 2.22$; $df = 9/162$; $p < .05$). The apparent difference in fighting frequency between killer and nonkiller rats during the ten sessions at 1 milliampere did not approach statistical significance. In addition, no differences between these groups emerged when the rats were then tested at a 2-milliampere shock intensity. While the first part of the second experiment was successful in producing a lower overall fighting frequency than the preceding experiment, it was no more successful in demonstrating differences in shock-elicited aggression between killer and nonkiller rats than the preceding experiment. As in the first experiment, both groups were characterized by extreme within-group variability.

The results of these experiments indicate the independence of predatory mouse-killing behavior in the rat and shock-elicited aggression in the rat. Thus, these experiments provide support for the positions suggested by Denenberg (chap. 2) and Moyer (chap. 1). Such results would seem to argue against attempts at wholesale extrapolations among different research paradigms, different operational definitions of aggression, and different data bases. In addition, such data argue against attempts at generating single, all-encompassing theories of aggression or theories of general aggressivity.

Individual Differences in Aggressivity

Individual differences have been considered in each chapter. In psychology there are two approaches to understanding differences manifested among subjects in a research population. One strategy is to assume that individual differences reflect errors of measurement, that the obtained differences stem from fallible measurement devices rather than true differences among subjects. The other position suggests that individual differences and the understanding of individual differences constitute the *sine qua non* of research. Both positions have their adherents, and both positions can be easily misrepresented. Individual differences can be a function of fallible assessment devices. At the same time, there is a literature supporting the bona fide nature of differences among subjects.

Aggression research would emphasize the importance of understanding the true differences among individuals. For example, Berkowitz (1962) and Feshback (1970) comment upon the importance of understanding individual differences in the analysis of aggression. Similarly, the recent Surgeon General's Scientific Advisory Committee on Television and Social Behavior (1972) stressed the importance of understanding why there were differences among children in responsiveness to the televised aggression. The conclusions of the committee repeatedly emphasized that the variables in question influenced *some* children. It seems that the understanding of individual differences in aggressive responding is a central theme in most aggression research.

An obvious source of individual differences in aggressive behavior involves genotypic variability among subjects, the heritability of aggressive behavior, and the manner in which the genotype and the environment interact to determine this behavior. McClearn and DeFries (chap. 3) have demonstrated the importance of genetics in influencing differences in aggressive behavior. In addition, along with Denenberg (chap. 2), they have demonstrated the degree to which the genetic composition of an organism may determine whether an environmental manipulation, such as cross-fostering, will be successful in influencing phenotypic aggressive responding. It is plausible that genetic sources of variability are operating, although unassessed and unmanipulated, in the other studies. Moyer (chap. 1) indicated that certain types of aggression are influenced by the sex of the subjects. Perhaps other less obvious but equally potent genetic influences operate in all eight kinds of aggression considered by him. Ulrich, Dulaney, Arnett and Mueller (chap. 4) based many of their analyses upon a literature that characteristically emphasizes data based upon the performance of individual subjects. That literature is replete with examples of individual organisms differing with respect to their behavior in aggression-test situations (see, e.g., Azrin, Hutchinson, and Hake 1963, 1966; Knutson 1970; Knutson and Kleinknecht 1970; Powell et al. 1969). While it is easy to hypothesize that genetic components determine these individual differences, the experimental investigation of genetic variables influencing these behaviors has not been undertaken. The inbred-strain methodology of the behavioral geneticist might be employed profitably in almost every aspect of aggression research. It is not sufficient to concede the influence of genetic variables; a systematic analysis is required.

The genetic determination of individual differences in aggression is not the only variable operating. Frequently, variables such as unique reinforcement histories, unique environmental situations, or unique conditioning experiences are offered to account for individual differences in aggressive responding. Conditioning history as a potent variable is consistent with the findings of Bandura (chap. 7); Berkowitz (chap. 5); Patterson and Cobb (chap. 6); and Ulrich, Dulaney, Arnett and Mueller (chap. 4). One interesting aspect of the Patterson and Cobb study is that the antecedent behavior "Talk" is a significant facilitator for social hostility in the sample of children with behavior problems. A priori, talk would be an unlikely candidate as a facilitator of hostility in most models of aggression. Unfortunately, the control-group children provided an inadequate number of observations to assess the hostility-facilitating influence of talk. However, it is possible to hypothesize that talk as a facilitator of hostility is only characteristic of the problem-behavior children, and that talk as a facilitator of hostility reflects a difference between problem and nonproblem children. It is possible that the semantic conditioning discussed by Berkowitz is involved in the development of talk as a facilitator of social hostility in problem-behavior children. With sufficient data, the Berkowitz model may determine whether the development of the behavior reported by Patterson and Cobb reflects differences among subjects or general characteristics of social aggressive behavior.

The theory of operant conditioning as a determinant of individual differences in aggressive behavior is well established. The reinforcement or punishment of intraspecific aggressive behavior can radically influence the resulting social hierarchy and aggressive behaviors of all members of the group of organisms (e.g., Radlow, Hale, and Smith 1958). Similarly, Patterson, Littman, and Bricker (1967) indicated that preschool children receiving the reinforcement for aggressive attacks on other preschoolers were more likely to continue to be aggressive. Children punished, or nonreinforced, showed a lower probability of subsequent aggression. Data reported here by Bandura (chap. 7); McClearn and DeFries (chap. 3); Moyer (chap. 1); and Ulrich, Dulaney, Arnett and Mueller (chap. 4) have offered additional support for unique reinforcement history as a potent determinant of individual differences in various aggressive responses. The importance of winning or losing as determinants of individual differences in the mouse aggression discussed by McClearn and DeFries is a vivid example of how noncontrived contingencies of punishment and reinforcement can influence subsequent aggressive behavior.

The acquisition of a unique response repertoire under stimulus conditions ordinarily associated with aggressive responding might constitute another source of individual differences in aggressive responding.

In two recent experiments in our laboratory (Hynan and Knutson, 1972; Knutson and Hynan, 1972) the probability of shock-elicited fighting was altered by training a behavior pattern in response to shock that was topographically incompatible with shock-elicited aggression. Thus, acquired behavioral differences under stimulus conditions ordinarily associated with aggression might result in aggression-frequency differences. Such an analysis could be used to account for the Powell and Creer (1969) data, which indicated that prior exposure to electric shock attenuated shock-elicited aggression.

The acquisition of responses incompatible with attack, genetic influences, and reinforcement and conditioning history might account for only some of the variables functioning as determinants of the individual differences reflected in these studies. Understanding the effects of these responses and other variables is essential in order to understand the laws controlling aggressive behaviors.

The Target as a Determinant of Individual Differences

Most research investigating individual differences in aggressive behavior have concentrated on understanding these differences in terms of variables associated with the aggressor. A much less frequently examined source of variability is the target, and the manner in which individual differences among targets interact with individual differences among subjects to determine aggressive behaviors. Moyer (chap. 1) indicates the importance of the target as a variable in determining aggression; that is, he has emphasized the importance of the appropriate target for a particular kind of aggression. However, there seems to be more involved than just having a suitable aggression-specific target available. Intermale aggression obviously requires a male conspecific target, but some male conspecifics might be better targets than others. There are a number of variables that could operate in determining whether an individual target is an optimal target.

The ethological literature has often considered the importance of target behaviors, such as stereotyped displays necessary to provoke aggressive responding (e.g., Lorenz 1966). Recently, a number of laboratory investigations of aggression have reported data indicating that individual differences in targets could be a potent variable in determining the level of the aggressive behavior. For example, Azrin, Hutchinson, and Hake (1963) presented data that seemed to implicate the importance of the behavior of the target in determining the frequency of pain-induced aggression in paired primates. It was observed that some pairs of squirrel monkeys displayed high frequencies of fighting when submitted to shock-elicited-aggression test sessions. Other pairs of squirrel monkeys displayed no fighting, regardless of shock intensity. Constructing a new pair using a high-frequency-fighting monkey and a member of a nonfighting pair resulted in markedly attenuated fighting behavior by the subject that had been highly aggressive.

This same effect was demonstrated by Powell et al. (1969) under conditions of pain-elicited aggression in rats. In addition, the Powell et al. (1969) study demonstrated that treating single members of rat pairs with chlorpromazine eliminated shock-elicited fighting. Thus, when only a single member of a fighting pair had been administered the drug, fighting was effectively eliminated. Knutson (1971) extended these findings by demonstrating that a single rat receiving shock is unlikely to attack a non-shocked rat. Thus, irritable aggression requires more than a conspecific target: it requires a conspecific target that displays particular response characteristics.

Ulrich, Dulaney, Arnett and Mueller (chap. 4) reviewed much of the literature on schedule-induced and extinction-induced aggressive behavior as it relates to the pain-aggression hypothesis. The extinction-induced- and schedule-induced-aggression research is frequently accomplished with pigeons, the literature on which reports marked individual differences among subjects in fighting frequencies (e.g., Azrin, Hutchinson, and Hake 1966; Flory 1969; Gentry 1968; Knutson 1970; Knutson and Kleinknecht 1970). Two standard target arrangements are used in this experimental paradigm. Some of the experiments pair an experimental subject with a single target, and that subject is always exposed to manipulations while paired with that one target (e.g., Knutson 1970). An alternative procedure is to provide a pool of target conspecifics, and each aggression-test session involves the use of a randomly chosen target animal (e.g., Richards and Rilling 1972). Under both experimental procedures the variability in aggression is attributed to individual differences in the aggressing subject. It is possible that in both procedures the variability among targets contributes to variations in obtained frequency of attack. In the procedure using randomly chosen targets, variations in targets would be manifested as within-subject variability between sessions. In the procedure using a single target with each aggressor, target differences are indistinguishable from aggressor differences. A recently completed experiment in this laboratory assessed the influence of target rotation on schedule-induced aggression in pigeons. The experiment was embedded in an ongoing investigation of extended exposure to fixed-time (FT) reinforcement schedules and the maintenance of schedule-induced aggression.

An FT schedule provides reinforcement to an organism independently of its behavior at specified fixed intervals. Thus, an FT 120-second schedule provides response-independent food to an animal every 120 seconds. Pigeons submitted to such reinforcement schedules have been shown to display high frequencies of attack when a restrained target pigeon was available (Flory 1969). For this reason, FT schedules were incorporated into this experiment.

Three adult-male homing pigeons and one adult-female homing pigeon served as experimental subjects (aggressors). Three adult-male homing pigeons and three adult-female homing pigeons served as targets.[1] The experimental birds, maintained at 80 percent free-feeding weight, had been exposed to over 150 sessions of schedule-induced-aggression testing with a single target. Fixed-time-induced-aggression testing was accomplished in a modified operant-conditioning chamber, which included a device for restraining a live target pigeon and recording blows in excess of 125 grams struck against the target. (See Azrin, Hutchinson, and Hake [1966] and Knutson [1970] for a description of this chamber.) During the assessment of the influence of the target upon the FT-induced aggression, all experimental birds were submitted to a series of target rotations involving at least two different targets and at least fifty-three sessions. Sessions lasted until the experimental subject had been provided thirty reinforcements consisting of a 5-second access to a hopper filled with food pellets.

Figure 8.2 shows the mean number of target displacements recorded during the 48-second period immediately following each reinforcement. This limited aggression-recording period is predicated on the fact that most schedule-induced aggression is in the postreinforcement period, and, with markedly different FT schedules, differences in overall performance can be more a function of different session lengths than attack-rate differences.

1. The pigeons were supplied as two-year-old males. Pigeon sexing is a difficult task, and the presence of hens among birds purchased as males from three different reputable suppliers atests to this difficulty or to the general unreliability of pigeon suppliers. The birds of this experiment were sexed anatomically after they had been sacrificed following the completion of the experiment. Postexperiment sexing results in a clear determination of sex, but unfortunately it cannot prevent unplanned male-female aggressor-target pairings.

Subject-153, a male, was tested with two hen targets *(T)*. It is obvious that during both FT 240 and FT 480 *T*-81 was struck much more frequently. Subject-155, a male, had targets changed unsystematically between sessions during FT 240. The targets were then rotated in successive blocks of sessions during FT 120

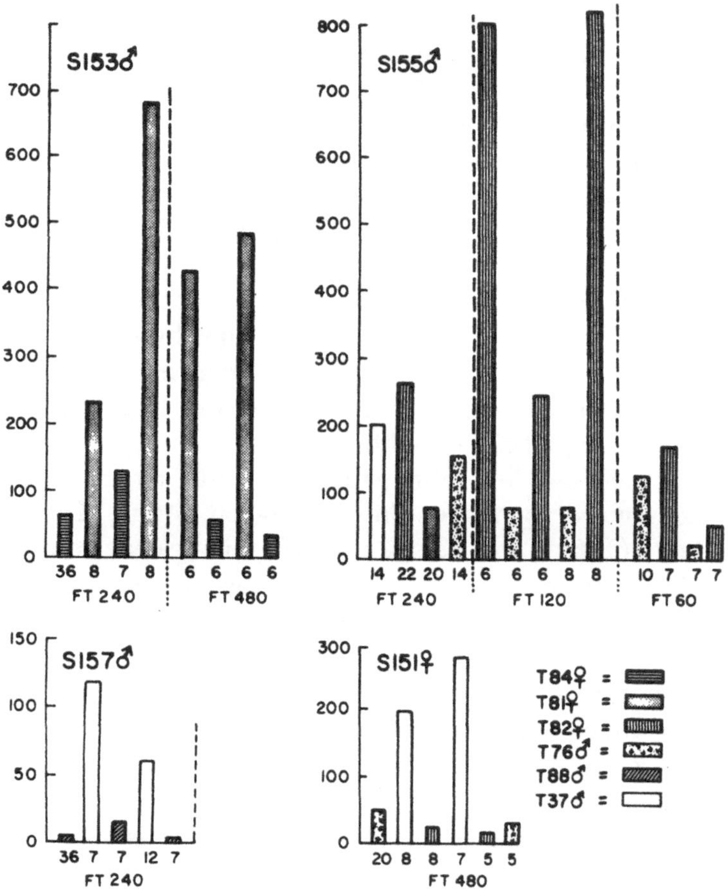

FIGURE 8.2. *Each bar shows the mean number of target displacements during the 48-second period following reinforcement when the subject was paired with the specific target indicated by the legend. The number beneath each bar indicates the number of sessions upon which the mean is based. Pairing changes were usually accomplished successively, as reflected in the left to right arrangement of the abscissas. The exception was the random rotation of targets with S–155 during the 70-session exposure to FT 240.*

and FT 60 with S-155. Under either condition, *T*-82, a hen, was the target most frequently attacked. Notice that an increased frequency of attack during FT 120 was only apparent with *T*-82. Target-76 was struck only infrequently by S-155 during FT 240, FT 120, and FT 60. Subject-157, a male, was paired with two male targets, *T*-37 and *T*-88. This bird aggressed against *T*-37 at a high rate, but rarely displayed attack with *T*-88. Subject-151, a hen, was paired with two male targets (*T*-37 and *T*-76) and one hen target (*T*-82). Target-37 was attacked at a high rate, but *T*-76 and *T*-82 were rarely attacked.

These data show the degree to which targets can determine the frequency of schedule-induced aggression in pigeons. In addition, data suggest that some targets (e.g., *T*-37) are almost always good victims, while other targets (e.g., *T*-76) are rarely attacked. Of course, there are probably other targets (e.g., *T*-82) that are attacked by some aggressors and not by others. The importance of these data resides in the fact that even under potent aggression-inducing laboratory conditions, the target determined the obtained frequencies of fighting.

This is not the first observation that the target determines schedule-induced aggression in the pigeon. Azrin, Hutchinson, and Hake (1966) and Knutson (1970) indicated, respectively, that only 25 percent and 20 percent of the pigeons tested would attack a taxidermically prepared target. It now seems that an optimal target is not just a living target, but rather is a living target displaying particular characteristics. It is essential for future research to direct some effort toward understanding the variables that predispose some targets to be good victims and others to be rather poor ones.

One possible characteristic of a good victim is the ability to provoke attack. Targets might have several aspects that would determine their aggression-provoking potential. Behavior is one. Recently, in an investigation of pain-elicited aggression in rats, Hynan and Knutson (1972) demonstrated that restrained, harnessed targets that received grid shock served as a stronger provocation to attack than did targets trained to display topographies in response to shock which were incompatible with shock-elicited aggression. Thus, attack frequency can be a function of the presence or absence of attack-provoking behaviors in the target's repertoire.

Just as genetics is an important variable in determining individual differences in the behavior of aggressors, it is an important determiner of individual differences in targets. McClearn and DeFries (chap. 3) reported data involving an inbred strain of mice that served as excellent victims in intraspecific aggression. This strain can be effectively used to give nonaggressive mice, or weak aggressors, fighting experiences that insure victory and that enhance the probability of subsequent aggression against more vigorously defensive targets. This strain of mice might be viewed as a universal good victim for intraspecific aggression in the mouse.

Perhaps the strain of the mouse determines the obtained frequency of mouse-killing behavior in rats also. Differences among laboratories in the percentage of rats that kill mice can be most easily attributed to differences among the rats of different laboratories. It is also possible that the strains of mice used determine the frequency of mouse killing. The Denenberg data (chap. 2) and the data from this laboratory suggest that mouse pigmentation does not influence the frequency of killing. These data do not rule out the possibility that genetically determined pheromones, or behaviors, uncorrelated with coat pigmentation might be variables in the mouse-killing research. Perhaps there are the good mouse victims and bad mouse victims of interspecific aggression as there are good and bad victims in intraspecific aggression.

A variable that obviously influences intraspecific aggression is the history of winning or losing. The round-robin procedure is a technique that explicitly takes into account successes and failures, as well as targets, as determinants of fighting. McClearn and DeFries reported changes in aggressivity in mice by engaging them in a series of graded fights with targets displaying varying degrees of aggressiveness, Low-frequency fighters became high-frequency fighters after repeated tests with increasingly vigorous but beatable targets. These data indicate the importance of the target in the winning and losing equation. The history of winning or losing a series of aggressive encounters and the characteristics of the target are probably involved in both the provocation to attack and the maintenance of attack. Hence, both variables are probably important in determining the degree to which a laboratory procedure induces or attenuates aggression behaviors.

Both Berkowitz (chap. 5) and Bandura (chap. 7) considered the interaction between the characteristics of the target and the history of the subject to be a variable in the control of aggression. Both authors infer that individuals with certain characteristics are more likely to be aggressed against than others. Berkowitz suggests that a conditioning process operates through an individual's experiencies and that this conditioning determines whether specific individuals or specific groups are good or bad targets. Similarly, Bandura notes that "people learn to dislike and to attack certain types of individuals on the basis of symbolic and vicarious experiences, as well as through direct encounters with them." Thus, for both human and infrahuman subjects, the history of the organism combines with target characteristics to influence the occurrence of attack behaviors.

Target characteristics might also determine whether the opportunity to aggress can serve as a reinforcement. Certain data indicate that under suitable conditions an organism will learn a new response or maintain behavior when the opportunity to attack is the response-contingent consequence. Azrin, Hutchinson, and McLaughlin (1965) demonstrated that aversively stimulated primates learned to operate a manipulandum when the reinforcement was access to an inanimate target. Dreyer and Church (1970) and Cole and Parker (1971) both demonstrated that aversively stimulated rats and pigeons would acquire responses when the reinforcement was access to a conspecific target. McClearn and DeFries (chap. 3) have reported mouse data indicating the reinforcing potential of the opportunity to aggress. Both Myer and White (1965) and Van Hemel (1972) demonstrated that target mice were effective reinforcers for mouse-killing rats. All these studies have suggested that histories involving winning or successful killing are potent determiners of whether the opportunity to aggress is reinforcing. In addition, the data suggest that target characteristics influence the reinforcing value of the opportunity to attack a target. Targets with the characteristics of past good victims should be potent reinforcers, and those with the characteristics of bad victims should be weak reinforcers. With respect to the schedule-induced-aggression data considered earlier, the targets that were aggressed against at a high rate would be more likely to be effective reinforcers than those that were rarely attacked. The present studies by Bandura; Patterson and Cobb; and Ulrich, Dulaney, Arnett and Mueller consider to some extent the reinforcing aspects of attack and the characteristics of the reinforcing target.

Closely related to the aggression-provoking characteristics and the reinforcing aspects of the good target are its aggression-maintaining qualities. The question is, Once a victim is attacked, what target characteristics determine whether it continues to be attacked? At an almost trivial level, one such characteristic is the degree to which the target can be overpowered. In the intraspecific, intermale aggression reported by McClearn and DeFries (chap. 3), the overpowered nondominant mice in the triad chambers continued to receive flank wounds as the victorious male mouse repeatedly attacked the unsuccessful fighters. Parallel data, indicating that the easy victim continues to be a victim, was reported by Patterson, Littman, and Bricker (1967): a preschool child who was easily overpowered continued to be the victim in aggressive encounters, while preschool children who were not easy victims were attacked less often.

One almost ubiquitous aspect of aggressive encounters is the display of pain cues by the attacked victim. Although there may be an absence of pain cues in the attenuation aggression associated with the nonshocked-target (Knutson 1971) or the drugged-target (Powell et al. 1969) procedures, pain cues as target variables have not been systematically investigated in animal-aggression research. In contrast, target pain cues are among the more frequently investigated target variables in human-aggression research. In spite of several studies investigating pain cues in human aggression, the influence of pain cues has not been unequivocally determined. Most of the data from human laboratories have suggested that pain cues displayed by targets serve as potent inhibitors of aggressive responding (e.g., Baron 1971*a*, 1971b; Buss 1966). However, Sears (1958) suggested that pain cues were reinforcing events in an aggressive encounter. In support of this position, Patterson, Littman, and Bricker (1967) demonstrated that nursery-school children responded in a manner that suggested that the pain cues displayed by a victim of an attack had reinforcing properties. Additional support for the reinforcing nature of pain cues was provided by Hartmann (1969).

These apparently contradictory results could be due to different kinds of aggression, or they could be due to additional variables such as subject differences. Research on aggression that could be classified under the categories of instrumental aggression and irritable aggression (frustration induced) have provided data indicating both the aggression-facilitating and the aggression-inhibiting roles of pain cues. Thus, the type of aggressive behavior does not account for these disparate conclusions. However, the subject population could be a variable in determining the different effects of target pain cues on human laboratory aggression. Those studies suggesting that pain cues were aggression inhibitors were accomplished with adult subjects (Baron 1971*a*, 1971*b*; Buss 1966). Data based upon children (Hartmann 1969; Patterson, Littman, and Bricker 1967) supported the aggression-facilitating role of pain cues. In two recent experiments, Mazzola (1971, 1973) examined the role that visible target pain cues played in the aggression-machine responding of both male college students and third-grade boys. In addition, the study distinguished between subjects that characteristically displayed high- or low-intensity aggressive responses on an aggression-machine task. In the initial study Mazzola (1971) demonstrated that the presence or absence of pain cues had no influence on the groups of low-aggressive adults, but that pain cues suppressed aggressive responding of the high-aggressive adults. In addition, the absence of pain cues increased the aggressive responding of the high-aggressive adult subjects. In the study using third-grade boys (Mazzola 1973), the presence of pain cues served as a facilitator of aggressive responding by some of the low aggressive groups. Thus, the influence of the presence or absence of target pain cues was a function of the differences among subjects in terms of age and characteristic response level in an aggression-machine task.

It is probably a safe generalization to state that individual differences in targets either directly determine differences in aggressive behavior, or interact with individual differences among subjects to determine aggression frequencies. An exploration of the target as a potent determinant of aggression seems indicated.

Implications for Clinical Psychology

These studies and the problems encountered in defining aggression reflect the complexity of the behaviors commonly subsumed under the nonspecific label of aggression. Aggression, in the broad sense of the term, involves too many multifaceted behaviors, under the control of too many divergent variables, to permit one to develop a single model applicable to the human situation. Only two chapters provide models that approximate a general understanding of human aggression. Bandura's social learning approach (chap. 7) and that of Ulrich, Dulaney, Arnett and Mueller (chap. 4), which combined the pain-aggression hypothesis with an operant analysis of behavior, are models which seem to be directed toward an analysis of human aggression in general. While both chapters, by means of a synthesis of data and theory, provide potentially productive models of human aggression, they do not purport to deal with all of the different kinds of aggression considered in research, nor do they exhaust the potential variables that could be important in an applied situation. The authors recognize the importance of the complementary and supplementary roles of additional variables. The models offered in other chapters are obviously important. The applied psychologist looking for a specific model to provide an understanding of aggression in general is likely to be very disappointed. Just as the molar general theories of learning have slipped into disuse, productive molar models of aggression are unlikely to be developed. The data are too diverse to be distilled into single programs. In view of this diversity, when he is asked what research can do to alleviate pressing social problems associated with aggression, the behavioral scientist has to reply with a question regarding the kind of aggression. Nevertheless, some implications for human behavior seem apparent in basic research.

Another aspect of aggression research that determines its applicability to man is the use of human or nonhuman subjects. Procedurally, there has been much to recommend the use of animals in aggression research. Not only has it been easier to accomplish solid operational definitions, but it is possible to observe and control the behavior to a greater extent. Many of the parameters investigated are probably not feasible for direct manipulation in human research (see, e.g., chaps. 1–4). By using parallels between animal and human data, Moyer (chap. 1); McClearn and DeFries (chap. 3); and Ulrich, Dulaney, Arnett and Mueller (chap. 4) all suggested that the animal data had implications for human aggressive behavior. Similarly, Denenberg (chap. 2) expressed optimism that there were implications for understanding human aggression in his data. Recently, Harlow, Gluck and Suomi (1972) discussed the problems associated with generalizations from nonhuman behavior to human behavior. They noted the difficulty in developing a formula for predicting generalization; generalizations will be made, but the important factors are the competence and data with which they are attempted. Whether the aggression data from animal laboratories will be useful to applied psychology probably depends on the development of human analogues of the animal research for testing the ideas emanating therefrom. Thus, the applicability of animal data will be determined to a large extent by the research of investigators interested directly in human aggressive behavior and by the skill with which they test hypotheses based upon animal data. The study by Ulrich, Dulaney, Arnett and Mueller (chap. 4) provided a human analogue of animal research, and Bandura (chap. 7) and Patterson and Cobb (chap. 6) offer some support for the potential generalization of animal data to human behavior. Some generalizations appear obvious, but whether they are functional must be established with data.

An additional variable determining the applicability of aggression research relates to whether the research is accomplished in a laboratory or in the natural environment of the subject. Most aggression research has been confined to the laboratory, and, as a consequence, the data are often considered to be irrelevant to applied problems. If the criterion validity of the laboratory definition has been established, the potential applied import of the data may be more obvious. However, even with validity of an operational definition of aggression, the effects of variables remain to be demonstrated in the natural environment in order for the data to be applicable. Unfortunately, the technology and sophistication of laboratory research has exceeded the available technology for research in the natural environment. For this reason, the generality of laboratory phenomena has not often been assessed directly. The paradigm offered by Patterson and Cobb (chap. 6) seems to be an important step in developing a research methodology for use in the natural human environment. This method could provide a basis for testing the generalizability of laboratory research since it offers the prospect of adequately investigating aggressive behaviors in natural environments. The importance of a rigorous methodology for the study of aggression in the natural environment cannot be overemphasized.

Despite the diversity of aggressive behaviors and the problems inherent in laboratory paradigms and subject populations, these chapters do reflect some degree of consensus and offer some implications for the control of human aggression. The most obvious point of consensus is at the level of distinguishing between the pathological or nonpathological essence of aggressive behaviors. While the potential deleterious consequences of aggressive behavior is recognized, all studies hold the position that aggressive behaviors are generally a function of the operation of variables that do not have overtones of psychopathology or abnormal behavior. Bandura (chap. 7) indicated that aggressive behaviors associated with delusional thinking accounts for only a small minority of human aggressive incidents. This comment by Bandura, and Moyer's (chap. 1) review of the biological manipulation of pathological aggression are the only considerations of abnormal behavior and aggression in this book. The thrust of these chapters suggests that an understanding of human aggression will be accomplished through an assessment of aggression and not through an assessment of syndromes and diagnostic categories of abnormal behavior.

While the pathological nature of aggressive behavior is not emphasized, the potential biological utility of the behavior is apparent in these chapters. Much of the current research has related aggression to the evolutionary history of the organism, the gene pool, dispersion, breeding, and predation. The biological importance of the Denenberg (chap. 2) and the McClearn and DeFries (chap. 3) data is obvious, and a case can be made for the biological utility of other kinds of aggression data as well. Data such as these could be erroneously viewed as support for the instinct-hydraulic theories of human aggression, and the inevitability of human aggression. Such a view is not consistent with the positions of any of the contributors. They all demonstrate that nonpathological, and perhaps biologically relevant, aggression is controllable behavior.

Technically, any of the variables considered could provide a basis for both the understanding and control of aggression. A few variables might be especially important in developing controlling variables. The pain-aggression hypothesis is an animal-based model that is beginning to get some support in human paradigms. Patterson and Cobb (chap. 6) indicate some support for this model in a paradigm using humans in a nonlaboratory setting.

The pain-aggression hypothesis deserves some comment with respect to the specification of the parameters involved. In addition to the definition of the aggressive response, this hypothesis requires a careful specification of aversive stimulation. Demonstration of the aversive characteristics of a stimulus is usually accomplished by demonstrating that an organism will respond to terminate the occurrence of the stimulus, or that the occurrence of that stimulus contingent upon a response serves to decrease the probability of the behavior. Unfortunately, such transituational specification of aversive stimuli is insufficient for the pain-aggression hypothesis. The stimulus intensities sufficient to maintain aggressive behavior (Powell et al. 1969; Ulrich and Azrin 1962) are far greater than those that have been demonstrated to be aversive (Campbell and Masterson 1969). Consequently, the pain-aggression hypothesis indicates that certain classes of events may result in aggressive behavior, but that the probability of attack being associated with a particular aversive stimulus depends on the intensity of the stimulus and a host of complicating subject and environmental variables (e.g., Azrin et al. 1964; Flory, Ulrich, and Wolff 1965; Hutchinson, Ulrich, and Azrin 1965; Knutson 1971; Lester and Cheses 1968; Morden et al. 1968; Powell and Creer 1969). The fact that aversive stimuli did not produce interspecific predatory aggression (Myer and Baenninger 1966) suggests that the pain-aggression hypothesis is not likely to account for all types of aggression. A reasonable conclusion might be that *some* human aggression is facilitated by antecedent aversive events.

Another approach to understanding aggression which received support from several contributors involved instrumental conditioning. Moyer (chap. 1) suggested that his category of instrumental attack was very much like other instrumental behavior. Berkowitz (chap. 5) suggested that an operant-conditioning or instrumental-conditioning strategy was overly emphasized in the literature, but he acknowledged its role in maintaining aggression. Bandura (chap. 7) and Ulrich, Dulaney, Arnett and Mueller (chap. 4) recognized the importance of contingencies of reinforcement for maintaining attack. Although it was not a central consideration in the Patterson and Cobb study (chap. 6), the role of instrumental conditioning was recognized. Aggression as another operant response has had considerable support in both the animal and human literatures. However, while many studies have demonstrated that attack behavior could be established by operant conditioning (Reynolds, Catania, and Skinner 1963; Stachnic, Ulrich and Mabry 1966; Ulrich et al. 1963; Willis, Michael, and Edwards 1966), the characteristics of the behavior are quite unlike other operant responses. For example, Azrin and Hutchinson (1967, p. 401) noted that the aggressive response established by food reinforcement and maintained on a fixed-interval-reinforcement schedule "appeared to have intrinsic momentum as evidenced by the failure to terminate attacks as soon as food was available." An apparent human parallel to this laboratory phenomenon can be found in reports of armed-robbery victims being assaulted and abused to a degree that appears to be far in excess of that required by the instrumental act of robbery. Laboratory data and popular reports suggest that, although operant-conditioning variables may play a major role in the development of the behavior, a simple instrumental- or operant-conditioning model does not adequately handle all the characteristics of instrumental aggressive behavior.

To some extent the pain-aggression hypothesis deals with variables that directly influence the momentary occurrences of aggression. Instrumental-conditioning analyses are concerned with both the momentary occurrences of aggressive responses and the acquisition of an aggressive repertoire. It is this latter phenomenon, together with the variables that influence the subsequent long-term probabilities of aggressive behavior, which poses a major problem in understanding human aggressive behavior, and most of the data are directed toward this particular aspect. The various physiological characteristics of aggressing subjects, considered by Moyer (chap. 1); the acquisition of aggressive responses, reported by Ulrich, Dulaney, Arnett and Mueller (chap. 4) and Bandura (chap. 7); the attenuation of aggressive behaviors, accomplished by Denenberg (chap. 2); and genetic influences, reviewed by McClearn and DeFries (chap. 3); may all constitute variables that influence the development of aggressive patterns or be factors that determine specific states of aggressivity. As such, the extent of their influence should be determined.

Sibling and peer interactions may influence subsequent aggressive behavior. Denenberg (chap. 2) and Patterson and Cobb (chap. 6) have strongly implicated siblings and peers as possible agents for the control of aggression. These influences, those of parents and significant adults (discussed by Bandura), and long-term conditioning through personal interactions and media presentations (see Berkowitz data) constitute a multiplicity of sources influencing human aggressivity. When these factors are considered in conjunction with genetic variables, instrumental aggression, pain-aggression phenomena, and target variations, the possibility of controlling human aggression seems remote. Yet, all the present contributors have been optimistic about the control of the kinds of aggression under their respective considerations. Their data suggest that such optimism is well founded, since the control of particular types of aggression has indeed been accomplished.

The implications are clear for behavioral scientists: we must identify the types of human aggression and help incorporate into society the parameters that influence them.

References

Azrin, N. H., and Hutchinson, R. R. "Conditioning of the Aggressive Behavior of Pigeons by a Fixed-Interval Schedule of Reinforcement." *Journal of the Experimental Analysis of Behavior* 10 (1967): 395–402.

Azrin, N. H.; Hutchinson, R. R.; and Hake, D. F. "Pain-induced Fighting in the Squirrel Monkey." *Journal of the Experimental Analysis of Behavior* 6 (1963): 620.

——. "Extinction-induced Aggression." 9 (1966): 191–204.

Azrin, N. H.; Hutchinson, R. R.; and MacLaughlin, R. "The Opportunity for Aggression as an Operant Reinforcer during Aversive Stimulation." *Journal of the Experimental Analysis of Behavior* 8 (1965): 171–80.

Azrin, N. H.; Rubin, H. B.; and Hutchinson, R. R. "Biting Attack by Rats in Response to Aversive Shock." *Journal of the Experimental Analysis of Behavior* 11 (1968): 633–39.

Azrin, N. H.; Ulrich, R. E.; Hutchinson, R. R.; and Norman, D. J. "Effect of Shock Duration on Shock-induced Fighting." *Journal of the Experimental Analysis of Behavior* 7 (1964): 9–11.

Barnett, S. A. *The Rat: A study in Behaviour*. London: Methuen & Co.; Chicago: Aldine Press, 1963.

——. "Grouping and Dispersive Behavior among Wild Rats." In *Aggresive Behavior*, edited by S. Garattini and E. B. Sigg. New York: John Wiley & Sons, 1969.

Baron, R. A. "Aggression as a Function of Magnitude of Victim's Pain Cues, Level of Prior Anger Arousal, and Aggressor-Victim Similarity." *Journal of Personality and Social Psychology* 18 (1971): 48–54. *(a)*

——. "Magnitude of Victims' Pain Cues and Level of Prior Anger Arousal as Determinants of Adult Aggressive Behavior." *Journal of Personality and Social Psychology* 17 (1971): 236–43. *(b)*

Berkowitz, L. *Aggression: A Social Psychological Analysis.* New York: McGraw-Hill Book Co., 1962.

Buss, A. H. *The Psychology of Aggression*. New York: John Wiley & Sons, 1961.

——. "Instrumentality of Aggression, Feedback, and Frustration as Determinants of Physical Aggression." *Journal of Personality and Social Psychology* 3 (1966): 153–62.

Cahoon, D. D.; Crosby, R. M.; Dunn, S.; Herrin, M. S.; Hill, C. C.; and McGinnis, M. "The Effect of Food Deprivation on Shock Elicited Aggression in Rats." *Psychonomic Science* 22 (1971: 43–44.

Campbell, B. A., and Masterson, F. A. "Psychophysics of Punishment." In *Punishment and Aversive Behavior*, edited by B. A. Campbell and R. M. Church. New York: Appleton-Century-Crofts, 1969.

Carthy, J. D., and Ebling, F. J. *The Natural History of Aggression*. New York: Academic Press, 1964.

Cole, J. M., and Parker, B. K. "Schedule-induced Aggression: Access to an Attackable Target Bird as a Positive Reinforcer." *Psychonomic Science* 22 (1971): 33–35.

Conner, R. L., and Levine, S. "Hormonal Influences on Aggressive Behaviour." In *Aggressive Behaviour*, edited by S. Garattini and E. B. Sigg. New York: John Wiley & Sons, 1969.

Daniels, D. N.; Gilula, M. F.; and Ochberg, F. M. *Violence and the Struggle for Existence*. Boston: Little, Brown, & Co., 1970.

Dollard, J.; Doob, L.; Miller, N.; Mowrer, O.; and Sears, R. *Frustration and Aggression*. New Haven: Yale University Press, 1939.

Dreyer, T. I., and Church, R. M. "Reinforcement of Shock-induced Fighting." *Psychonomic Science* 18 (1970): 147–48.

Feshbach, S. "The Function of Aggression and the Regulation of Aggressive Drive." *Psychological Review* 71 (1964): 257–72.

——. "Aggression." In *Carmichael Manual of Child Psychology*, edited by P. H. Mussen. New York: John Wiley & Sons, 1970.

——. "Dynamics and Morality of Violence and Aggression: Some Psychological Considerations." *American Psychologist* 26 (1971): 281–92.

Flory, R. "Attack Behavior as a Function of Minimum Inter-Food Interval." *Journal of the Experimental Analysis of Behavior* 12 (1969): 825–28.

Flory, R. K.; Ulrich, R. E.; and Wolff, P. C. "The Effects of Visual Impairment on Aggressive Behavior." *Psychological Record* 15 (1965): 185–90.

Gentry, W. D. "Fixed-ratio Schedule-induced Aggression." *Journal of the Experimental Analysis of Behavior* 11 (1968): 813–17.

Hamby, W., and Cahoon, D. D. "The Effect of Water Deprivation upon Shock-elicited Aggression in the White Rat." *Psychonomic Science* 23 (1971): 52.

Harlow, H. F.; Gluck, J. P.; and Suomi, S. J. "Generalization of Behavioral Data between Nonhuman and Human Animals." *American Psychologist* 27 (1972): 709–16.

Hartmann, D. P. "Influence of Symbolically Modeled Instrumental

Aggression and Pain Cues on Aggressive Behavior." *Journal of Personality and Social Psychology* 11 (1969): 280–88.

Hutchinson, R. R.; Ulrich, R. E.; and Azrin, N. H. "Effects of Age and Related Factors on the Pain-Aggression Reaction." *Journal of Comparative and Physiological Psychology* 59 (1965): 365–69.

Hutzell, R. R.; and Knutson, J. F. "A Comparison of Shock-elicited Fighting and Shock-elicited Biting in Rats." *Physiology and Behavior* 8 (1972): 477–80.

Hynan, M. T. "The Influence of Target Variables upon Shock-elicited Aggression in Rats." Master's thesis, University of Iowa, 1971.

Hynan, M. T., and Knutson, J. F. The Influence of Target Variables on Shock-elicited Aggression in Rats. Paper presented at the Iowa Academy of Science, June, 1972.

Kahn, M. W., and Kirk, W. E. "The Concepts of Aggression: A Review and Reformulation." *Psychological Record* 18 (1968): 559–73.

Kaufmann, H. "Definitions and Methodology in the Study of Aggression." *Psychological Bulletin* 64 (1965): 351–64.

——. *Aggression and Altruism*. New York: Holt, Rinehart & Winston, Inc., 1970.

Karli, P. "The Norway Rat's Killing Response to the White Mouse: An Experimental Analysis." *Behaviour* 10 (1956): 81–103.

Kelly, J. F., and Hake, D. F. "An Extinction-induced Increase in an Aggressive Response with Humans." *Journal of the Experimental Analysis of Behavior* 14 (1970): 153–64.

Kimbrell, G. M. " 'Fighting Response': A Definitional Problem." *Psychological Record* 18 (1968): 639–40.

Knutson, J. F. "Aggression during the Fixed-Ratio and Extinction Components of a Multiple Schedule of Reinforcement." *Journal of the Experimental Analysis of Behavior* 13 (1970): 221–31.

——. "The Effects of Shocking One Member of a Pair of Rats." *Psychonomic Science* 22 (1971): 265–66.

Knutson, J. F., and Hynan, M. T. "Influence of Upright Posture on Shock-elicited Aggression in Rats." *Journal of Comparative and Physiological Psychology*, 81 (1972): 297–306.

Knutson, J. F., and Hynan, M. T. "Predatory Aggression and Irritable Aggression: Shock-induced Fighting in Mouse-killing Rats." *Physiology and Behavior*, in press.

Knutson, J. F., and Kleinknecht, R. A. "Attack during Differential Reinforcement of a Low Rate of Responding." *Psychonomic Science* 19 (1970): 289–90.

Lagerspetz, K. *Studies upon the Aggressive Behaviour of Mice*. Helsinki: Suomalainen Tiedeakatemina, 1964.

Lester, D., and Cheses, K. T. "Effects of Deprivation upon Aggression in Rats." *Psychological Reports* 22 (1968): 1129–33.

Lorenz, K. *On Aggression*. New York: Harcourt, Brace, & World, 1966.

Mazzola, J. A. "The Presence and Absence of Visible Pain Cues as Possible Conditioned Stimuli for High and Low Aggressive College Males." Master's thesis, University of Iowa, 1971.

——. "The Influence of Visible Pain Cues and Intermittent Reinforcement on the Aggression Machine Responding of Third Grade Boys. Ph.D. dissertation, University of Iowa, 1973.

Morden, D.; Conner, R.; Mitchell, G.; Dement, W.; and Levine, S. "Effects of Rapid Eyemovement (REM) Sleep Deprivation on Shock-induced Fighting." *Physiology and Behavior* 3 (1968): 425–32.

Moyer, K. E. "Kinds of Aggression and Their Physiological Basis." *Communications in Behavioural Biology* 2 (1968): 65–87.

Myer, J. S. "Early Experience and the Development of Mouse Killing by Rats." *Journal of Comparative and Physiological Psychology* 67 (1969): 46–49.

——. "Experience and the Stability of Mouse Killing by Rats." *Journal of Comparative and Physiological Psychology* 75 (1971): 264–68.

Myer, J. S., and Baenninger, R. "Some Effects of Punishment and Stress on Mouse Killing by Rats." *Journal of Comparative and Physiological Psychology* 62 (1966): 292–97.

Myer, J. S., and White, R. T. "Aggressive Motivation in the Rat." *Animal Behaviour* 13 (1965): 430–33.

Panksepp, J. "Effects of Hypothalamic Lesions on Mouse-Killing and Shock-induced Fighting in Rats. *Physiology and Behavior* 6 (1971): 311–16.

Patterson, G. R.; Littman, R. A.; and Bricker, W. "Assertive Behavior in Children: A Step Toward a Theory of Aggression. *Monographs of the Society for Research in Child Development*, vol. 32 (5, serial no. 113) (1967).

Paul, L.; Miley, W. M.; and Baenninger, R. "Mouse Killing by Rats: Roles of Hunger and Thirst in its Initiation and Maintenance." *Journal of Comparative and Physiological Psychology* 76 (1971): 242–49.

Peterson, G. "The Relationship between Fixed-Ratio Schedules of Reinforcement and Aggression in Children." Ph.D. dissertation, Louisana State University, 1970.

Powell, D. A., and Creer, T. L. "Interaction of Developmental and Environmental Variables in Shock-elicited Aggression." *Journal of Comparative and Physiological Psychology* 69 (1969): 219–25.

Powell, D. A.; Francis, J.; Braman, M. J.; and Schneiderman, N. "Frequency of Attack in Shock-elicited Aggression as a Function of the Performance of Individual Rats." *Journal of the Experimental Analysis of Behavior* 12 (1969): 817–23.

Radlow, R.; Hale, E. B.; and Smith, W. I. "A Note on the Role of

Conditioning in the Modification of Social Dominance." *Psychological Reports* 4 (1958): 579–81.

Reynolds, G. S.; Catania, A. C.; and Skinner, B. F. "Conditioned and Unconditioned Aggression in Pigeons." *Journal of the Experimental Analysis of Behavior* 6 (1963): 73–74.

Richards, R. W., and Rilling, M. "Aversive Aspects of a Fixed-interval Schedule of Food Reinforcement." *Journal of the Experimental Analysis of Behavior* 17 (1972): 405–11.

Scott, J. P., and Fredericson, E. "The Causes of Fighting in Mice and Rats." *Physiological Zöology* 24 (1951): 273–309.

Sears, R. R. "Personality Development in the Family." in *The Child,* edited by J. M. Seidman. New York: Holt, Rinehart, & Winston, 1958.

Singer, J. L. "The Influence of Violence portrayed in Television or Motion Pictures upon Overt Aggressive Behavior." In *The Control of Aggression and Violence: Cognitive and Physiological Factors,* edited by J. L. Singer. New York: Academic Press, 1971.

Stachnic, T. J.; Ulrich, R. E.; and Mabry, J. H. "Reinforcement of Aggression through Intracranial Stimulation." *Psychonomic Science* 5 (1966): 101–2.

Surgeon General's Scientific Advisory Committee on Television and Social Behavior. *Television and Growing Up: The Impact of Televised Violence.* Washington, D.C.: Government Printing Office, 1972.

Tinbergen, N. *Social Behavior in Animals.* New York: John Wiley & Sons, 1953.

Ulrich, R. E.; and Azrin, N. H. "Reflexive Fighting in Response to Aversive Stimulation." *Journal of the Experimental Analysis of Behavior* 5 (1962): 511–20.

Ulrich, R. E.; Johnston, M.; Richardson, J.; and Wolff, P. "The Operant Conditioning of Fighting Behavior in Rats." *Psychological Record* 13 (1963): 465–70.

Van Hemel, E. E. "Aggression as a Reinforcer: Operant Behavior in the Mouse-killing Rat." *Journal of the Experimental Analysis of Behavior* 17 (1972): 237–45.

Whalen, R. E., and Fehr, H. "The Development of the Mouse-killing Response in Rats." *Psychonomic Science* 1 (1964): 77–78.

Williams, J. F.; Meyerson, L. J.; Eron, L. D.; and Semler, I. J. "Peer-rated Aggression and Aggressive Responses Elicited in an Experimental Situation." *Child Development* 38 (1967): 181–90.

Willis, F. N.; Michael, G.; and Edwards, J. "Persistance of Conditioned Fighting in a Hen Pigeon." *Psychonomic Science* 5 (1966): 323–24.

Author Index

Subject Index